and thank goodness the dreary rain ceased last night, though I am sopping wet and have no change of clothes. Colonel's rheumatism was aggravated by the cold penetrating damp in the dismal hours before dawn today. His eyes often ask when are we going home to our warm stable and good hay. I doubt, my dear, he'll see them again, poor fellow. As we ploughed our way through deep mud searching out the officers with orders for this morning's movement, eerie miasmal mists swirled around us, and both of us were soaked and chilled clean through until the marrow in our bones chattered like the ague. Most of the men are miserably wet, hungry, and have been for days.

In such state I came upon two men more bedraggled than two old roosters; looking more forlorn than Romeo and Adonis standing under fast dripping eaves. They had gotten as much fire going as you could hold in the hollow of your hand, and were trying to make coffee from a handful of rye they must have foraged. When I asked them where their captain and company were they told me that they were all left of their company after yesterday's engagement. I took it upon myself to assign them to what was left of Frank Lynn's (do you recollect him?) company, hoping he would have mounts for them.

Please send some of my old hunting shirts and some under clothes, everything I possessed was lost last week. It has been unusually cold this early spring. Ask Uncle Rob if he can spare

A PAGE FROM A SERGEANT'S LETTER

From this we learn nought of Confederate handguns but can understand much of the indo[m]
Confederacy and of the times in which these arms were used.

Against discouraging obstacles of supply, overwhelming and increasing odds in combats
"*Cause*" is found within the lines of this neatly penned page and is magnificently reflecte[d]
Woodson.

CONFEDERATE HANDGUNS

JOSIAH GORGAS

Brigadier General, Chief-of-Ordnance,
Provisional Army of the Confederate States.

CONFEDERATE HANDGUNS

CONCERNING THE GUNS
THE MEN WHO MADE THEM
AND THE TIMES OF THEIR USE

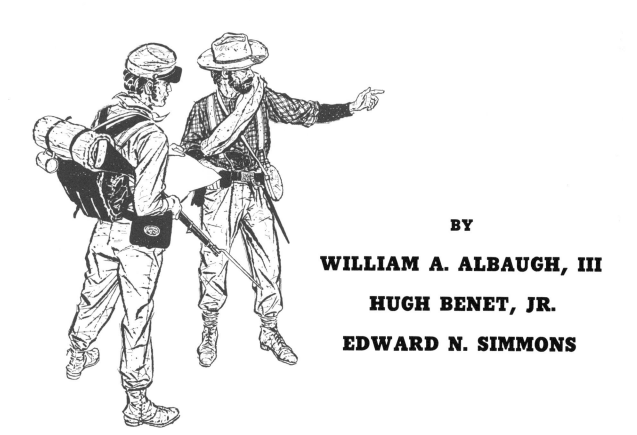

BY

WILLIAM A. ALBAUGH, III

HUGH BENET, JR.

EDWARD N. SIMMONS

RILING AND LENTZ

PHILADELPHIA, PENNSYLVANIA • 1963

PUBLISHED BY RILING AND LENTZ
6844 GORSTEN STREET, PHILADELPHIA 19, PENNSYLVANIA

Produced in the United States of America

Color end papers by Everett Waddey Company, Inc., Richmond, Virginia.
*Text set in Linotype Caledonia with display in Stymie Bold by
Ruttle, Shaw & Wetherill, Philadelphia, Pennsylvania.*
Offset printing by The Meriden Gravure Company, Meriden, Connecticut.
Binding by Russell-Rutter Company, Inc., New York, N. Y.
Designed by Ray Riling, Philadelphia, Pennsylvania.

Library of Congress Catalog Card Number: 63-10982

A. M. D. G.

Respectfully dedicated to

the men who made the arms
and to

the men who used them

in the war

for Southern Independence

FOREWORD

HIGH tribute was paid to my deep-rooted love of the Confederacy by the request to write the foreword to this important study of the handguns used by the armed forces of the Confederate States of America. I am deeply grateful.

To me, the War between the States will always be *"The* War." There never was, nor has there been, another war quite like it. It was a personal war, yet it was most impersonal, and I doubt that any two people can ever come to complete agreement on its many facets and contradictions. Be that as it may, this is no Sumter—I but offer a few lines in sincere appreciation of this valuable and timely work which so competently presents factual evidence of the South's Herculean efforts in organizing its industrial power to produce and develop the sinews of war.

When I was four, in 1908, I would play storekeeper and "sell" my grandmother sugar for supper from an old powder keg in the pantry at Harvie Street, and it must have been then that subconscious thoughts began to mold my love and compassion for the South and her people. "Your grandfather," she would tell me, "brought that keg home the night Richmond was burning . . . the night your Aunt Nora was born."

It was many years before the significance of what she had said dawned on me, and I could connect Aunt Nora's birthday and the evacuation of Richmond, along with ever so many memories and feelings that were kindled within Granny. She was one of those valiant women of the South whose ideals and beliefs suffered defeat and heartbreak when their men laid down their arms with Lee at Appomattox.

Did the Confederacy manufacture arms? Of course she did! And she continued to make them throughout The War in spite of the blockade and the loss of valuable territory containing the natural resources so vital to success in the field, and to her economy. The people were united; they were determined, and no ordeal or pain of personal sacrifice was too great. Goodness knows, toward the last there was precious little to cheer about, but cheer they did, even as individuals gave up their last treasured possessions, especially those made of metal. Their belief and faith in "Marse Robert" was inflexible, and they wrung some sort of comfort from the knowledge that in making their great sacrifice The War might be ended the sooner.

The price of all commodities, especially food, soared sky-high; there was actual physical suffering, but the people of the South proved that there is practically no limitation to human endurance. Again and again, as materials necessary to ordnance manufacturing were lopped off remorselessly by the enemy, each new call was answered by continued sacrifice until, at last, Appomattox put an end to it all. Dreams and hopes of a resumption of their former way of life went up in smoke on that April day, yet they breathed a sigh of relief as they thanked God that the bitter fighting was over at last. Of course the end of the struggle would not return their loved ones killed in battle, nor give back a wedding ring or sacred memento. But The War was over! They found solace in knowing that through their heroic efforts, high morale and unimpeachable courage the South had kept over half a million men under arms, had sustained them continuously for four long years, and finally lost only through an overwhelming force of circumstances.

Of all that I have written, the reader will find the essence more technically expressed by three most competent authors in their masterful portrayal of the production of Confederate handguns during a disastrous and anguished era.

Through eyes burning with tears of soul-searing frustrations the South surveyed a ravished land, then faced the unknown and unchartered future with unconquered spirit. "What we have to do, our children will continue; with these hands we will build anew." And this we have done by uniting in the construction of a wondrous and mighty land, an undivided nation—The United States of America.

Richmond, Virginia

FRANKLIN SHEPPERSON

INTRODUCTION

DEPENDING upon where one was born or raised, American history between the years 1861 and 1865 is known variously as the Civil War, the War between the States, the War for Southern Independence, or simply The War. Regardless of what it is called, interest in this period has been so great and so continuing, that books dealing with this broad subject have been published at a conservative estimate of one per day since the first shot was fired at Fort Sumter. And if this is so, the ratio of one volume for each participant therein must be fast approaching.

These publications cover many aspects of the war but, strangely, only a few have dealt with Confederate industry, and of this small handful most have been forthcoming only within the past ten to twenty years. Possibly this omission is due to the generally accepted opinion that prior to the war the South had no industry worthy of the name and that with hostilities what little there was fell apart. Nothing could be more incorrect.

It is an irrefutable fact that from first to last the Confederacy had well over 500,000 men under arms, and that she was able to sustain continuously from three to four armies in the field as well as a navy. It would appear then that the South was in fact making (or having made) and issuing vast quantities of arms, munitions, clothing, etc.; for despite shipments from Europe it cannot be held that these imports were her main source of supply. Most of her war material was home-grown.

That the South survived four years of history's bloodiest war is of course a high tribute to the courage, morale and leadership of her people. We believe it is also indicative of the industrial potential that lay within her borders, without which this newly-formed nation would have collapsed long before Appomattox, if indeed it could have outlived even the first year of the blockade.

While the industrial, economic and military might of the Confederacy cannot be compared to the industrial potential or power-in-being in the North, she nevertheless did possess industry before the war. This was a complex geared to an agricultural economy but sufficiently flexible that, with the advent of hostilities, it could and did convert the ploughshares of peace into the swords of war. Similar conversions made possible the minie balls, canister, grape, spherical and solid shot, along with the guns that fired them.

There are as many phases of manufacturing as there are of human ingenuity, and in the latter the Southern people were certainly not lacking. This study attempts to touch on only one small facet of Southern industry—the manufacture of handguns—and is a summary of the wartime efforts of such men as Samuel Griswold, who quickly changed a cotton gin works into a revolver factory; or an erstwhile cotton broker, Thomas Leech, who ventured into the same field of endeavor; and many others whose courses lay roughly parallel. Our stories are by no means complete but are an attempt to put between two covers all that is presently known on the subject.

Before discussing those pistols and revolvers used by the armed forces of the Confederate States and the militia of the various states that comprised this ill-starred nation, a few bench marks must be established and a few terms defined. Accordingly, we have broken our subject into three main categories: Primary, Secondary and Associated. We have made our own definitions for each. There may be some who will disagree with the standards we have set, but this is beside the point. They are only intended for this work and do not necessarily apply to any weapons other than those under discussion.

It is our opinion that only pistols or revolvers made expressly for the Confederate States of

America, either by contract with the government or by the government itself, can be considered as *Primary*. These are the guns that were issued fresh and new as government property.

Into our *Secondary* class fall those martial handguns made abroad for the various Southern states or the Confederate Government. Note our inclusion of the word "martial." We might also add that such guns were made in some quantity, uniformly and according to a fixed pattern.

The *Associated* classification comprises those pistols or revolvers that are simply Southern made or which bear Southern markings. These may or may not have seen actual service or even have been handled by a Confederate soldier. They are included, however, because of the distinct possibility that any or all may have been so used. It would be impossible to prove or disprove such use of most of the weapons in this category.

For the sake of organization we have divided the book into four parts. Part I concerns those Primary handguns made in the South. Part II also relates to martial pieces which were made abroad. They should not be confused with the heterogeneous weapons purchased by both sides all over Europe. Part III deals exclusively with an associated class of Secondary arms. Part IV consists primarily of a directory of persons and places connected with the manufacture, repair, purchase or sale, of Southern or Confederate pistols and revolvers before, during and after the war. No attempt has been made to include all of the gunsmiths or dealers who operated south of the Mason-Dixon line, but only those who are definitely known to have had some connection with the making, sale or repair of handguns during the war. Concise Bibliographical Notes and an Addendum, which presents Confederate patent records, conclude Part IV and our work of nineteen chapters.

The authors are not unaware of the gaps that appear here and there in the material which follows. In extenuation, we can only say that in some cases a lack of specific information has of necessity required reliance upon theory, deduction or assumption rather than the documented facts which of course we would have preferred.

We would like to remind those interested that their state, county and city archives and libraries are filled with gold for those who have the initiative to dig for it. Court records are also invaluable and include municipal, county, state and federal material. Newspapers frequently not only furnish valuable clues but also lead to the location of still more information.

It is to be hoped that interested persons everywhere will take heart and investigate the possibilities that exist right in their own locale. Such research will undoubtedly change tenuous theory and unsupported assumption into the documented facts which should be both the foundation and keystone of all historical studies.

We trust that the pages to follow will engender a climate conducive to further study and appreciation of handguns of the Confederacy.

July 29, 1962

WILLIAM A. ALBAUGH, III
HUGH BENET, JR.
EDWARD N. SIMMONS

ACKNOWLEDGMENTS

THE authors wish to gratefully recognize the assistance they have received from many collectors and other interested persons, for without their help this book never could have been. In preparing a list of those whose aid and advice was so freely and cheerfully given, we were struck by the fact that many whose names appear below are members of the American Society of Arms Collectors or The Company of Military Collectors and Historians, or of both. This in itself speaks highly of the manner in which these organizations and their members foster and aid research.

The following have helped to make *Confederate Handguns* a worthy record:

Richard B. Abbott, Sanger, California
John T. Amber, Chicago, Illinois
Lawrence Austin, Bloomington, Illinois
William Bacon, Richmond, Virginia
W. Herbert Bahlke, Chesterton, Indiana
John Beck, Fort Worth, Texas
Dr. Vergil Bedsole, Baton Rouge, Louisiana
Mrs. Christie Benet, Columbia, South Carolina
Dr. George Benet, Columbia, South Carolina
Harry D. Berry, Baltimore, Maryland
Robert Berryman, East Point, Georgia
Frank W. Bishop, Old Church, Virginia
Eugene Bond, Holland, Ohio
William A. Bond, Vernon, Texas
Monty Bonner, Inglewood, California
Francis Borowyk, Philadelphia, Pennsylvania
E. Berkley Bowie (Deceased)
John W. Boyle, Chester, Pennsylvania
Richard T. Brady (Deceased)
Charles L. Bricker, Ferndale, Michigan
Lee Brigham, Excelsior Springs, Missouri
Eleanor Brockenbrough, Richmond, Virginia
Dr. S. Traner Buck (Deceased)
E. Milby Burton, Charleston, South Carolina
Forrest E. Coburn, Bryn Mawr, Pennsylvania
William E. Codd, Monkton, Maryland
Richard S. Cofer (Deceased)
Mrs. Richard S. Cofer, Norfolk, Virginia
Peter F. Copeland, Washington, D. C.
Floyd Cox, Bradenton, Florida
Colonel Alston Deas, Mt. Pleasant, South Carolina

Ciro DeGennaso, Omaha, Nebraska
Oscar DePrato, Quaint Acres, Maryland
Joseph W. Desserich, Foster, Ohio
F. Theodore Dexter, Poplar Bluff, Missouri
Charles Dienthal, Chicago, Illinois
Charles L. Dufour, New Orleans, Louisiana
Colonel George B. Dyer, New Hope, Pennsylvania
Dr. J. H. Easterby (Deceased)
Mrs. Eugenie Le Mat Eggleston, Washington, D. C.
Alan Emanuel, Anaconda, Montana
Robert A. Erlandson, Baltimore, Maryland
E. Norman Flayderman, Greenwich, Connecticut
Victor Friedrichs, Austin, Texas
Colonel Charles W. Fritz, Norwood, Ohio
Claude E. Fuller (Deceased)
H. L. Gaidis, Baltimore, Maryland
Harry B. Garden, Rockingham, North Carolina
T. Price Gibson, Charlotte, North Carolina
Fred M. Gloth, Jr., Baltimore, Maryland
Craddock R. Goins, Washington, D. C.
E. J. Gray, Los Angeles, California
Howard W. Gwaltney, Smithfield, Virginia
Mrs. Joseph Halligan, Baltimore, Maryland
Ashley Halsey, Jr., Philadelphia, Pennsylvania
Frank M. Hancock, Scotland Neck, North Carolina
T. Sherman Harding, Arcadia, Florida
Richard Harwell, Chicago, Illinois
Dr. Paul Hess, Kansas City, Kansas

Miss Marie Hoeck, Baltimore, Maryland
Carroll C. Holloway, Longview, Texas
Gayle P. Hoskins (Deceased)
Robert I. Howard, Richmond, Virginia
Walter J. Howe, Arlington, Virginia
Edgar M. Howell, Washington, D. C.
Dr. George W. Huckaba, Memphis, Tennessee
E. Harold Hugo, Meriden, Connecticut
Julius Hulff, Reseda, California
S. L. Hutcheson, Greenwich, Connecticut
E. L. Inabinett, Columbia, South Carolina
Colonel and Mrs. Leon C. Jackson, Dallas, Texas
Paul C. Janke, Houston, Texas
Colonel Catesby Jones, Richmond, Virginia
Manuel Kean, Philadelphia, Pennsylvania
Frank J. Kelly, Lee, Massachusetts
John F. Kerr, Philadelphia, Pennsylvania
Robert Klinger, Arlington, Virginia
George Knight, Alexandria, Virginia
Harry C. Knode, Dallas, Texas
Robert Krumdick, Chicago, Illinois
Colonel R. C. Kuhn, Chicago, Illinois
Bruce Kusrow, Tacoma Park, Maryland
E. M. Lander, Jr., Clemson, South Carolina
Mrs. Ann Lange, Baltimore, Maryland
Dorothy Lawton, New Orleans, Louisiana
Colonel Alfred M. Leonard, Columbus, Georgia
Edward R. Leonard, Birmingham, Alabama
John W. Lentz, Bryn Mawr, Pennsylvania
Colonel Berkeley R. Lewis, Vista, California
Mrs. Joseph Liles, Baltimore, Maryland
William M. Locke, Cincinnati, Ohio
Herschel C. Logan, Salina, Kansas
Andrew F. Lustyik, Middletown, New York
J. Joseph May, Richmond, Virginia
Sam McClaren, Richmond, Virginia
Robert McDonald, Dearborn, Michigan
W. L. McDowell, Jr., Columbia, South Carolina
Carl Metzger (Deceased)
B. G. Miller, Kansas City, Missouri
Robert L. Miller, Arlington, Virginia
Bernard J. Mitchell, Falls Church, Virginia
James F. Moser, Jr., Orange, Virginia
Dr. Robert Nelson, Chicago, Illinois
Waldo E. Nutter, St. Louis, Missouri

H. Hume Parks, Nashville, Tennessee
Thomas Parvin, Lombard, Illinois
C. Meade Patterson, Washington, D. C.
Harold L. Peterson, Arlington, Virginia
Mrs. Frank H. Pinkerton, Norfolk, Virginia
W. C. Phillips, San Bernardino, California
Carl J. Pugliese, Yonkers, New York
F. A. Purvis, Alexandria, Virginia
Mrs. Harriet Quigley, Baltimore, Maryland
John J. Rawls, Vienna, Virginia
H. Collis Reed, Jr., Louisville, Kentucky
J. J. Reen, McLean, Virginia
Mrs. Mary M. Rigley, Merchantville, New Jersey
Joseph R. Riling, Wyncote, Pennsylvania
Ray Riling, Philadelphia, Pennsylvania
Ray Riling, Jr., Philadelphia, Pennsylvania
James Robertson, Norwalk, California
James G. Robinson, Baton Rouge, Louisiana
Frank Russell, Fort Lauderdale, Florida
Lawrence D. Satterlee (Deceased)
Herman Schindler, Charleston, South Carolina
James E. Serven, Santa Ana, California
Franklin Shepperson, Richmond, Virginia
Fred Slaton, Jr., Madisonville, Kentucky
Jim Smalldon, Arcadia, California
Samuel E. Smith, Markesan, Wisconsin
W. Thomas Smith, Richmond, Virginia
Wyman Spalding, San Francisco, California
Miles W. Standish, Kansas City, Missouri
Richard D. Steuart (Deceased)
William C. Steuart, Baltimore, Maryland
Henry M. Stewart, Jr., Wynnewood,
    Pennsylvania
Herman Strumpf, Cincinnati, Ohio
Dr. Lloyd Sutherland, Union, South Carolina
Mr. and Mrs. K. D. Sykes, Oceanview, Virginia
India Thomas, Richmond, Virginia
Mrs. Clayton Torrence, Richmond, Virginia
Eric Vaule, Providence, Rhode Island
Lee Wallace, Arlington, Virginia
Charles W. Waterman, Newbury, Massachusetts
Jac Weller, Princeton, New Jersey
Reverend Charles F. Wells, Macon, Georgia
James S. White (Deceased)
James F. Whitmore, Philadelphia, Pennsylvania

Donald Winer, Montgomery, Alabama

H. L. Woodlief, Alhambra, California

Jack Woodson, Richmond, Virginia

Charles G. Worman, Dayton, Ohio

Robert H. Wright, Cleveland, Ohio

Honorable Ralph W. Yarborough, Tyler, Texas

M. Clifford Young, Boston, Massachusetts

Fred H. Zerble, Houston, Texas

A considerable amount of our effort was directed toward obtaining clear illustrations. To say the job was difficult would be putting it mildly, but again we were given splendid assistance by everyone concerned, and the results speak for themselves. Here, particular thanks are given to Harry C. Knode, Miles W. Standish, William E. Codd, Ray Riling, Jack Woodson, John F. Kerr, Franklin Shepperson and Peter F. Copeland for their invaluable help.

We were also impressed by the manner in which various state and local archives and libraries cooperated in tracing down what, in many cases, were necessarily vague and sometimes chimerical queries. The help we received from these and private organizations was heartwarming, and the information and assistance was priceless.

Battle Abbey, Richmond, Virginia
Charleston Museum, Charleston, South Carolina
Chicago Historical Society, Chicago, Illinois
Confederate Museum, Richmond, Virginia
Enoch Pratt Free Library, Baltimore, Maryland
Historical Commission of South Carolina, Columbia, South Carolina
Kean Archives, Philadelphia, Pennsylvania
Louisiana State University Archives, New Orleans, Louisiana
Maryland Historical Society, Baltimore, Maryland
Meriden Gravure Company, Meriden, Connecticut
Montgomery Museum of Fine Arts, Montgomery, Alabama
National Rifle Association of America, Washington, D. C.
Norfolk Public Library, Norfolk, Virginia
Richland County Public Library, Columbia, South Carolina
Ruttle, Shaw & Wetherill, Inc., Philadelphia, Pennsylvania
Smithsonian Institution, Washington, D. C.
South Carolina Archives Department, Columbia, South Carolina
Standard Paper Manufacturing Company, Richmond, Virginia
Texas Agricultural and Mechanical College, College Station, Texas
The Boston Athenaeum, Boston, Massachusetts
The South Caroliniana Library, Columbia, South Carolina
The Virginia State Library, Richmond, Virginia
Tulane University, New Orleans, Louisiana
United States Archives, Washington, D. C.
University of Alabama Press, University, Alabama
University of Texas Press, Austin, Texas

We hope that any unintentional error or omission will be viewed charitably and that all who have contributed even a small scrap of information to *Confederate Handguns* are assured that the authors are deeply grateful.

The Authors

CONTENTS

xv

ILLUSTRATIONS

PART I

CHAPTERS 1 through 6

PRIMARY MARTIAL HANDGUNS
MADE IN THE CONFEDERACY

Only those handguns made by, or under contract with the Confederate Government within the Confederacy, 1861-1865

CHAPTER 1

Augusta Machine Works

THE newspapers of the eighteen sixties, North and South, were no better or worse than they are today. They were properly patriotic and loyal to the side or cause they supported and sufficiently biased to please the readers whose money kept them in business. At times they tended to become a little too enthusiastic over a proposed venture, particularly if said venture lay, so to speak, in their own back yard. Thus it is that historians do not place complete reliance in newspaper accounts alone but seek additional corroboration.

In looking over Southern newspapers of the war period, it is not at all uncommon to read an account which usually starts: "We were today shown a revolver invented by our prominent citizen, Mr. Firenze B. Rimstone which shoots fifteen times without reloading. Its finish and workmanship is far superior to that of Colonel Colt's famous, but now out-dated, six-shooters. Mr. Rimstone expects to have his plant in full operation within a very short time and it is anticipated that five hundred revolvers will be forthcoming every month. Etc., etc. . . ."

In the majority of cases this one article is the end of Firenze B. Rimstone as far as the newspaper, Confederate records and the historian are concerned. It is a swan song before he sinks back into the oblivion from whence he came. Disheartening, but true. Occasionally, however, a Rimstone will pull himself up by his boot-straps and actually produce x number of revolvers (pistols, swords or carbines), thereby aiding the Confederacy to the extent of the

items made. By so doing, he has reserved for himself a place in posterity, to be exalted and almost worshiped by today's collectors of old metal with a Civil War connection. Such a person was Thomas Cofer of Portsmouth, Virginia, whose x number of revolvers are now a cause of much speculation and adoration among the demented brotherhood known loosely as gun collectors. The proceeds of the sale of one such revolver on today's market would almost have armed an entire company of Confederate infantry.

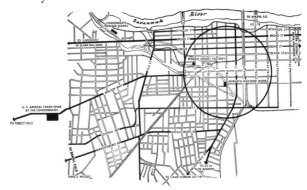

MAP OF MODERN AUGUSTA, GEORGIA

Showing the locations of the Augusta Machine Works and the Rigdon and Ansley factory.

Occasionally guns of Confederate manufacture appear in such number as to indicate a sizable operation. It is particularly exasperating to the historian to have indisputable evidence of an enterprise and not to be able to tie the product to the manufacturer. So it was with Griswold and Gunnison, whose products were

3

known for years only as "Confederate brass-framed Colts." The fact that they were made by two gentlemen named Griswold and Gunnison was not established until the nineteen thirties.

As it was with Griswold, so it is still with the Augusta Machine Works of Augusta, Georgia. We know that this firm was engaged in revolver making but have not as yet been able to definitely match the product to the maker.

To establish that this plant actually made handguns during the war, let us first turn to the inevitable newspaper account which appeared in the Augusta *Chronicle and Sentinel* of September 11, 1861. According to this source: "We are pleased to see that the Confederate Government has taken steps for the immediate manufacture of materials of war on a large scale. Augusta has been selected as the site, and it is designed to construct, forthwith, spacious buildings and suitable machinery for the manufacture of everything pertaining to ordnance, such as carriages, chassis, caissons, harness, etc., and for the manufacture of gunpowder.

"For the former purpose, extensive additions are to be made to the Arsenal on the Sand Hills, some three miles from the city. We had an opportunity of inspecting some days ago, in the offices of Messrs. Fulton & Miller, engineers and architects of this city, who have the work in charge, the drafts of the new improvements. The MACHINE WORKS, when completed, will be 505 feet at the front and 42 feet in depth, etc. (sic).

"The MACHINE WORKS will comprise a carpenter shop, manufactory of small arms, as well as everything pertaining to ordnance; the whole machinery to be of the most improved patterns and driven by an engine of 75 horse power. The foundation was commenced Wednesday last, and a large force will be put to work so as to complete it at the earliest day practicable. The work is in charge of Lieut. Col. Gill of the Confederate States Army. . . ."

The editor of the *Chronicle and Sentinel* reluctantly admits that the source of the above information was the Savannah *Republican* and expresses deep sorrow "that the news of these matters should have come from sources outside of Augusta." In other words, the *Chronicle and Sentinel* had been scooped by its closest competitor and liked it about as much as does the Washington *Post & Times Herald* when it is scooped by the *Daily Worker*.

The account of the Machine Works, regardless of its source or authenticity, is clear; a government manufactory was underway in Augusta which would manufacture small arms, among other things. Is this just another example of a local Firenze B. Rimstone and his fifteen-shot revolver, or did the Augusta Machine Works actually get into operation, and if they did, were handguns a part of their output?

Mr. Samuel C. Wilson, Secretary, Department of Public Health, City of Augusta, seems to think so, because in 1918 he wrote to E. Berkley Bowie[1] ". . . Pistol factory at Augusta between Jackson & Campbell, Adams & D'Antignac Streets, now occupied by the Augusta Lumber Company was operated by the Confederate Government under a Major N. S. Finney, Chief of Ordnance on the staff of Gen'l B. D. Fry, commanding the Department of Augusta. The pistol was long-barreled, six-chambered, percussion cap, paper cartridge, similar to Colts, and considered at that time one of the best in our service. . . . "

James W. Camak, Esq., an attorney-at-law at Athens, Georgia and an early gun collector also thought so, for in March, 1915, he wrote: "The Confederate Government owned a pistol factory at Augusta, Ga., where pistols were made. Also some few arms made at the Augusta Arsenal. W. D. Bowen of Augusta also made rifles and pistols for Confederate service. His plant was a small one.

"I am now trying to make some inquiries in regard to the Augusta Confederate Pistol Works, but so far can find no one who has any personal knowledge of the matter."

A deposition which adds additional confirmation on the subject is here included:

Deposition, State of Georgia, Richmond County.
    Personally appeared before me Mr. J. B. Patterson of Augusta, State of Georgia, who says that he was born in that city of Augusta, State of Georgia, in the year 1860, that he had a brother to work in the "Old Pistol Factory" which was situated between the second and third levels of the Augusta Canal on the west side of Marbury St., Augusta, Ga. on the spot now occupied by the Georgia Iron Works. That it was discontinued before the end of the War Between the States, that he distinctly remembers the people of Augusta when they expected Sherman's Army to pass

Courtesy Robert A. Erlandson

AUGUSTA MACHINE WORKS REVOLVER
Showing right and left sides. Serial K appears on all parts.

through Augusta, flocked to the Foundry properly known as the Augusta Machine Works, where also guns, cannon, heavy machinery and pistols were made, this being the property of the Confederate States Government, to remove anything left of value. That the first people to occupy the pistol factory, now Georgia Iron Works, after the war were Day and Phillips, who used it for a Foundry and Machine shop, Phillips selling out his interest about 1866 to Isaac Hopkins. After several years they also went out of business; Amos Clark, who afterwards founded the present Globe Cotton Mills operated the old foundry or pistol factory as a cotton mill known as Southern Cross Cotton Mills, until he purchased land and built and founded the Globe Cotton Mills, then the foundry or pistol factory stood idle for several years; then J. P. Coats & Co., thread people, operated a yarn mill until the wooden building was burned. The Georgia Iron Works having purchased this property and built on the old site about 1899 or 1900. He further states positively that the pistol factory was only operated about eleven months, and not until the end of the War, as his brother-in-law, William P. Phillips, and John Day obtained the machinery to start up the old pistol factory into the foundry from the Government Pistol Factory or Augusta Machine Works and the manufacture of pistols had already been discontinued then. They obtained the machinery when they thought Sherman's Army was coming through Augusta.

(signed) J. B. Patterson Sr.

Sworn to before me the 11 day of May 1928.

In his deposition, Mr. Patterson refers to two pistol factories in Augusta—first, the Rigdon-Ansley plant which we know without question was located as he describes it on the west side of Marbury Street between canal levels. The second pistol factory referred to is the Augusta Machine Works or "the Government Pistol Factory."

A few years ago we had occasion to spend several months in Augusta. Quaint, charming and still old-fashioned, the city is one easy to love. Although fast modernizing, sufficient of the old remains that ghosts of the sixties are still plentiful and often in twilight walks along the thickly treed streets we had occasion to bow gravely to Charles H. Rigdon and his partner Jesse Ansley. It is easy to bow to the past in almost any Southern city at eventide, but Augusta is one of the few where the bow is returned. Times without number the site of the Rigdon-Ansley revolver plant was visited, but nothing is to be found there but the ghosts which will always live on.

Inquiries as to the location of the "Government Pistol Factory" to older residents resulted in consistent referral to the Augusta Lumber Company located just where Mr. Samuel Wilson said it was, although the street names have changed and it is presently 903 8th Street. The original building dates back to the war and in size corresponds to the structure described by the *Chronicle and Sentinel*. A large cupola caps its center, as was the custom for most armories of that period.

Talking with old workmen we were told that revolver parts were still occasionally dug up but we found no parts nor complete guns.

When percussion revolvers first made their appearance they contained a feature that was most unsafe and yet peculiar to the arm. This was the apparent necessity for allowing the hammer to rest upon the nipple of one of the capped and loaded chambers. To avoid this many owners of six-shooters always kept one chamber unloaded and uncapped so that the hammer might safely rest thereon. Those who did not sometimes discovered that a sharp accidental blow on the hammer was sufficient to explode the cap and discharge the loaded chamber. Such a chain of events often resulted in the loss of a toe and at times even an organ more vital.

The old master, Samuel Colt, partially solved this problem by inserting small projecting pins in the rear of the cylinder between the nipples to engage a small slot in the hammer itself. This method worked while the gun was new but the pins were subject to wear and they often failed to secure the hammer which could then drift over on one of the capped nipples.

The Colt cylinder contained six cylinder stops. These stops (slots in the side of the cylinder itself which were engaged by a rising bolt in the frame) locked the cylinder in position so that when the hammer was drawn back it would fall squarely upon the nipple and not between nipples, which of course would cause a misfire. In 1859 the Manhattan Arms Company of Newark, New Jersey, patented and brought out an improved safety feature on their revolvers which consisted of twelve instead of six cylinder stops. By such means the hammer, down, could be locked securely between the nipples without danger of slipping over onto a capped nipple.

This was a decided improvement over the Colt safety-pin method and except for its patent protection undoubtedly would have been adopted by many manufacturers. Untroubled by fear of suit for patent infringements, the South liberally "borrowed" any Yankee patent they thought worthy of using and it will be noted that a distinguishing feature of the Rigdon-Ansley revolver is the twelve-stop cylinder.

Now it is known that when Leech and Rigdon dissolved their partnership and Rigdon removed to Augusta to set up a new shop, he was merely continuing the original contract and that the guns he made were identical to those previously made at Greensboro. After turning these out for several months he switched to a twelve-stop cylinder. Why? Possibly because this type of revolver was already being made by the Augusta Machine Works.

Several six-shot, full octagon barrel, twelve-stop revolvers are extant, obviously of American manufacture but as yet unidentified as to maker. Generally they conform to the Colt Navy but parts are not interchangeable. A detailed des-

cription of one such gun is as follows: Six-shot, full octagon barrel, .36 caliber, fine workmanship throughout, originally browned. Barrel length $7^{11}\!/_{16}$ inches. The serial number 4 is on the rear of the barrel lug. It appears twice on top of the loading lever plunger, the barrel wedge, the rear of the cylinder between the nipples, the hammer and inside of the trigger guard. It also appears once on the bottom of the main spring, the back of the frame on either side of the hammer slot, the front of the frame between the locking studs, the inside of the backstrap and five times on the cylinder pin on the rebated area. All screws are without excep-

Courtesy William M. Locke

ANOTHER AUGUSTA MACHINE WORKS REVOLVER

With twelve-stop cylinder.

tion round-headed and extend well beyond the surfaces into which they are set. The barrel has noticeably faint rifling, with a slight right twist and six lands and grooves. The hammer spur is finely checkered. The cylinder is of the twelve-stop variety, $1^{11}\!/_{16}$ inches long. There is a deep oval brass trigger guard and a brass backstrap. The frame is $3^{3}\!/_{16}$ inches long. It is noted that some guns fitting this description use letters such as *J*, *O* or *Y* in place of a serial number. Another known specimen is serial No. 48.

At least two specimens identical in measurement and method of marking but made with only six cylinder stops are known. They are serial No. 7 and *U*, respectively. They are obviously of the same manufacture and we can only assume that these were made prior to the adoption of the twelve stops. It is our opinion that these revolvers are all products of the Augusta Machine Works.

FOOTNOTE REFERENCE

1. E. Berkley Bowie was one of the first collectors to link the collection of Confederate Arms with their history. Mentor and associate of Richard D. Steuart, Bowie was known and respected far beyond his native Baltimore, Maryland. A representative portion of his extensive collection may be seen at Fort McHenry in Baltimore, which, although the inspiration of "The Star-Spangled Banner," was used as a Federal prison for political prisoners during the Civil War.

CHAPTER 2

The Columbus Fire Arms Manufacturing Company,
also known as L. Haiman and Brother

STRATEGICALLY located at the head of navigation on the east bank of the Chattahoochee River is Columbus, Georgia. During the war of secession it was second only to Richmond as a Confederate ordnance center. Here were extensive government works in addition to numerous private contractors engaged in making or supplying articles necessary for the war.

The hub of these activities was the Columbus Iron Works, which had been established in 1850 by W. Riley Brown. During the war it was leased to the government and operated as the Confederate States Naval Iron Works. The plant, located on the southwest corner of Short and Dillingham Streets, was a three-story red brick building, three hundred feet long and forty feet wide. To its immediate rear was the old steamboat landing where the Chattahoochee river packets first began to dock in 1828. To the right was the Muscogee Railroad and its freight depot and shops.

The Columbus Iron Works were under the supervision of the Navy Department. At first, the Department of Army Ordnance was represented only by an agent in the person of Captain F. W. Dillard. In 1862, an ordnance Depot, under the command of Captain (later Major) Frederick C. Humphreys was established but under the administrative jurisdiction of the Atlanta Arsenal. The Depot developed into an Arsenal which had under its administration an armory. The main activities of the Arsenal appear to have been the inspecting and receiving of arms and war material manufactured by the various contractors in the vicinity. Humphreys remained in command of the post until replaced by Colonel Moses Wright, who had been the Commandant of the Arsenal in Atlanta until the fall of that city in 1864. Rifles and carbines are frequently found bearing on their breech the initials *F. C. H.*, those of their inspecting officer, Frederick C. Humphreys.

The C.S. Armory was located at Franklin and Oglethorpe Streets on the corner opposite the Muscogee Iron Works and was under the command of Captain (later Major) James Harding. The C.S. Arsenal lay between the ammunition plant and the Muscogee Railroad Shops. Greenwood and Grey's factory was on Oglethorpe Street between Franklin and Bryan while J. P. Murray was at Warren Street. John D. Gray's foundry was at the foot of Franklin Street at the river.

The machinery for the armory was mostly from Baton Rouge, Louisiana, to which had been added that from Demopolis, Alabama, and in 1864 that from Atlanta. Although General Gorgas, Chief of Confederate Ordnance, reported on December 31, 1864 that the capability of the Columbus, Georgia, Arsenal and

9

Armory "at full strength was 4,000 rifles per month," there is no record of guns actually being made at the armory and so it is assumed that this figure represents the entire activity of the Columbus area contractors and not just that of the Arsenal-Armory itself. However, at one time the government evidently planned to produce rifles, because, according to the Daily Richmond *Examiner* of October 24, 1861: "Columbus (Ga.) Iron Works will soon be in full blast casting cannon and car wheels. The building being built in which to manufacture the celebrated Mississippi rifle is fast pushing forward to completion. The rifling machinery will go into operation next week."

The manufacture of cannon referred to appears to have resolved itself into one breech-loading piece which was not cast, but bored from the steel shaft of the river steamer *John C. Calhoun*. It is said that this cannon is still to be seen in the iron works building. It is also said that this gun, although the first of its kind, was nevertheless like Hudibras' in that "Aimed at duck or plover, it shot wide the mark and kicked its owner over."

By April the Columbus Iron Works appears to have been in full operation with 12 to 15 large and small lathes, a foundry and a new blacksmith shop one hundred feet long. Here were built the engines and machinery for the gun boats *Muscogee* and *Jackson*. Belonging only in part and not attached was a large foundry, some 60 feet square, where brass field pieces were made for the State of Florida and also shot and shell for C.S. Ordnance. Attached to this was a rolling mill for the purpose of making iron suitable for gun barrels. Here were also cast small brasses for gun and sword mounts.

Also close to all this activity was the shop of Louis and Elias Haiman. These two brothers were born in Colmar, Prussia, and at a tender age were brought to Columbus, Georgia, which was then a small village. They grew with the town itself and enjoyed a modest success as

tinners. Early in 1861, however, they turned their attention to sword making.

The Columbus *Times*, September 2, 1861, contains their advertisement as follows: "WAR! WAR! WAR! Made to order: Brass Buckles and Plates, for Belts and Cartridge Boxes, and Mountings for Bayonet Scabbards. All tin and Sheet Iron Furniture for Camp Stores, which are manufactured and sold at Reasonable prices. Officers' and Sergeants' Swords, finished in the best style. Cavalry Sabres, etc. We also put bayonets to double barrel Shot Guns and Rifles. L. Haiman & Bro., next door to Dr. Ware's Drug Store."

Those interested in pursuing the sword-making activities are referred to *Confederate Edged Weapons* (Harper & Brothers, 1960)[1], but here, suffice it to say this venture was highly successful and from it the brothers branched off into associated fields. On April 1, 1862, they purchased the Muscogee Foundry and Machinery Co. from the Columbus Iron Works. The property was lot No. 124, situated at Oglethorpe and Franklin Streets and the price was $5,000.00. In this way their enterprises were enlarged to include a blacksmith shop with trip hammers, a saddle shop, a foundry and a sewing shop. These were quite an addition to the original sword factory, which was now advertising: "SWORDS! SWORDS! The best quality of Swords are now made and for sale at the Confederate States Sword Factory of Columbus, Georgia, by L. Haiman & Bro., who have large contracts for the Confederate Government. They will furnish officers swords with belt for $25 or for $22 where as many as four are ordered in one lot. Every sword is tested according to rules laid down in the manual of War."

According to Federal General Winslow's report at the time of capturing Columbus, the ". . . Muscogee Iron Works consisted of a foundry, machine shop, small-arms manufactory, blacksmith shop and 30 forges, large saddlery shop, 100 sets of flasks and one 30 HP engine."[2]

The success of the Haiman brothers con-

REVOLVER BY COLUMBUS FIRE ARMS MANUFACTURING CO.

Serial number 23, with detail of cylinder marking.

tinued. Lots to the north of their plant were purchased and a building was erected for the manufacture of revolvers. On August 26, 1862, they entered into a contract with the Confederate Government for "10,000 Colt's Navy pistols," and were advanced $50,000 by the government on the strength of the contract and their posting bond for the fulfillment of the contract. From this we gather that their enterprise had grown to such an extent that it was necessary to set up a subsidiary concern to handle the pistol-making end of the business, i.e., the Columbus Firearms Company in whose name the bond was posted.

Just previous to the revolver contract, the Columbus *Daily Sun*, of August 18, 1862, contained the following: "PISTOL FACTORY—We intimated a few days since that there was a good prospect for the establishment in our city of a manufactory of Colt's celebrated repeaters. From the advertisement of Messrs. Haiman, Bro. & Co. in another column for Machinists we are glad to chronicle the enterprise as a fact soon to be put in operation. We hail this additional branch of industry to our busy little city as an omen of coming wealth, an extension of mechanical ingenuity and enterprise. It gladdened our hearts sometime since to learn that Colt's repeaters were being manufactured at Griswoldville, Ga., on the Central railroad. But we are more glad that now so enterprising a firm as Messrs. Haiman, Bro. & Co. have brought this branch of industry nearer home. The establishment of this enterprise in connection with others in our City, suggests a thought for parents who have sons, and particularly widowed mothers.

Place your sons in some one of these shops and let them learn how to be useful to themselves, the community and a blessing to you. There are now openings for industrious boys and youths through the length and breadth of the land which parents should not permit to pass unimproved."

The same day and in the same paper, appeared an advertisement by Haiman & Brother: "Twenty-five good machinists wanted. Good wages and steady employment given."

For several months we hear nothing of the pistol making and can only assume that the firm was readying its building and facilities for this purpose. However, on March 20, 1863, another advertisement was to be seen in the Columbus *Daily Sun*: "100 gunsmiths and machinists wanted at our pistol factory in Columbus, Ga. Piece work will be given and all who remain with us over three months will have their traveling expenses refunded. Haiman, Bro. & Co." Some twelve papers were named to copy this advertisement and to send their bill to Haiman.

This would indicate that the firm had about completed tooling up and was ready to start manufacture. This is further borne out by a notice in the Montgomery *Weekly Advertiser* of May 6, 1863: "The Columbus papers state that Mr. Haiman of that city is now engaged in the manufacture of repeating pistols equal in every respect to the celebrated Colt pistols."

About the actual manufacture of the revolvers little is known, the only account being found in two letters to E. Berkley Bowie from a David Wolfson, a relation of the Haimans and a former employee in the Haiman plant. The first letter is dated May 22, 1924.

All I can give you is about the Haiman sword factory, as I was connected with them and know all the particulars. They made swords, sabres and army revolvers. We employed over five hundred people. The first sabres we made were for Clanton's regiment of cavalry of Alabama. We also made swords for officers. We had two people from Virginia who were experts in the manufacture of Colt's revolvers or pistols. They built

machinery to make the several parts of these pistols and we made quite a large number of them, in exact imitation of the Colt's army pistol. The demand for work was so large that we had to annex leather works to make the boxes and straps to carry the cartridges and also opened a foundry to make cooking utensils for the army. The proprietors of the establishment were Louis and Elias Haiman. Both are now dead. Elias Haiman went to Europe and sent material over here through the blockade.

These works were carried on until the close of the war, when the Federals came in, as the last battle of the war was fought just across the river here at what is called Alabama Heights, and they destroyed the works at that time. [April 16, 1865.]

In a later letter to Bowie dated December 14, 1929, in response to questions concerning the revolver making, Mr. Wolfson wrote:

Size of building three story brick 65 x 85 feet (pistol factory), 385 employees in all departments, manufactured only small quantity of pistols, from 300 to 500. None of the works of Haiman & Bros. was bought by the Confederate States or anyone else, they were the sole owners. The machinery and factories were burnt by Wilson when he captured the city on his raid. It was never moved out of Columbus, Ga. They manufactured cavalry sabres, 150 daily; they also made saddles, bridles, wagon covers, bayonets, mess plates, tin cups, etc. The different buildings consisted of Sword Factory, Blacksmith Shop with trip hammers, etc. Saddle Shop, Foundry, Sewing Shop. The pistol was made with round barrel and every part made by machinery. The inspecting officer was a man in Capt. Humphrey's office, I do not remember his name. I do not know if they put an "H" on the barrel of the pistols or not. Capt. Humphreys had nothing to do with the works except the detailing of the employees and receiving the finished products.

When one considers that these letters were written almost sixty-five years after the end of the war by one of its participants, the wonder is not that any of his information is wrong but that man can retain for so long a time any information that is correct. In many aspects Mr. Wolfson appears to be entirely correct but judging from the six specimens that are extant, his estimate that from 300 to 500 revolvers were made seems high. Existing examples bear the serial numbers *7, 9, 23, 46, 67* (mixed with Colt parts) and *94.* From this it might be judged that only a hundred or so were made. Otherwise it seems odd that none bearing a serial over 100 has yet appeared.

In addition to those named, several others of decidedly questionable background are known whose original parentage was definitely Samuel Colt.

The measurements of those that are still with us are: 13½ inches overall, 7½ inch barrel, of which the breech is octagon, the remainder round, rifled 7 grooves right, 6 shot, .36 caliber, brass backstrap, trigger guard and front pinsight. One has a full octagon barrel, but the remaining five are dragoon type. The markings on these guns are somewhat varied. For example: Number *46* has stamped on the barrel, *Columbus Firearms Manuf. Co./Columbus.* This is a two-line address and note that *Ga.* is not in-

Courtesy Paul C. Janke

OCTAGON BARREL BY COLUMBUS FIRE ARMS MANUFACTURING CO.

Numbered 94 and joined to a Colt frame, with detail of barrel marking.

cluded. Number *46* is found on trigger guard and cylinder, *468* on the left side of the loading lever, *S* on the bottom of the wooden grips, and *C.S.* on the trigger guard. Neither the firm name nor the serial appears on the cylinder.

Gun number *23* is stamped *Columbus, Ga.* on the barrel, and *Columbus Firearms Manuf. Co./Columbus, Ga.* on the cylinder. The serial *23* appears on various parts. The stamping on all guns, incidentally, is only about ³⁄₆₄ of an inch in height.

Also illustrated is a full octagon barreled gun which is stamped *Columbus Firearms Manuf. Co./Columbus Ga.* on the barrel. This barrel is joined to a Colt frame. The serial on the barrel is *94*.

In his letter Mr. Wolfson rather emphatically denies that any portion of the Haiman enterprises were purchased by the government. In this instance, however, records indicate that he is mistaken.

Colonel J. H. Burton comments in his diary on being in Columbus, on January 19, 1864, to inquire and report upon the expediency of purchasing the pistol factory of Haiman & Brother. At this time he reported on the subject to General Gorgas and estimated its value at $80,000. As we shall see the revolver plant was, in fact, purchased by the government in the spring of 1864 although the exact details of the sale have not been found.

The question immediately rises as to why Haiman & Brother disposed of the plant. A definite reason cannot be given but a reasonable assumption seems to be that some portion of the manufacturing process proved difficult and beyond their power to correct in a manner financially profitable. This follows if from the time they started pistol making (about May 1863) until the purchase by the government in early 1864, they had managed to turn out only about one hundred revolvers. Considering that $50,000 was initially invested, this volume does not reflect the probability of profit.

We may assume that by February 11, 1864, the purchase of the Haiman factory was an accomplished fact because of a letter by Colonel Burton, who, having been appointed by General Gorgas as the supervising officer for all revolver manufacturing, wrote Major F. C. Humphreys, the Commandant of the Columbus Arsenal, Columbus, Georgia, as follows: "Please oblige me by obtaining from Mr. L. Haiman the name and address of the person who supplied him with stocks for pistols and send it to me."[3] Note that Burton uses the past tense, saying "who supplied him with stocks." Colonel Burton wanted this information for the Spiller and Burr revolvers which he was then making for the government at Macon. Major Humphreys' reply was that one Gideon Black of Dadesville, Alabama, was the person who had previously supplied Haiman.

On February 25, 1864, W. D. Copeland, foreman of the machine shop at the Macon Armory, sent his application to Captain James Harding "in charge of pistol factory attached to the C.S. Arsenal at Columbus, Ga." for a position in said factory. Captain Harding referred Copeland's application to Colonel Burton who gave his blessing to the transfer, saying that Copeland's duties would cease as far as Macon was concerned on February 29.[4]

Shortly thereafter Captain Harding was promoted to Major, for he is so addressed by Burton on March 15 in a letter stating that Burton had "no drawings of the pistol rifling machine from the pistol factory of Spiller and Burr." He adds that he has no extra rifling machinery to send to Harding but "the machine itself is at your service to copy."[5] From this we infer that Haiman's major source of trouble may have been rifling barrels and that Harding was having the same trouble.

Upon receipt of this letter Harding then asked Burton for any extra pistol parts he might have. Burton obliged (May 14, 1864) by stating that there "is at hand at this armory (Macon) quite an assortment of components in various stages for small arms for which there is no present use here. I will turn them over to you at once."[6] That he did so is shown by an invoice sent to "The C.S. Pistol Factory, Columbus, Ga." consisting of eleven boxes of ordnance stores weighing 2,961 pounds.

On July 11, 1864, upon an additional request to Burton for machinery, Harding was sent one large gear cutter, one planer, one screw cutting lathe "No. 12," all from the Macon Armory. The cutter and planer, according to Burton, were both originally from the Atlanta Arsenal, but "should be taken up on the property return of the MSK as loaned to the C.S. Government by the State of Virginia for use during the present war."[7] This last is important as it shows that some of the Harpers Ferry machinery, seized by the State of Virginia, was sent to Atlanta and before that city fell, to Macon and finally to Columbus, Georgia.

The attempt on Harding's part to overcome whatever the basic deficiency was that caused the lag in pistol making continued for several months, but on September 13, 1864, Colonel Burton wrote the Chief of Confederate Ordnance, General Gorgas, expressing doubt whether it would be advisable to "continue the effort to complete this set of machinery and tools for pistol manufacture in view of the considerable amount of preparation yet necessary consequent upon the very limited amount of machinery tools, etc., which were on hand especially adapted to the purposes intended and which were purchased of Haiman & Brother." Burton thinks the machinery might be better applied to the Columbia, South Carolina Armory for the making of rifles. He does not think it advisable to move the Columbus pistol works to Macon as "more or less difficulty would result from the manufacture of two models in the same establishment."[8]

We have already established the approximate time the C.S. government took over the Haiman

plant. The letter confirms the fact that it was actually purchased from Haiman & Brother. It further makes plain that Burton had little faith in getting the pistol project off the ground.

In November, Colonel M. H. Wright, who had replaced Major Humphreys as commanding officer in charge of the Columbus Arsenal, wrote Burton requesting, "Ten milling machines for the service of the pistol factory under my charge." Burton replied saying that all his spare machinery had been sent to Savannah for safekeeping but he would try to get some of it back.[9]

COLUMBUS FIRE ARMS MANUFACTURING CO.
ROUND BARREL REVOLVER
Serial number 7.

Meanwhile, Confederate activities in Columbus were being reported to the Federal Army by a Lieutenant Commander Simpson, USN: "A tailor named Farrell has come in from Columbus, Ga. He says it is a place of 12,000 inhabitants and has in operation the Naval Iron Works employing 400 white hands. Haiman's factories, one of which is devoted to the manufacture of pistols and the other to swords and bayonets employs 175 white hands. The Ordnance Works of Major Humphreys is in two parts, one for shot and shell and the other makes saddles, harness, etc., for artillery."[10]

By the end of January, 1865, still no pistols were forthcoming, but by this time it was apparent, even to the Confederates, that the soft underbelly of the South was ripe for slitting. General Gorgas wrote Burton suggesting that the pistol factory be removed to Tallassee, Alabama, site of the C.S. Carbine factory. Burton dissented, saying that there were no buildings or workmen at Tallassee for such an establishment.[11]

The first indication that the activities of the Columbus pistol factory might prove fruitful comes on March 26, 1865, when Burton advises Major Harding that he is sending him a sample of the packing case used for the Spiller and Burr pistols made at the Macon Armory. He warns, "That while they are of navy size they were not of Colt's pattern," showing plainly that the guns planned at Columbus were of Colt's pattern. In a footnote he adds: "Pleased to hear you have a good prospect of turning out some pistols this month."[12]

A few days later, Federal General Winslow captured Columbus, Georgia, and the war was over. General Winslow reports: "I destroyed at Columbus, Ga.: The Muscogee Iron Works—foundry, machine shop, small arms manufactory, blacksmith shop of 30 forges, large saddlery shop, 100 sets of flasks and one 30 HP engine; Columbus Iron Works—sabres, bayonets and trace chains made here and 1,000 stand of small arms found there; Haiman's Pistol Factory—this establishment repaired small arms, made

locks and was about ready to commence making revolvers similar to the Colt's army pistol."[13]

Except for the fact that on March 25, 1865, Colonel Burton had written Major Harding that he was "Pleased to receive the sample pistol,"[14] we would conclude that no pistols were ever actually produced by the Confederate Government at Columbus, but Burton's letter gives proof that at least one was made.

It seems very unlikely that just one gun was produced and we would suppose that the "sample" gun received by Burton was one of an undetermined but small number.

We are not prepared to say categorically whether or not any of this original number still survive, nor to identify one if it were brought to us. However, we know that it would be navy caliber and Colt's pattern. It would be safe to suppose that in general it would follow the lines of the Columbus Firearms Manufactory revolvers already described, although we doubt that it would be so marked. Possibly the gun would be marked *CSA* but this is supposition. In all likelihood the serial marking would have been done with the original Haiman number stamps which are considerably smaller than those usually encountered.

FOOTNOTE REFERENCES

1. William A. Albaugh, III, *Confederate Edged Weapons* (New York, 1960), pp. 56-63.
2. *War of the Rebellion:* A Compilation of the Official Records of the Union and Confederate Armies (Washington, D. C., 1880-1901), Series 4, Vol. XLI, p. 486; hereinafter *O.R.*, followed by the SERIES, VOLUME, PART and PAGE(s). See Bibliography.
3. *Captured Rebel Ordnance Records,* MSS in National Archives, Vol. 31, 2-11-64. Hereafter: *C.R.O.R.*, Volume, date of entry.
4. *Ibid.*, 2-25-64.
5. *Ibid.*, 3-15-64.
6. *Ibid.*, 5-14-64.
7. *Ibid.*, 7-11-64.
8. *C.R.O.R.*, Vol. 49, 9-13-64.
9. *C.R.O.R.*, Vol. 29, 11-64, Vol. 31, 11-64.
10. *War of the Rebellion:* A Compilation of the Official Records of the Union and Confederate Navies (Washington, D. C., 1894-1922), Series 2, Vol. XVII, p. 773. Hereinafter: *O.R.* NAVIES, SERIES, VOLUME, and PAGE(s).
11. *C.R.O.R.*, Vol. 29, 1-30-65.
12. *C.R.O.R.*, Vol. 29, 3-26-65.
13. *O.R.*, Series 4, Vol. XLIL, p. 486.
14. *C.R.O.R.*, Vol. 29, 3-25-65.

CHAPTER 3

The Fayetteville Armory

IN MARCH 1896, Matthew P. Taylor, ex-Major, 6th Battalion, Armory Guard, wrote in the Wilmington *Messenger* (North Carolina):

The Confederate States Armory was located on what is known as Hay Mount and no trace remains, having been totally destroyed by Sherman. It overlooked the old city and was constructed by the U.S. Government prior to the war, under the immediate supervision of a Mr. William Bell as architect, who was also in charge of various army officers of high distinction as Commandants of the post. It was one of the loveliest spots anywhere in the South, was very often visited by strangers from various States and greatly admired.

Conspicuous octagonal high brick and stone towers were located at the four corners of the enclosure, while symmetrical walls and massive iron railing and heavy iron gates surrounded the premises. Handsome two-story brick and stone buildings for officers' quarters and the accommodation of the troops adorned the front and sides, while in the centre, rear and both sides were large commodious buildings used for the storing of small arms, fixed ammunition, commissary and quartermaster supplies. In the centre of the enclosure were the gun-carriage and machine shops, the former with Mr. T. S. Barratt as superintendent, who had served the U.S. Government formerly at Old Point Comfort for a number of years before the war; in the rear part of this enclosure was a large rifle-factory, containing all the rifle works brought from Harpers Ferry, Va., and handsome frame dwellings for various officers' quarters. With the exception of these last, all the other buildings were constructed of brick, trimmed with stone. Mr. Bell, a Scotchman of

national reputation, continued during the entire war as architect of all buildings. Some 100 yards from the rifle-factory were two large brick magazines for storage of powder and fixed ammunition.

Captain John C. Booth, an old army man, was placed in command of the arsenal following its surrender to the C.S. authorities by Lieutenant DeLagnel, who returned North, gave up his commission and then joined the C.S. Army. Booth enlarged the buildings and added an armory for the rifle machinery. He became ill from over-work and died, but previous to his death and, while ill, was promoted to rank of major. At his death, Captain Charles P. Bolles assumed command until Lieutenant Colonel J. A. DeLagnel was placed in command three weeks later. DeLagnel remained at the post for about six months when he returned to the field, being relieved of command by Colonel F. L. Childs who continued in command until the close of the war . . .

The authors have never seen a breakdown of what arms were on hand at the Fayetteville Arsenal at the time of its seizure from the Federals by North Carolina State troops, but the Official Records of the Union and Confederate Armies notes that, on May 25, 1861, Governor Ellis wired Confederate President Jefferson Davis: "The arms in the Fayetteville Arsenal, 27,000 stand, are placed at your disposal."

Let us now jump a bit geographically from North Carolina some two hundred miles to the northern boundary of Virginia and the confluence of the Shenandoah and Potomac rivers. On the peninsula thus formed is the little town of Harpers Ferry. The spot had gained some slight notoriety in 1859, but had been known for over half a century previous as the site of the U.S. Armory and Arsenal.

Virginia seceded from the Union on April 19, 1861. The evening before, Lieutenant Roger Jones, commanding the U.S. Armory and Arsenal at Harpers Ferry had been warned that an attempt would be made by southern military companies in the neighborhood to capture the place. He made the decision to abandon the works. After taking what he thought were the steps necessary to destroy the plant by fire, Lieutenant Jones and his forty-five United States soldiers retired to Maryland. The ensuing damage was extensive but local citizens loyal to Virginia and militiamen extinguished the fires and valuable machinery and tools as well as quantities of material and many thousands of gun parts were saved, all of which were of priceless value to the Confederacy at a later date.

General Joseph E. Johnston, C.S.A., in his narrative, states that by order of the authorities at Richmond he took charge of Harpers Ferry, May 23, 1861. Steps were taken to remove the machinery and material that had been captured to a place of safety. It was sent first by rail to Winchester, terminus of the railroad, thence by wagons to Strasburg where it was transferred to the Manassas Gap Railroad and sent to Richmond. It was not until June 18 that all of the material had been removed, but from the time of its capture by the State of Virginia in April until its removal, manufacture of arms from component parts continued.

As early as April 22, 1861, Major General Kenton Harper, commanding at Harpers Ferry, wrote to Governor Letcher of Virginia:

"From the information I have of the condition of the guns in progress of manufacture, there are components to fit readily for use from seven to ten thousand stand of arms, exclusive of those rescued uninjured from the flames. I have employed artificers to put these together, and am turning out daily several hundred minie muskets." The guns are said to have been assembled

at the Hall's Carbine factory on the south side of the peninsula which had been undamaged.

To all the material that was captured Virginia rightfully laid claim. For her own use she retained all muskets and the musket machinery which was installed in the Virginia Manufactory. The balance of the machinery, components, etc., was loaned to the Confederacy for the duration of the war. Some went to George Morse in Nashville, Tennessee, but the rifle machinery was sent to Fayetteville, North Carolina. On May 31, 1861, General Robert E. Lee, commanding Virginia State troops, wrote Governor Ellis of North Carolina:

> It has been determined by the Governor and Council of this State to send to Fayetteville machinery from the Harpers Ferry works for the manufacture of small arms. I will endeavor to expedite its delivery. Most of the machinery is at Winchester or Strasburg. The former Superintendent of the Harpers Ferry Arsenal has been sent to Raleigh to arrange for its transportation.[1]

By June 18, 1861, the Richmond *Dispatch* could report that "all the rifle works recently at Harpers Ferry have been boxed and removed to the armory at Fayetteville, N. C., where fabrication and alteration of guns will be immediately commenced."

On November 27, 1861, the Richmond *Daily Examiner* announced that "Two 75-horsepower engines have been completed for the Fayetteville Armory by James M. Talbott & Bro. The armory is to have a capacity of 5,000 rifle muskets per month."

By August 9, 1862 the Richmond *Dispatch* was able to report: "The Confederate Arsenal and Armory at Fayetteville, N. C., may be said to be in full blast; at least there is nothing pertaining to the Minie rifle and the sabre bayonet that cannot be manufactured on the spot and equal to any in the world. A few days since a large lot of rifles, manufactured at the Armory, were sent to the Chief of Ordnance, Richmond, Va. Besides making new ones and altering old ones, the force at the Armory has been engaged lately in

Courtesy Thomas Hall, Curator

THREE MODEL 1855 PISTOL CARBINES, CALIBER .58

From top to bottom, a Harpers Ferry, a Springfield and a Fayetteville. These fine specimens are presently in the Winchester Arms Museum at Hartford, Conn.

restoring and putting in order several thousand Enfield and Belgian rifles, swords, sabres and bayonets, and also several boxes of pistols received from the *Modern Greece* (a blockade runner) considerably damaged. They will soon be restored to their original appearance and condition by the industry and skill of the mechanics engaged."

This book, however, is not primarily concerned with the rifles or bayonets but with handguns, and in this particular instance, with the single-shot pistols bearing the Fayetteville mark.

Militarily speaking, by 1861 the single-shot pistol was as obsolete as the spear. Yet in her desperation for any type of weapon, the South made use of both. Fowling pieces and "Tennessee" rifles were carefully gathered up to be placed in the hands of the infantry while double-barreled shotguns and single-shot pistols were eagerly collected to arm the cavalry.

If there be doubts as to the extent that single-shot pistols were used in the early part of the war, a quick look at cartridges issued by the C.S. Ordnance Depot, Dalton, Georgia, to Captain S. H. Reynolds, Knoxville, Tennessee, on April 24, 1862, should be noted: "13,500 Navy pistol cartridges, 7,600 Army pistol cartridges and 10,000 holster pistol cartridges."[2]

From this report it would appear that as of this time there were about twice the number of Navy caliber .36 revolvers in use as the Army caliber .44. It also appears that almost a full half of the cartridges required were for single-shot holster pistols.

Three months later, on January 4, 1863, the Dalton Ordnance Depot shipped to Murphreesboro "10,000 pistol cartridges, caliber .54 and 35,000 holster pistol cartridges caliber .54."[3] The distinction between the two is not known.

By the Spring of 1863, the Confederate Ordnance Department was operating smoothly and much of the deadwood, which included single-shot pistols began to disappear. By March, Colonel Oladowski, General J. E. Johnston's Chief of Ordnance, reported the following arms on hand: "Infantry—11,869 percussion muskets, 19,942 rifled arms; Cavalry—1,363 percussion muskets, 4,649 rifles of various calibers, 1,469 carbines and musketoons, 773 double-barreled shotguns, 1,566 Colt's pattern revolvers and 42 single-shot pistols."[4] Forty-two single-shot pistols out of a total of 41,673 arms seems to speak for itself. However, the single-shot pistol, the shotgun and the flint muskets were never completely dropped from the Confederate Army, and many a Southern soldier fought through the entire war armed with nothing better.

There were a few military men in 1861 who were not fully aware that the single-shot pistol was as obsolete as the percussion pistol is today,

but nevertheless it was used to a certain extent. It is absurd to think that the Confederacy entertained any idea of producing them on any large scale any more than they considered making flintlock muskets. It is equally absurd to believe that the ingenious Southerners would have discarded single-shot pistol locks, stocks or barrels simply because they were not as desirable as the components for revolvers.

The U.S. pistol-carbine, Model 1855, is still encountered with reasonable regularity, although somewhat less than 4,000 were made at the Springfield, Massachusetts, Armory in 1856 and 1857. These pistols were .58 caliber with a 12-inch round barrel, rifled with three broad grooves. Overall length was 17¾ inches, weight three pounds, thirteen ounces. The barrel is stamped with the customary U.S. markings, i.e., *V.P.* and an eagle's head, and the date of manufacture is stamped on the tang of the breech plug. It has a blade foresight and a folding triple-leaf rear sight. The metal ramrod is of the swivel variety. All mountings are brass except for the steel lanyard ring in the butt and a steel sling swivel on the single barrel band. It is full stocked in walnut. The detachable brass-mounted shoulder stock is also of walnut. Assembled, the complete arm is 28¼ inches overall with a weight of five pounds, seven ounces. The left side of the pistol stock is stamped with an inspector's mark as are all United States military arms. Numerous assembler's numbers appear on the metal and brass parts, even on the breech end of the barrel and breech plug itself, which peculiarity also extends to the Model 1842 arms. The butt-plate tang on the detachable shoulder stock is stamped *U.S.* The lock bears the customary Springfield Armory stampings which include the name of the armory, a spread eagle on the Maynard primer cover, *U.S.* and the date behind the hammer.

Experimental production of the pistol-carbine was first undertaken at the Harpers Ferry Armory. Although the exact date has as yet to be established, it was apparently in 1854 or

1855, but judging from a comparison of the component parts of the Harpers Ferry pistol-carbine and those made at Springfield, it is likely that many, if not all, had a common parentage to the point that when disassembled, it would be impossible to say whether any one part was made at Harpers Ferry or Springfield. Identical die or assembly stamps are common to the two.

The .58 caliber Harpers Ferry pistol had a 12-inch barrel, semi-octagonal at the breech, rifled with three broad grooves. The overall length was 18 inches, brass mounted and full stocked. As can be seen, the two pistols were essentially the same. The only basic difference was that the lock on the Springfield contained a Maynard primer while the Harpers Ferry lock did not. Thus, the inletting of the stock behind the lock plates on the two guns was different, it being unnecessary in the Harpers Ferry to accommodate those lock portions which activated the primer. If records exist relative to the production of the Harpers Ferry pistol-carbine, they have not been found and if the survival ratio is indicative, production must have been small.

First published notice of the Fayetteville pistol-carbine appeared in an article in the December, 1911, issue of the *Magazine of Antique Firearms* by the late Richard D. Steuart, dean of all Confederate researchers. According to this source, a fine specimen was to be found in the "Lawrence" collection. Since the publication of Steuart's article, mention has been made of similar guns from time to time but on an infrequent basis.

The Fayetteville pistol follows the Harpers Ferry model in all particulars with the exception of its markings. The barrel does not and never did bear the familiar *V.P.* and eagle U.S. marking. Instead it is stamped at the breech with the letters *E.P.* (or *E.F.*). The identification of the initials is unknown. The underside of the barrel is stamped *D.A.* and the interpretation of these initials is also unknown. Although various as-

sembler's stamps appear on the metal work, there is no inspector's stamp on the stock itself.

The lock is of the highwall variety such as is found on the Richmond muskets or Fayetteville rifle of 1862 but is of course considerably smaller. It was never milled for the Maynard primer and the stock does not indicate that it was ever inletted for the primer mechanism. The lock is deeply stamped with a spread eagle, but this is not identical to that found on the 1863 Fayetteville rifle. Moreover, the Fayetteville eagle faces to the right, while the eagles on the U.S. models face left. Beneath the eagle

Courtesy William A. Albaugh, III

FIRST MODEL FAYETTEVILLE "HIGHWALL" RIFLE LOCK

are the letters *CSA*. These letters are not stamped with the same die as appears on the 1863 rifles but are identical with the stampings on early Fayetteville highwall rifles of 1862. It is noted in this stamping that the *S* is not inverted and the letters are all in line, not staggered. Forward of the eagle is *Fayetteville*, apparently stamped with the same die as used on all rifles. Behind the hammer is the date *1862*, but not stamped with the same die as used on the 1862 or 1863 rifles. The butt-plate tang does not appear to have ever been stamped *US* nor is it stamped *CSA* as are the rifles. The gun has a two-leaf rear sight at the juncture of breech and barrel, the long leaf containing a sighting aperture.

In summary, close examination leads to the conclusion that the Fayetteville could not have been made from a Springfield pistol, but could only have been made from Harpers Ferry parts which must have been shipped to Fayetteville along with the rifle parts and machinery.

Mention of the Fayetteville lock plates bearing the eagle with *CSA* beneath it, recalls a letter to the editor of the *National Tribune* of January 21, 1904, by W. J. Nelson, formerly A.A.Q.M., 23rd Corps, U.S.A. who assisted in the capture of Fayetteville in May, 1865. Mr. Nelson writes:

. . . May 6, at General Schofield's headquarters I met a citizen named Silas Burns, who came from Chatham County to inform General Schofield about the machinery from the Fayetteville Armory which had originally been the property of the Harpers Ferry Arsenal. May 8, I was directed to proceed to Chatham County and procure this arsenal property. Accordingly, on the morning of May 9 I took 98 six-mule teams and started for Egypt (N.C.), arriving there on May 11, where I caught Colonel Northrop, formerly Commissary-General, C.SA., trying to escape armed with three revolvers. I assured him that peace had been declared.

I found most of the Arsenal property and loaded it on my wagons to move to Raleigh. I found also other stores including one 12-pounder Napoleon gun, together with one load of musket barrels without stocks.

I notified the Philadelphia capitalists and former owners by wire, and hauled the arsenal property to Raleigh where it was loaded on cars for Washington. While gathering together the machinery, dies, etc., I found the die used to impress the image of the eagle on the Fayetteville rifle lock. It was the one used at Harpers Ferry for the same purpose but the "U.S.A." had been plowed out, and in type form "C.S.A." had been keyed in, making it read C.S.A. instead of U.S.A.

On October 27, 1904, in response to numerous inquiries, Mr. Nelson supplied the following additional information regarding the disposal of the Fayetteville (Harpers Ferry) machinery.

Now as to the machinery taken by me at Egypt I cannot find any retained copy of my report; it must be on file at the War Department. There were 98 six-mule loads of it, and it consisted of all kinds of machines for manufacturing arms, both wood and metal.

The only railroad between Fayetteville and Egypt was a coal road and on Sherman's approach to Fayetteville this machinery was loaded on coal and flat cars and carried to Egypt and was there unloaded and secreted. My diary shows that 20 wagons were loaded at Gulf and Sapona Iron Works and the balance of the 98 wagons were loaded in and around Egypt. All the natives declared it all to be the old Harpers Ferry machinery; so said also, Malette and Brown, residents of Fayetteville, lessees of Egypt's coal mines, as well as Silas Burns, a native of Cumberland County.

Upon my arrival at Raleigh, General Schofield directed me to make written report and wire General Halleck for instructions. My detailed report if it can be found will give number and kind of machines as far as I could name them. E. C. Trobridge was my master of transportation and Colonel McDonald with the 47th N.Y. acted as guard.

It would be interesting to know if any of the Harpers Ferry-Fayetteville Armory machinery still survives.

FOOTNOTE REFERENCES

1. *O. R.*, Series I, Vol. 1, part II, p. 122.
2. *C.R.O.R.*, Vol. 113, 4-24-62.
3. *Ibid.*, 1-4-63.
4. *O.R.*, Series I, Vol. XXIII, part II, p. 762.

CHAPTER 4

Griswold and Gunnison

NO STUDY of primary confederate revolvers would be complete without the story of a transplanted Yankee named Samuel Griswold, who supplied more revolvers to the Confederate Army than any other maker—and did it without fuss or muss, subsidy or bond and with almost religious regularity after he got started.

The enterprising Mr. Griswold had actually retired from a long and successful career of manufacturing cotton gins, when, in 1861, he first made pikes, then one of the most famous and certainly now one of the most cherished, of Confederate handguns. This was variously called the *Griswold and Grier, Griswold and Gunnison,* and for short, the *Griswold,* but more properly *The Griswoldville Revolver.*

Sam Griswold arrived in Clinton, Jones County, Georgia, from Windsor, Connecticut, in 1822, accompanied by his wife and the first of what was to be a large family. Having been born in Burlington, Connecticut, on December 27, 1790, Sam was then 32 years old.

The state of his finances can best be judged from the fact that he became a clerk in a store while Mrs. Griswold did tailoring work. Sam was possessed of "natural shrewdness in business and soon put up a shop and began on his famous gins." The latter were for cleaning cotton and not what some might think. It seems only natural for a man from Connecticut to have had mechanical ability and business acuity of no mean order. It is to Windsor and its environs that the beginnings of the Machine Tool Industry in this country can be traced and any

collector knows that New England was the birthplace of the famous Mississippi rifle of Mexican War fame and may recall the tales of wooden nutmegs, over which a veil of charity might be drawn.

In company with a Daniel Pratt, formerly of New Hampshire, he set up a plant in Clinton to make his cotton gins, also a sawmill and a grist mill. Mr. Pratt departed for Alabama and went into business alone at some undetermined date, although it is known that he founded the town of Prattville and designed the State Capitol Building in Montgomery.

Clinton, while a pleasant place to live, was somewhat off the lines of communication when the Central Railroad of Georgia was surveyed in 1835. For this practical reason, Sam bought 4,000 acres on the right of way, approximately nine miles south of Macon, and there established Griswoldville. Here were erected the buildings of a small but important manufacturing center—a foundry, a planing mill, saw and grist mills, a post office, a soap, tallow and candle factory, his gin plant, a laundry and 50 or more cottages for his slaves and white employees. His residence—said to be a three-story, twenty-room affair—his barns and stables, a church, a commissary and homes for three sons and five daughters completed the picture. It is said that everything used in the manufacture of cotton gins was made on the spot, with more than 100 slaves hard at work.

The foregoing is a correlation and winnowing of letters from Mrs. Ellen Griswold Hardeman, niece of Giles G. Griswold and Mrs. Claude B. Wilson, a granddaughter of Samuel Griswold, checked against excerpts from "Georgia Landmarks, Memorials and Legends," as well as the notes of Mr. Charles F. Wells, an amateur historian of some consequence in Macon.

The first evidence that Sam Griswold was interested in munitions of war is to be found in his manufacture of what have come to be known as Georgia pikes, in 1862. The war found the individual States, as well as the Confederate Government, sorely in need of weapons and on February 20, 1862, Governor Brown of Georgia appealed to the patriotism of mechanics and manufacturers to furnish the State with "pikes on a 6-foot staff." Backing up the appeal to patriotism was the added inducement of $5 for each pike finished. Evidently farsighted enough to know that cotton gins would hardly be in demand at this particular time, Sam Griswold converted his plant to the manufacture of pikes, a simple enough proposition for one of his means and facilities, because in those days most machinery could be termed "all purpose." The Confederate military records of Georgia enumerate the number of pikes received by the State of Georgia, listing each manufacturer, number and date received.[1]

On April 3, 1862, a little over six weeks after Governor Brown's appeal, it is noted that Samuel Griswold sent in 16 pikes. Evidently he was just getting started. The entry for April 15 shows 90 pikes and one week later, April 22, 100. Sam was getting into the swing of things. Further supply dates list May 17, 300; May 27, 97; June 2, 201; a grand total of 804 pikes. For two months' work at $5 per, this was no doubt a good piece of business.

Several of Sam Griswold's pikes have survived the years. All we have seen have been of the "cloverleaf" variety; a 6-foot tapering shaft with a round knob on the butt and a 3-pointed blade of which the center is 10 inches long and pear-shaped. The side blades are 3½ inches each from

center to point. The blade is stamped *S. Griswold* or *Griswold*. One is to be seen in the Battle Abbey, Richmond, Virginia. The State records of pikes received continued all through the year 1862, but Griswold's name does not appear after June 2.

From what we know of Sam, he was too good a businessman to let such a profitable undertaking cease from lack of interest and this date probably marks the time when his interest became focused entirely on revolver making. The records bear us out on this. An article appeared in the Macon, Georgia, *Telegraph* on August 5, 1862:

MANUFACTURE OF COLT'S REVOLVERS

We were equally surprised and gratified on Saturday last, at the sight of a Colt's Navy Repeater, made at the machine shops of Messrs. Griswold, at Griswoldville, about 12 miles from Macon.

The weapon had just passed the inspection of the Confederate Superintendent of Armories at this place, and a contract had been made for as many as the manufacturers could produce, which they thought would be, for the present, about five a day. The pistol, to our inexperienced eyes, was as well finished as those made by the patentee himself and we have no doubt equally as efficient. These weapons are designed for the cavalry service.

The specimen before us was the first fruit of the skill and inventive ingenuity in elaborating machinery and tools for the purpose of men who had never seen a pistol shop, or a single tool or piece of machinery for making them. The machines now in use have all been contrived and built since last March, and the force of the establishment diverted from the manufacture of cotton gins to the making of Colt's revolvers, with the well-known resources and enterprise of the concern. We need not say the business under their hands will grow to meet any demand likely to be made upon them. . . . This is a strong illustration of the power of the South to supply her

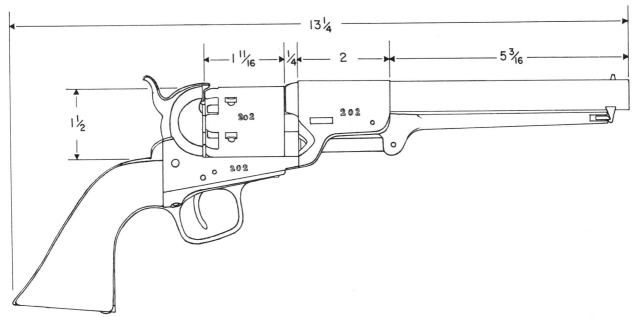

Drawn by W. E. Codd, from the Collection of Hugh Benet, Jr.

A GRISWOLD AND GUNNISON REVOLVER

Serial number 202 was used as the model for this drawing, and it seems to be the exception that proves the rule, in some respects. It is marked with cryptic mark K on frame, cylinder and barrel, according to the system generally used. The serial number is used as both a primary and secondary number, appearing on the right side of the frame and the rear of the barrel housing, inside the grips and on the hammer, on the rear flat of the rammer lever, on the barrel key, the trigger guard and the butt. Figure 2 is found on the trigger and the hand, and G is stamped between the holes for the frame studs on the barrel housing. The "fault" lines or twist of the cylinder may be seen only under a magnifying glass, and then only by exercising the imagination. Obviously, number 202 was made while Griswold was still developing his system of production, and certain refinements in markings were bound to occur in later weapons. This is the earliest numbered Griswold and Gunnison for which the authors have a complete description.

own wants. We certainly had no idea that a manufactory of Colt's pistols would spring up near Macon in 1862.

Spring of 1862 brought a serious threat to Savannah from the sea and fearful lest valuable ordnance stores there fall into enemy hands, Colonel (later General) Gorgas, Chief of Confederate Ordnance, ordered their removal to Macon, Georgia, 183 miles inland.[2]

Later, Macon was to become one of the largest Confederate Ordnance centers, but in the early part of 1862 there were no government establishments there.

It now becomes necessary to introduce another character into the story. This is Captain Richard E. Cuyler, who in 1861 and 1862 was in charge of C.S. Ordnance at Savannah, Georgia.

Captain Cuyler arrived in Macon around May, 1862, and purchased the old Finlay Iron Works, lock, stock and barrel, even to the mechanics and timekeeper[3] and went about setting up the C.S. Arsenal as he had been instructed to do. He also took over the establishment of D. C. Hodgkins and Sons who were gunsmiths.[4] Walter Hodgkins, one of the "Sons," was to become one of his most valued employees and later it was he who was responsible for the inspection of the Griswoldville revolvers.

After locating in Macon, it is probable that one of the first things Cuyler did was to seek contracts for arms, accouterments, etc. Less than a month after his arrival, he wrote Gorgas concerning a proposed revolver manufactory at Griswoldville. We do not have this letter, but we do have Gorgas's reply which is dated May 19, 1862: "Capt., You are hereby authorized to receive from Messrs. Griswold & Gunnison, all the revolvers they can make in eight months, and pay $40.00 for each complete; they must stand the usual tests, and be of good workmanship."[5]

Cuyler passed this information on to Griswold and received this reply: "Dear Sir, In answer to your communication of yesterday would say that we shall not be able to deliver you more than a specimen of our revolvers within the next two months. After then, we expect to finish and deliver between 50-60 per week regularly. As required by our contract we shall endeavour to make an article that will stand your thorough test, and of as good workmanship as the hands we have and can procure, can give them. Very respectfully, Griswold & Gunnison."[6] After reading so many contracts which promised any amount of anything, to be delivered at anytime starting tomorrow, we find the letter of Sam Griswold particularly refreshing. Sam makes no promises except that he will do his best.

A most illuminating document comes to us in the form of a letter to Captain Cuyler from Walter Hodgkins dated July 16, 1862.

Dear Sir: According to your instructions I repaired to Griswoldville yesterday noon for the purpose of showing defects in Colt's Pattern Pistol exhibited to you, and to give such other information as would be necessary to make the pistols efficient and suitable for ordnance purposes. After making the necessary comparisons of the components I proceeded to examine their mode of construction. I found 22 machines worked by 24 hands, 22 of whom are Negro slaves. They have about 100 pistols in progress.

The barrels are forged from ordinary 1-inch-square bar iron. The cylinders are cut from ordinary round bar of sufficient size. I cannot approve of this process, but the proprietors feel confident that they will stand the required test. At their request I have brought up barrels and cylinders which I will subject to severe proof with your permission.

I demonstrated to the foreman the process of case hardening, tempering springs, and tinning steel without the use of acids and described the manner of blueing. I also enjoined on them the importance of high polish on the inside of the barrel to prevent the ball slipping and reducing the liability to foul.

I think they will require the services of more practical mechanics, particularly for the assembling and also think it will be necessary to subject each pistol to proof, and close examination.[7]

From this we know that on July 16, 1862, Sam Griswold had about 100 pistols underway, that he had a factory housing 22 machines operated by 24 hands of which 22 were slaves. This then was the original plant arrangement with which he hoped to turn out fifty to sixty revolvers a week and most amazingly, he did!

On July 18, Hodgkins set about the "proving" of the barrels and cylinders, and on this date wrote to Cuyler:

Sir, By your direction I proceeded this morning to prove the Colt's pattern cylinders and barrel. I had prepared false breech and clamps (weight 4 pounds) for the barrel which rested upon the ground. 1st Charge, 55 grains rifle powder, 2 round balls, and 2 wads. Results favorable, but discovered opening between breech and barrel, causing windage on top of resistance.

2nd Charge, 82 grains rifle powder, 2 conical balls and 2 wads. Result—bursted. The cylinder rested upon an iron ring (to avoid the ratchet)—perpendicular. Each chamber stood the proof of 27 grains and one ball. When we found it impossible to fire the whole together, and to cause some additional resistance, we placed 2 pounds of weight upon the ball and top of chamber. 1st chamber stood, 2nd—bursted.

I present herewith both cylinders and barrel that the nature of the iron may be properly inspected. I will also state the English proof charge is 120 grains Provisional (before the barrel is turned), 75 grains Definitive (after finished).[8]

Recommendations were evidently made and followed, for in the proving of August 4, considerable improvement is noted in a letter of Hodgkins to Cuyler: "By your direction I proceeded this day to prove 3 gun barrels forged at the Arsenal, also the Colt's pattern pistol barrel furnished by Messrs. Griswold & Gunnison. The gun barrels stood all the tests we gave them up to 465 grains with 2 wads and 2 balls. 232 grains is all that is required. The pistol barrel also stood every test we gave it from 55 grains to 165 grains (the latter filled the barrel to within about ¾ inch of muzzle) with 2 balls well packed. Believing it impossible to burst either of the above by fair means, we deemed the above sufficient."[9]

Although some "100 revolvers were underway" as far back as July, 1862, the finished product was not forthcoming until October 14. On this date, Lieutenant R. Milton Gary, later in charge of the C.S. Arsenal, Belona, Virginia, near Midlothian, Virginia, but then Inspecting Officer, Artillery and Ordnance, wrote Cuyler:

I have the honor to report that in obedience to your verbal order of the 12th, I on that day, and on yesterday, inspected twenty-two revolving pistols mfged. after the model of the Colt's Navy Pistol and submitted by Messrs. Griswold and Gunnison.

Each pistol was taken apart and each part carefully inspected. They were then subjected to the following powder proof. Each barrel was fired separately with 54 grains of powder and 2 bullets.

Such as stood this test were then adjusted to the cylinders and the pistols fired, some with 1 bullet and some with 2 bullets, the cylinders being charged to their fullest capacity.

The barrels of three of the pistols bursted. One was found deficient because of a defect in the casting of the base, another because of a broken

hand spring, another for a bursted tube or cone and another because the ramrod catch was broken off.

The deficiencies of the last mentioned three will be repaired so as to pass inspection.

I therefore report that 18 out of the 22 pistols inspected by your order, as above, have passed inspection.

Numbers on pistols inspected: 3, 5, 9, 10, 11, 12, 15, 19, 20, 21, 22, 23, 24, 25, 26, 27, 28, 29, 30 (1), 30 (2), 31, 32. Numbers 18, 20, 22, and 32 rejected.[10]

Courtesy Miles W. Standish

CYLINDER MARKING

This Griswold and Gunnison cylinder clearly shows twist or "fault" lines.

There were numerous gaps between the serials up to No. 19, an indication of considerable trouble at first and probably a large number of discards. From No. 19 on, the numbers run consecutively, showing that the manufactory was getting into more efficient operation. Two pistols were numbered 30, differentiated by secondary numbers 1 and 2.

On October 22, 1862, another letter from Lieutenant Gary to Major R. M. Cuyler, C.S.A., Commander of the Arsenal at Macon, Georgia, said:

On Monday last, the 20th, Messrs. Griswold & Gunnison submitted for inspection, 22 of their pistols, numbers from 30 to 54 both inclusive. I have completed the inspection on the following results. Nos. 36, 39, 41, 48 and 52 found to be fit for service. The cylinder of No. 40 burst in proof. The remainder were rejected for various defects in their parts such as want of temper in hand springs and bolts—a broken hand spring in proof—ratchet too short—main spring too short so as to be displaced by the recoil on discharge of pistol, or an improperly secured basepin. The proof (powder) was the same hithertofore applied to a similar lot by your order.[11]

The Griswoldville plant was desirably located, being on a railroad deep in southern territory, and so comparatively safe from enemy raids which so often interrupted other operations. But like all other Confederate enterprises, Griswold and Gunnison were plagued by lack of material. In the letter from Superintendent Hodgkins to Captain Cuyler, dated July 16, 1862, already cited, Hodgkins verbally shook his head over Griswold and Gunnison's extensive use of iron for their revolvers in place of steel.

Another letter dated December 1, 1863, from recently promoted Lieutenant Colonel Cuyler to Major W. R. Hunt, of the Nitre and Mining Bureau, seems to vindicate the far-sighted Sam Griswold, and throws a good deal of light on the capacity of Confederate basic industry:

The foregoing bill of iron is urgently needed at this Arsenal to supply Messrs. Griswold & Gunnison, contractors for making Navy revolvers. When the iron is furnished please let me know cost price. From Shelby County Iron Works, Shelby County, Alabama. 7,000 lbs. 2-inch round iron, 11,000 lbs. 1-inch square iron, 2,000 lbs. 1½-inch square iron, 3,000 lbs. 1¾ x ⁷⁄₁₆ iron, 1,200 lbs. ¾ x ½ iron, 1,800 lbs. ¾ x ⅜ iron, 2,000 lbs. 1 x ½ iron, 600 lbs. ⅝ x ¼ iron, 400 lbs. ⅝ x ³⁄₁₆ iron, 1,000 lbs. ½ inch-square iron, 4,000 lbs. ½-inch round iron, 5,000 lbs. 5-inch round iron.[12]

The fact was that iron was not plentiful, even in the small quantities Cuyler wanted for Griswold. On August 15, 1862, Cuyler wired Gorgas as follows: "Will you give Messrs. Griswold & Gunnison, Contractors for Colt's Revolvers, an order on C. T. McRae, Selma, for iron?"[13] It was September 4 before McRae, Agent, could reply, "Capt., Absence for 3 weeks from this place has been the cause of my not answering your letters of the 16th and 18th ultimo. I have today forwarded to the Shelby Co. Iron Works your order for the wrought iron for Messrs. Griswold & Gunnison, and will ship you 8 tons (a carload) of pig metal by the 1st boat after tomorrow. The Shelby Iron Co. is putting up a new furnace to run with cold blasts. It will be done in about 60 days, when they will turn out 7 tons No. 1 cold blast charcoal iron per day."[14] A receipt dated September 29, shows that Cuyler paid $327.60 for a carload of pig iron whose weight was 16,380 pounds, and $22.60 for railroad freight from Selma.[15]

The difficulty in transportation was not a minor item either. Cuyler's standard form letter for coal, coke, or iron from Selma was as follows:

I have sent in charge of a special messenger crates to be filled with (coal, coke, or iron) in Selma, Alabama. The crates will be loaded in platform cars, four on each, and are mounted on wheels so that they may be hauled across (Montgomery or Columbus) and put on board a steamer for Selma. In this way I will avoid breaking bulk at Montgomery and Columbus. Should the agent have any difficulty in getting cars on which to load the crates at (Montgomery —Columbus), I beg that you will assist him to get them. It is a matter of utmost importance to have (coal, coke or iron) at this Arsenal.[16]

Iron was not the only metal that was hard to come by. Upon first reaching Macon, Cuyler was in such urgent need of brass that he requested permission from Richmond to appeal to the patriotism of the local churches to "loan" their church bells for Arsenal purposes. On May 7, he was told by Gorgas, "Capt., Your letter of the 30th ulto. has been received and contents noted. Get your works at Macon into operation as soon as possible, and get up 12, 4 gun batteries complete. Bells may be called for to be replaced at the close of the war."[17]

Accordingly, the local churches were solicited to donate their bells to "The Cause." The results were gratifying. To quote a few, Cuyler received a welcome note from J. E. Evans, Pastor, Methodist Church, May 12, "This is to inform you that by order of the Methodist E. Church Mulberry St., of this city, their church bell is hereby placed at the control of the War Dept. of the Confederate States of America. It will be delivered when called for by a duly authorized agent."[18]

And to Cuyler from J. L. Jones, of Christ Church, Macon, May 26, "At a meeting of the wardens and vestry of Christ Church held this P.M., it was unanimously resolved to tender to you for the use of the Govt., their church bell. It is therefore at your disposal whenever you consider the exigencies of the country requires it."[19]

It is no wonder that Woodrow Wilson in speaking of the Confederacy said, "No cause not of a religious nature had ever been so passionately or wholeheartedly embraced by a people." These bells were gladly accepted by the Arsenal, melted down to make cannon and sword and bayonet hilts, and undoubtedly a portion of them went to supply Sam Griswold's factory. Those fortunate enough to own one of these revolvers may have a portion of these church bells in their possession.

During the three-year period that Griswold and Gunnison were in operation (October, 1862 to November, 1864), average production was about 100 pistols per month, for which the Government paid $40 at first, later raising the price to $50.

In Volume No. 33, Captured Rebel Ordnance

Records, the entry dated January 1, 1863, gives an "estimate of funds needed for purchase of Navy revolvers" at the Macon Arsenal:

Needed for April, 1863 ....$ 6,000
Needed for May, 1863 6,000
Needed for June, 1863 6,000
Needed for July, 1863 6,000
Needed for August, 1863 10,000
Needed for September, 1863 12,000
Needed for October, 1863 12,000
Needed for November, 1863 10,000
Needed for December, 1863 10,000
Needed for January, 1864 10,000

The total of these monthly estimates divided by $50 for each revolver to be purchased would indicate that 1,760 revolvers would be delivered in the latter 10 months of 1863. During this period, however, the Macon Arsenal was also purchasing the .36 caliber Navy revolvers made by Spiller and Burr in Atlanta, and so the rough figure of 1,760 revolvers probably would apply to the total produced by both Spiller and Burr and Griswold and Gunnison.

As we know Spiller and Burr's output during this period was in the neighborhood of 760, the balance of 1,000 is probably a pretty close estimate of the number of guns turned out by Griswold and Gunnison during the 10-month period.

This 100-per-month production appears to have been more or less steady throughout the entire three-year period the firm was in operation.

By interpreting the reports that have survived and by means of simple arithmetic, it would appear that the actual date of delivery of any revolver to the C.S. Government can be determined. Making due allowance for rejects, but with the knowledge that all weapons were numbered consecutively, the following should be of interest to the owner of a Griswold, and date its delivery within three months.

1862	Guns per day	Guns per month	Delivered Serial Numbers Total
July	2	25	25
August	3	75	100
September	3	80	180
October	3	100	280
November	4	105	385
December	4	120	505
1863			
January	5	135	640
February	"	"	775
March	"	"	910
April	"	"	1045
May	"	"	1180
June	"	"	1315
July	"	"	1450
August	"	"	1585
September	"	"	1720
October	"	"	1855
November	"	"	1990
December	"	"	2125
1864			
January	5	135	2260
February	"	"	2395
March	"	"	2530
April	"	"	2665
May	"	"	2800
June	"	"	2935
July	"	"	3070
August	"	"	3205
September	"	"	3340
October	"	"	3475
November	"	"	3500

On November 1, 1864, Atlanta, Georgia, was occupied by General W. T. Sherman, U.S. Army. On this date Sam Griswold also was exhibiting the same farsightedness which to this point had brought him success. Sam saw the shadow of coming events, and so seeing, took his pen in hand and wrote Colonel Burton of the Macon Armory to the effect that he no longer saw any benefit to be gained from ownership of his pistol factory. He preferred that the C.S. Government either rent or lease his "machinery and Negro workmen, etc., for the manufactory of pistols."

On November 1, Burton wrote Gorgas, Chief of Ordnance, enclosing the "letter from Mr. Samuel Griswold."[20] Burton was against the government taking over this factory but proposed instead, "To raise the prices paid to Griswold to justify his continuing of the work. I know the price paid hithertofore for pistols made at these works is much under that paid to other contractors."

On November 11, 1864, General Sherman began his destructive march from Atlanta to the Sea. His columns were spread to a width of 40 miles. Their effect on anything in their paths was very much like that of a railroad train coming in sideways. Damage done by his raiders is beyond calculation, and even after almost one hundred years the effects remain, spiritually and physically.

A small division of Confederate General Joe Wheeler's cavalry pegged away at the advancing columns, and at Macon a forlorn hope of Georgia Home Guards and Militia made a fruitless attempt to cut the huge serpent in two. Included in this force were the Rigdon Guards of Augusta, Georgia. The serpent was not cut, but it recoiled and Macon was spared the torch.

The State Militia was composed of workers, old men and boys against veteran U.S. soldiers! The battle of Griswoldville was fought on a little knoll, about a mile east of the town. The dead were buried on a nearby hillside and were never disturbed after that, remaining there to this day in unmarked graves. The fighting was fierce, the casualties heavy on the southern side, light on the northern side, and there never was any doubt of the ultimate result.

In the Official Records of the War of Rebellion we find a report that, "The pistol factory at Griswold Station was destroyed by the 10th

Ohio Cavalry," and Colonel Murray, 3rd Union Kentucky Cavalry, reports, "We destroyed a pistol factory at Griswoldville." General Kilpatrick writes, "The pistol factory at Griswoldville that we destroyed was very large and valuable."[21] There can be no question that the pistol factory was thoroughly destroyed, regardless of who did the actual job.

A newspaper account of the time states, "Every house in Griswoldville was burned by the enemy except Mr. Griswold's house, the residence occupied by Col. Grier, a few Negro houses bordering on the branch and a small frame building occupied by one of the operatives of the mill." One wonders how these escaped the torch. Certainly it was not through compassion. The best reason seems to be that the large houses were used as division headquarters with staff horses stabled on the verandas.[22]

The battle of Griswoldville Station was fought November 22, 1864, and this date marks the end of all pistol manufacturing. However, on February 21, 1865, three months later, General Gorgas wrote Colonel J. H. Burton of the Macon Armory, placing him in charge of various Confederate armories and private contractors.[23] Included in this list is the name of the Griswold and Gunnison contract revolver plant. Remember, however, communications were slow in those days. Evidently Gorgas was not aware that the factory had been destroyed beyond all hope of resurrection.

A month later, or on March 21, 1865, we find a letter from Burton to Colonel Cuyler, Commander C.S. Armory, Macon, Georgia, advising Cuyler that "the pistol manufactory of Mr. A. W. Gunnison" is being placed under his supervision by the "Chief of Ordnance" (Gorgas). Burton is "sure you will cooperate with me in getting Gunnison started again."[24]

On March 29, 1865, Burton again comments to Colonel Cuyler on the possibility of restarting Griswold & Gunnison, but this is the last

official reference found.[25] As this was written less than two weeks before General Robert E. Lee's surrender of the Army of Northern Virginia at Appomattox, Virginia, there is slight likelihood that operations were ever resumed at Griswoldville and it is pretty certain that the last revolver was turned out prior to November 20, 1864. In view of the destruction that followed the battle of Griswoldville, no other conclusion is possible. In one last letter from Burton, however, written March 31, 1865 to "Messrs. Rigdon & Ansley, Pistol Mfgrs., Augusta, Ga." he notes that ". . . your establishment has been placed under my supervision by Col. Gorgas, making me responsible for the amount of work produced by your firm. . . ."[26]

Burton wants to know if Rigdon-Ansley ". . . are now actively employed, and if so, what is the number of pistols turned out weekly or monthly, and what assistance do you require to produce maximum results?"

We have the advantage of time over Burton and we know (although he did not) that the operations of Rigdon and Ansley were as dead as those of Griswold. We also know from his record that Colonel Burton was no fool and must have seen the handwriting on the wall as clearly as did old Sam Griswold. One cannot help but feel an intense admiration for a man who can write such letters so close to the obvious end.

Having heard something of their background, let us take a look at the revolvers themselves. Except for an unimportant deviation, all known Griswolds conform to type. All are .36 caliber, 6-shot brass-framed imitations of the third model Colt dragoon. All had round barrels and most had the dragoon-type part octagon barrel housing, although it was round in the early model. This is the only distinguishing difference between any of them for otherwise they are as alike as any hand-finished items can be. The standard measurements of all Griswolds known, making due allowance for minor variations

Courtesy Tom Parvin

TOP AND BOTTOM VIEWS OF A GRISWOLD

Serial number 1455. These show the location of primary serial numbers, and the bottom view shows the location of a secondary serial number.

which crept in during manufacture and those due to the wear and tear of war and approximately 100 years, are as follows:

The barrel was round and 7½ inches in length, somewhat roughly finished, with numerous tool marks. It was rifled with six lands and grooves with a right gain-twist. Compare this with a Colt or Leech and Rigdon. The barrel frame was round or part octagonal, 1¹⁵⁄₁₆ inches long. The foresight was a brass pin. The barrel wedge was made without a spring and had a secondary serial number. The loading assembly closely resembles that of a Colt navy, with a Navy-type catch. Because the cylinders were made of twisted iron, the twist is usually quite apparent. They are 1¾ inches long with a diameter of 1⁹⁄₁₆ inches. The twist, incidentally, always runs from left to right. A safey device consists of pins between the cylinder nipples, similar to those used on Colt's pistols.

The frame was cast red or yellow brass, without a capping channel, and generally shows tool marks. Trigger guards and backstraps are also cast red or yellow brass, with no polishing out of tool marks. Hammers were provided with rollers. Grips were made of walnut, evidently not properly seasoned, for in most cases surviving guns are found with grips that appear to be

too small. This is believed to be due to the shrinkage of the wood through the years. The full serial number of the gun is usually to be found penciled or stamped on the grip under the backstrap and, in some cases, the secondary serial is stamped on the butt.

The overall length of these weapons is about 13 inches. The handle of the weapon is usually at a greater angle to the frame than is that of a Colt, giving the impression that the gun has been used as a club, although the angle varies from piece to piece. The measurements are so nearly the same on all surviving guns that one wonders why collectors believed for years that the weapons were the products of many factories or plants throughout the South rather than having all come from one place. This erroneous theory was corrected by Richard D. Steuart's article "The Confederate Colt" which appeared in *Army Ordnance*, September, 1934.

Ever since it has been established that all these revolvers came from Griswold's factory they have been referred to as "Griswold and Greers," this label having been given them by E. Berkley Bowie, one of the first serious Confederate collectors, in the late 1920's. The name comes from information Mr. Bowie had received from Mrs. Ellen Griswold Hardeman of

Macon, Georgia. Mrs. Hardeman, niece of Giles G. Griswold, one of Samuel Griswold's three sons, wrote Mr. Bowie March 13, 1923, to the effect that immediately after the Confederacy was formed, "Uncle Giles" had been sent to Montgomery, Alabama, to lease the Griswold plant to the Confederate Government. According to this source, "Uncle Giles" died on his way home and "my uncle-in-law, E. C. Grier, took charge of the whole business."

Research into E. C. Grier was not productive and what part, if any, he played in revolver making is not known. We do find record of a Grier and Masterson who on March 28, 1862, delivered 80 pikes in response to Governor Brown's proclamation of February 20, 1862.

There is no further mention of Grier and Masterson after April 10, 1862, when they delivered 33 additional pikes. Whether the "Grier" of this firm be the one in question we are not prepared to say.

While we hesitate to change such an established label as "Griswold and Grier," we feel compelled to say that there is no official correspondence that refers to them by this name. Officially, that is by Confederate Ordnance Officers, they are referred to only as "Griswold and Gunnisons," and that is what they should be called.

Gunnison had long been in Griswold's employ and in such a responsible position that as early as 1855 he was empowered to sign all the

Courtesy J. L. Robinson

GRISWOLD AND GUNNISON REVOLVERS

An exceptional pair, consecutively numbered 1037 and 1038.

firm's official correspondence, *Sam Griswold/per Gunnison.* It would seem likely to us that it was Gunnison who was in charge of actual production at the Griswoldville plant. Of the man personally, nothing is known.

Griswold and Gunnison markings are more or less standard, so the word "all" is used in describing them, although in the list of serials which follows will be found exceptions from which the reader may draw his own conclusions. All are stamped with the full serial number on cylinder, barrel frame and lock frame. Some are stamped on the right side, others on the left. From ordnance reports, it would seem that each serial plainly applies to the total number of revolvers made up to the time of stamping—although not necessarily accepted by the C.S. Ordnance Department.

Most guns also bear a sub-serial number which is usually the last, last two, or first and last numbers of the primary serial. For example, if a gun's serial were 3421, the sub, or secondary serial, will be either 1, 21, or 31. This secondary number is to be found on all the following parts —underside of trigger guard, backstrap, loading lever, cylinder pin, barrel wedge, even on the hammer and hand. It will not be found on those parts stamped with the full serial number. This secondary number can have but one meaning. The three main parts were first put together— barrel, frame and cylinder. To these main parts were fitted the balance of the smaller parts, each being stamped with a portion of the initial serial to show that it definitely belonged to that particular gun.

Close examination reveals that, in general, all brass parts contain a "bench-mark" in the form of a Roman numeral. This is cut or chiseled into the brass with a sharp-pointed tool. It is not stamped. This numeral can be found on the side of the backstrap and on the underside of the trigger guard and frame. As it appears only on brass parts, it probably applies to some method

of brass casting. We have never found this numeral to be higher than XXXV (35). The early pieces do not all show such marks. It is believed that this marking applies in some way to the number of brass castings which had been made from a particular mold. Possibly the frame, trigger guard and backstrap (for any one gun) were all cast at the same time in different but corresponding molds. Each casting was then given a bench mark. After thirty or more castings of each series, a new mold was made and the process repeated.

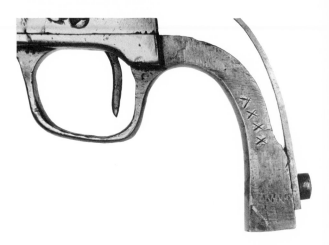

Courtesy Miles W. Standish

ROMAN NUMERALS ON TRIGGER GUARD
EXTENSION

These marks were concealed by the grip. Serial number 2860.

There is still another mark to be found on all guns. In at least one instance, this mark has positively identified a gun (otherwise devoid of markings) which was declared by many who should have known better to be a "fake." It is an initial found on all major parts; on the barrel it appears on the underside near the loading lever lug; it is found on the side of the backstrap, on the underside or rear of the frame and on the upper part of the trigger guard where it joins the frame as well as on the cylinder between the nipples near the safety pin. All weapons bear this cryptic mark throughout. There is

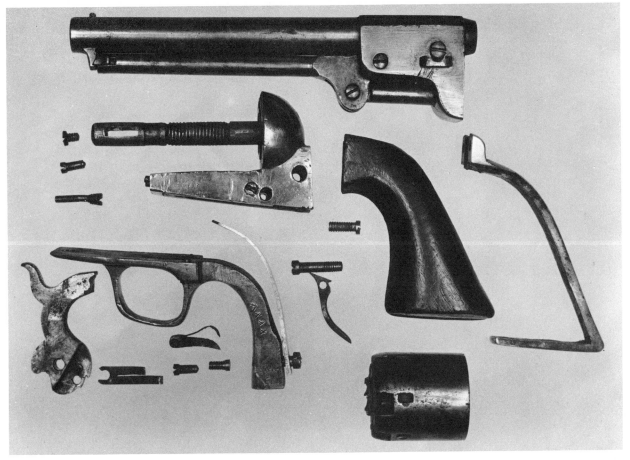

DISASSEMBLED GRISWOLD

Serial number 2860, showing components.

no mixing of this mark as is sometimes found to be the case with the numbers.

The term "cryptic" is used to describe this stamp because while it has been found in some cases to be a plain large letter *A*, more usually it takes the form of a capital letter backwards. In one case it is noted as *S* (on its side) *AM*, and in another case it is found to be a series of four dashes which retain the same geometric pattern on each part. This cryptic mark has been a source of great conjecture. It was first concluded to be the C.S. Ordnance Inspector's stamp, but if so, why would it not appear on all parts of other C.S. weapons?

The assembly line of today was unknown in the 1860's. Men worked alone or in small groups. We know from accounts of other revolver manufactories that if 50 men were working in a factory, all 50 did not work on the same arm continuously until it was completed. On the contrary, first a number of rough barrels, frames and cylinders were made. After these "roughs" were completed the men were formed into several groups or teams. One man was placed in charge of each team and was held responsible for the revolver on which his team was working.

The roughs, that is, barrel, frame and cylinder, were drawn from some central storeroom in a semi-finished condition. After they were completely finished by the team, they were laid on either their right or left sides and a serial number was stamped on each of the three parts. As the balance of the parts were fitted to that particular gun, they were stamped with a portion of the serial. A four digit serial was too large to stamp on the smaller parts so the secondary serial was used. After the gun was completed, it was disassembled and the foreman closely inspected every part. He then placed his own stamp or cryptic mark upon each major part, for, remember, he was responsible for the proper working of the weapon.

Many years ago when Griswold and Gunnisons were supposed to have been made all over the South, collectors believed the cryptic mark *A* to have denoted the gun having been made at the Augusta Armory, that the *R*-backwards showed it had come from Richmond, that the *F*-backwards came from Fayetteville, and so on. This logic is not bad and naturally supported the other erroneous theory that these guns were all made at different points.

To bear out our thesis, however, is a portion of a personal letter from Edwin Pugsley, on the letterhead of the Winchester Arms Co., dated January 11, 1934:

> . . . answering your question as to what the letters stamped on the barrels and frames of the Confederate Colt's might be, would say that I have no guess. It is conventional in more or less modern arms plants to stamp a code letter on a gun signifying the man who assembled that particular arm. This is a practice that has been used at Winchester for many years from time to time and I know that it has happened in other plants. Records are kept of these various letters in case of complaints about the operation of the arm. . . .

A complete list of all Griswold and Gunnisons, giving serial numbers, both primary and secondary, Roman and cryptic marks and the side upon which the serial appears together with other miscellaneous marks, would be a welcome addition to any collector's store of data. It is, however, manifestly impossible to prepare one, if only because many Griswoldville pistols exist that we have not seen or heard of.

Griswold and Gunnison Serials are: 8, 19, 45, 46, 70, 105, 114, 117, 133, 135, 174, 202, 262, 301, 307, 365, 414, 608, 696, 752, 763, 776, 786, 817, 906, 949, 973, 993, 1041, 1101, 1146, 1209, 1321, 1369, 1415, 1471, 1472, 1474, 1477, 1486, 1493, 1505, 1510, 1514, 1516, 1550, 1554, 1564, 1576, 1635, 1720, 1750, 1782, 1802, 1822, 1844, 1852, 1862, 1863, 1915, 1934, 1978, 2040, 2044, 2093, 2096, 2110, 2116, 2127, 2145, 2184, 2198, 2231, 2246, 2273, 2282, 2363, 2365, 2389, 2394, 2419, 2437, 2457, 2470, 2614, 2651, 2695, 2696, 2708, 2763, 2855, 2860, 2909, 2922, 2941, 2987, 3085, 3094, 3106, 3193, 3235, 3334, 3355, 3399, 3424, 3447, 3606.

Cryptic marks noted are as follows: *R* (backwards), *AA, I, L* (backwards), *11-11, BB, L* (upside down), *JJ* (backwards), *M, S* (backwards), *H, K, N, A, S,* (on their side), *AM, DD, CC, J. O* and *G.* A very few weapons are found stamped *CS* or *CSA.*

Based upon known serials as compared to the total production of the factory, it appears that the survival rate of these scarce weapons is 4.1 per cent.

The war ended, the Grand Army paraded down Constitution Avenue in Washington and everyone went home. Sam Griswold, aged 75, surveyed the ashes of his holdings and said, "If I were 10 years younger, I would start again."[27] As it was, he sold his land, the grass grew over the scattered bricks of the factory walls and vines climbed the lonely stack of the foundry, standing all alone and cold in the ruins. In September, 1867, Sam passed to his reward.

In 1928, the last R.F.D. delivery was made from Griswoldville, and the Post Office founded in 1835 with Samuel Griswold as its Postmaster, ceased to be. Today Griswoldville is hard to find. It is located in an extremely isolated spot, five miles from the nearest paved road, and consists only of a few widely scattered houses. There is no store or filling station and it is literally an intersection of two narrow dirt roads by the side of a railroad whose trains no longer stop and for which there is no station. One deserted house stands at the southeast corner of this intersection. This house, about 50 years old, is built on the foundations of the old Griswold home which burned some years after the war. A mile or so to the west of what was once the town, lie the brick foundations of a large building. This in 1861-65 had been a soap manufactory.

The revolver factory stood near the northwest corner of the intersection, on the north side of the railroad. The site is now an empty field which has been plowed and replowed many times. No trace of the factory remains, although a life-long resident pointed out where the old foundry chimney had stood—all that was left of the plant after it was destroyed in 1864.

Spurred by the account of a nearby farmer having plowed up various revolver parts, several hours were spent closely examining the area. The search was rewarded by kicking up a female die from which was struck rough hammer blanks. Being of fine tool steel, it is in remarkably good condition for having lain in the ground for 90 years. This prize was well worth the hours spent. Iron revolver parts are still being found in the vicinity of Griswoldville and, thanks to Mrs. Joe Etheridge and Mr. Charles Benton, we have in our possession a number of barrels, cylinders, hammers, triggers, cylinder pins, etc. Most appear to be discards, being imperfect in one way or another. Others, however, seem perfect—only unfinished. The latter show signs of having been exposed to intense heat or fire and might possibly be parts which were in the process of being finished when the factory was burned in November, 1864.

Brass parts are rarely found. It is assumed that if a barrel or cylinder was improperly bored the piece was tossed onto the scrap pile, but an imperfect brass part was probably thrown back

into the brass pot to be melted and recast. Speaking of the brass pot, while at Griswoldville we were shown where "a large cast iron pot full of brass" had stood for many years after the war, finally to be rolled away and cast into an unused well "to get it out of the way." Undoubtedly it was this "pot" that contained the brass used for the frames, trigger guards, etc.

An enterprising young man of this section has mounted on a board the various revolver parts that he has personally uncovered at Griswoldville. At this point he has a complete revolver except for the backstrap and grips. We hasten to add, however, that all such parts are either unfinished or are obvious discards and that their original poor condition has not been improved by being in the ground so long. The cylinder is in marked contrast to the rest of the parts, being in reasonably good condition, and clearly showing its serial number, *114*.

It will come as a distinct shock to collectors to learn that the frame of this artifact is not brass at all, but iron. It is badly warped and never could have been finished, quite obviously having been a discard. Nevertheless, the fact remains that it is iron, thus proving beyond doubt that an attempt was made to manufacture these revolvers with iron frames. Whether this attempt was successful or not, we are not prepared to say, but should an iron-framed Griswold appear one of these days, it might be well to examine it closely before denouncing it as a fake.

The scarcity and desirability of Sam Griswold's revolvers today is best shown by the indisputable fact that they are being reproduced, not in ones or twos, but by the hundreds, under a different name, and in another country. Several have fallen into the hands of tinkerers, or restorers, or fakers—call these gentry what you will. These weapons now masquerade as legitimate Griswolds, but even a cursory examination will reveal them for what they are.

A quick check to make is simple but revealing. The reproductions are lighter in weight and smaller in dimensions than the original. Secondly, the barrel lug is different, as is the barrel wedge. No "restoration" examined has been correctly marked and, sad to admit, the reproductions are made out of much better materials and to more exacting tolerances than the originals.

FOOTNOTE REFERENCES

1. Clement A. Evans, ed., *Confederate Military History, Georgia* (Atlanta, Georgia, 1899), Vol. II, p. 352.
2. *C.R.O.R.,* Vol. 36, 4-25-62.
3. *Ibid.,* 4-28-62.
4. *Ibid.,* 5-27-62.
5. *Ibid.,* 5-19-62.
6. *Ibid.,* 6-2-62.
7. *Ibid.,* 7-16-62.
8. *C.R.O.R.,* Vol. 4, 7-18-62.
9. *Ibid.,* 8-4-62.
10. *Ibid.,* 10-14-62.
11. *Ibid.,* 10-20-62.
12. *C.R.O.R.,* Vol. 101, 12-1-63.
13. *C.R.O.R.,* Vol 6, 8-15-62.
14. *Ibid.,* 9-4-62.
15. *Ibid.,* 9-29-62.
16. *C.R.O.R.,* Vol. 101, 1-6-64.
17. *C.R.O.R.,* Vol. 36, 5-7-62.
18. *Ibid.,* 5-12-62.
19. *Ibid.,* 5-26-62.
20. *C.R.O.R.,* Vol. 29, 11-1-64.
21. *O.R.* Series 4, Vol. XLIV, pp. 54, 368, 508.
22. Charles F. Wells, MS in Macon Historical Society; letters to the authors, 1959. Hereafter: Wells.
23. *C.R.O.R.,* Vol. 29, 2-21-65.
24. *Ibid.,* 3-21-65.
25. *Ibid.,* 3-29-65.
26. *Ibid.,* 3-31-65.
27. Wells.

CHAPTER 5

Leech and Rigdon, Rigdon and Ansley

A HISTORIAN given access to all American history up to 1861, could have easily predicted the Civil War and that the South would lose the contest. But how many could imagine that the Confederacy, poorly prepared, ill-armed, few in numbers, would be able to stand off the overwhelming forces of the North for four long years? Superior leadership of Southern soldiers may account in part for the length of the struggle, but the heart of the fight lay with the people themselves. Private citizens, doctors, merchants —all contributed their share. Those men who made arms using iron where steel should have been used, then brass for iron, were as surely important as the men at the front.

Of these arms makers, the products of Thomas Leech and Charles H. Rigdon are eagerly sought by present-day collectors as classic examples of Confederate revolvers. They are among the best that were made in the South and, except for minor variations, they all conform to type. They closely resemble the Colt Navy model of 1851 from which they were copied. The major difference was their "dragoon type" barrel, made part round instead of fully octagon because it took less time to produce and was easier to assemble. All are six-shot, .36 caliber, with iron frames and brass backstraps and trigger guards. Most are stamped *Leech & Rigdon CSA* on the top of the barrel. Because the letter *L* in Leech and the *d* in Rigdon are almost always indistinct, beginning collectors were unable to properly decipher the stampings; therefore these arms became erroneously known as "Beech and Riggons."

Thomas Leech of the Memphis Novelty Works, a well-known sword manufacturer, was not recognized as the *Beech* in "Beech and Riggon" until the nineteen-thirties. Several letters from early dealers and collectors offering these guns exist, and in one of these the writer apologizes because the marking seemed to be "Leech & Rigdon" instead of "Beech & Riggon."

The following facts are now mentioned casually, but they should be remembered because they have a definite bearing on material to follow. Early models have the pin and ball type catch on the loading lever, which was later replaced with the usual Colt-type rammer latch. Leech and Rigdons with high serial numbers are found without the safety pins between the nipples on the cylinder. Some of the revolvers made by Rigdon, Ansley and Company, successors to Leech and Rigdon, have twelve stops on the cylinder rather than the usual six. Otherwise they are almost identical, and well they should be, having been made with the same machinery and by the same workmen.

RIGDON IN ST. LOUIS

The story of the Leech and Rigdon revolver begins before the Civil War in St. Louis, Missouri. Thomas Leech does not come into the picture at this time, but Charles H. Rigdon, machinist and scale maker, does. Rigdon was in some way connected with one Wilhelm Abel Schalk, an inventor from Cincinnati, who had Anglicized his name to Abel Shawk. On January 26, 1856, *The Daily Missouri Re-*

publican of St. Louis ran a news item entitled "The Trial of a Steam Fire Engine." That this could have any possible connection with revolver making in the South seems remote, and yet this date and the event itself mark the start of a chain of circumstances that six years later led to the partnership of Leech and Rigdon and the manufacture of their famous Confederate revolving pistols.

The paths of Charles H. Rigdon of St. Louis and Abel Shawk of Cincinnati had been approaching one another for several years, but on this date in 1856, and with this newsworthy event, we establish that their ways merged and for a time ran together because Rigdon was the engineer of the fire engine aforesaid while Shawk was the inventor-builder.

Missouri in the eighteen-fifties was wild and woolly, rough and ready for anything. In 1849 gold was discovered in California and the rush was on. Some went by sea, but those that took the overland route went through St. Louis, the last city in which one could be outfitted for the long trip West. The brewing trouble between North and South was fast approaching a boil and St. Louis was the gateway between North and South as well as between East and West.

In such a town and at such a time, a gun was a mighty handy thing to own. One might think opportunities for a gunsmith in such a locale were unlimited. A glance through the city directories shows that others were of the same opinion. A few of the gunsmiths and dealers were Jacob and Samuel Hawken, Wiget, Friede, Albright, Meier, Caspari, Kleinhern, Basler and Denk, Gemmer, Gibbons, Altinger, Freligh, Brenan, Miller, and Folson and Dimick.

Neither Abel Shawk nor J. K. McLanahan, a partner, was a Confederate sympathizer and they never purposely made any revolvers or other arms for the Southern cause. We are concerned with Messrs. Shawk and McLanahan only because of the relationship between Abel Shawk and Charles H. Rigdon, and because there is a

distinct possibility that the machinery which made the Shawk and McLanahan revolver was later used, in part at least, to fashion the Leech and Rigdon revolvers.

Rigdon first appears on the scene in Cincinnati, Ohio. He is listed in the 1843 directory of that city as a partner in the firm of Rigdon and Harmstad, scale beam manufacturers. He must have left Cincinnati shortly thereafter, for that is his first and last listing in that city.

Turning to the St. Louis directories we find Rigdon listed in 1844 as a scale manufacturer, at 14 North Second Street. According to directories that follow, his occupation as scalemaker remains unchanged although his street address changes to 75 North Second, to 5 Green, to 82 North Second and finally to 56 North Second. In 1857, however, he is listed as a machinist at 137 North Third Street, as well as a scale manufacturer at 6 North Third, and also under "Machinery and Machinists" at 6 North Third.

His advertising in the St. Louis *Daily Missouri Republican* starting on January 5, 1847, and running until December 5, 1850, states: "St. Louis Scale Manufactory, 291 North Main Street, between Green and Morgan. C. H. Rigdon, St. Louis, Mo. Manufacturer of all kinds of scales, etc. Platform scales, of all sizes, Platform counter scales, of all sizes. Platform counter scales. Hay and car scales of any size, brass and iron beams, of all sizes. Druggists and Prescription balances of all kinds. N. B. Balances, Rules, Measures, and all apparatus necessary for state or county standards, weight proved and warranted to be correct. Repairing done at shortest notice."

After all, scales cannot be made with a set of wrenches, a file and a hacksaw. His name appears in the St. Louis directory of 1859 as "Engineer, Steam Fire Engine No. 2, residence 134 Washington," with no mention of a machine shop.

The records of St. Louis and Cincinnati contain ample accounts of Abel Shawk, but perhaps a letter dated February 16, 1932, from his grandson, Harry A. Shawk, of San Francisco, California, will throw as good a light as can be found, both on the man and on the revolver known as the Shawk and McLanahan.

...As a boy living in the city of Carondelet, at 6610 Virginia Avenue, I can well remember the old revolvers which you speak of, the rifling machine of which my grandfather was the inventor, and the old rapid fire rifle which weighed some 55 pounds and was intended for use during the Civil War but which Grandfather was unable to have Congress adopt up to the close of the Civil War.

Grandfather was in business under the name of Shawk and McLanahan, for a short time in the City of Carondelet. They proposed to build revolvers but did not stay in the partnership any great length of time. This was due to the fact that my grandfather I think, sold out his interest and devoted himself to the manufacture of Steam Fire Engines, of which he was the inventor. I am in the possession of the picture of Young America, a Steam Fire Engine which grandfather built in the City of Cincinnati, same being the first type of Fire Engine ever placed on the market. This engine threw a stream of water under 200 pounds pressure, for a distance of 186 feet, with a 4-inch nozzle. When grandfather made his appearance at a large fire in the City of Cincinnati, the volunteer fire department were very much annoyed and attempted to destroy the engine, with the result that grandfather turned this powerful stream of water on them with remarkably disastrous effects.

Getting back to the firearms venture, I would like to make a statement; there seems to be some error in regard to the information that this revolver was called a Confederate Model. Abel Shawk was an ardent Unionist, a man who struggled continuously and faithfully for the preservation of the Union during the Civil War. In fact the Civil War just about finished grandfather financially as he lost the entire family fortune in the deflation which followed this unfortunate controversy between the North and South.

The old revolver which you have is very familiar to me. As a boy I had several of these models in a partially completed stage and one finished article. This gun I carried for many years on camping trips through the Ozark Mountains and I am familiar with every portion of it. This revolver was a muzzle loader of percussion type. The cylinder was bored for six charges. The barrel was seven inches long, with the rammer lever fastened directly under the barrel. The stock skeleton and main frame were made of red brass and the stock itself of black walnut.

As a young man I went to sea and followed Marine Engineering, and during the move of the family from Carondelet, to the West Coast, these valuable old family possessions were lost. I am ashamed to state that I do not possess a single memento of any of grandfather's Firearms.

Abel Shawk was a man of great character and ability. Born of Quaker parents in the state of Pennsylvania, he immigrated to the City of St. Louis with his parents. These early settlers, among whom were Pierre Chouteau and Henry T. Blow, carved out homes for themselves in the little French settlement known as Carondelet. This settlement was originally called by the settlers "Empty Pockets," which was significant of its financial state at that time.

In accordance with the customs of the times, grandfather was induced to serve an apprenticeship as a blacksmith. He and four brothers were all blacksmiths, and from what information I have been able to obtain I understand they were all experts in their line. Being big, powerful, puritan trained, they were forceful characters with deep religious instincts and well-formed ideas of right and wrong. Grandfather was a very stern man; he was not a fluent talker, but was a deep student and thinker. At the age of thirteen he made his own rifle, which was a smooth-bore gun of about .38 caliber, with a 42-inch barrel. You might be interested to know, that he drilled the bore with a flat drill which he made himself, and his motive power in accomplishing this job was a very ordinary brace. As the barrel was drilled he carefully reamed it out to make it true. The rifle, when finished, was the entire work of his own hands, and my father who is now deceased told me that he had killed squirrels with it himself in the hills back of St. Louis.

I believe that Mr. Abel Shawk is the grandfather of the present-day rapid-fire gun. The weapon which he tried to induce Congress to accept during the Civil War was a mechanical masterpiece, its only drawback being its tremendous weight as a shoulder weapon. It evidently was ahead of its times. If I remember correctly, the Henry Rifle, which was afterwards purchased by the Winchester Company, was the principal obstacle in preventing grandfather from interesting the War Department in his invention.

For a little additional information on Shawk, an article in the *Carondelet News,* of September 10, 1920, tell us: "East of the railroad tracks, and fronting on the Market Street, was the two-story stone building of the Shawk foundry and machine shop. William Shawk was a machinist and built the first steam fire engine (in Cincinnati). It was called the 'Baltic.' The apparatus was too heavy for the unimproved streets, and in running to a fire would frequently get stuck in the mud. During the Civil War, the government took over Shawk's foundry and machine shop and manufactured guns and bayonets there. . . ."

There is nothing to link Abel Shawk and Charles Rigdon prior to Shawk's arrival in St. Louis, but our theory that the two men were more than acquaintances is borne out by a letter dated March 20, 1919, from Joseph Boyce of St. Louis, former officer of the 1st Missouri Infantry, C.S.A., and also president in 1917 of the Volunteer Firemen's Historical Society of St. Louis. Mr. Boyce knew both Rigdon and Shawk. Among other things Mr. Boyce writes: ". . . Mr. Shawk built in Cincinnati, the first steam fire engine for St. Louis, of which Mr. Rigdon was engineer, and he (Rigdon) made several changes which added much to its efficiency. He and Rigdon were great friends. . . ."

About this time Shawk became connected with one J. K. McLanahan and contracted with

authorities at Carondelet, which was then a suburb of St. Louis, to build a large machine shop. Existing records cover this phase in detail, but are not included here, as they have but little bearing on the activities of Charles Rigdon. Suffice it to say that McLanahan was evidently out for Shawk's money and patent rights. Records would indicate that he got them, leaving Shawk in considerable financial straits. Their connection and joint activities were severed by court order in July of 1861.

Three questions which the records do not answer and which still remain a mystery are: (1) Who made the so-called Shawk and McLanahan revolver? (2) With whose machinery were they made? (3) What happened to the machinery afterward?

A purely conjectural answer to these questions, but one which seems logical is that Shawk, assisted by Rigdon, turned out the revolvers on machinery which belonged to Rigdon and which was rented or leased to Shawk and McLanahan. Following this same line of reasoning it is assumed that when Rigdon left St. Louis in 1859 or 1860, he took this machinery with him.

From St. Louis, Rigdon went to Memphis, Tennessee, and is listed in the 1860 directory of that city as "Charles H. Rigdon, Foreman, Pressman, Enquirer Office. Scale Manufacturer, N. S. Poplar bet. Main and 2nd, H.N.W.C. Mulberry and Pontotos."

MEMPHIS, TENNESSEE

According to Memphis directories, the arrival of Thomas Leech in that city preceded Rigdon's by several years. Leech is listed in 1855 as a clerk at 35 Front Row. The next directory, dated 1859, lists him as follows: "Leech, T. & Co., Cotton Brokers, 35 Front Row." War fever was running high then, and under "Guns and pistols etc.," we again find him as "Leech, Thomas, of Leech T. & Co., Elliott, bet. Hernando and Desoto." That Leech ever actually made any

pistols or revolvers at this time is extremely unlikely. In all probability he acted only as agent
for some Eastern firm or firms, and at least one
imitation derringer has shown up bearing the
inscription: *Thomas Leech & Co., Memphis,
Tenn.*

Obviously, with the outbreak of war Leech
found the arms business more lucrative than
cotton brokering, as witness the following advertisement in the Memphis *Appeal*, August 29,
1861: "Wanted. 10,000 lbs of old zinc, copper,
and brass immediately for military purposes.
Send it in from the country, we will pay a full
price. Thomas Leech & Co., 35 Front Row."
This advertisement plainly indicates that
Thomas Leech was about to embark on arms
making on a large scale.

It did not take Leech long to get into operation once his course was decided upon. On September 18, 1861, less than three weeks after his
initial advertisement for old brass, the following
appeared in the Memphis *Appeal*:

Memphis Novelty Works/Thomas Leech &
Co./Corner Main and McCall Sts./Memphis,
Tenn.

Established primarily for the Manufacture of
Army cutlery and brass castings of all kinds.

We are now prepared to receive and fill orders
for the following orders, viz.: Infantry swords,
cavalry swords, and sabres, artillery cutlasses
and knives. Bowie knives of every description,
bayonets for shotguns and rifles. Stirrups and
spurs of the latest and most approved patterns,
bullet moulds of all kinds. Brass mountings for
saddlery. Special attention paid to the repairs
of printing presses. Light machinery and machine blacksmithing generally. We have engaged
the services of competent workmen and will
warrant our work to give complete satisfaction.
All orders will meet with prompt attention. We
will pay a high price for all the old copper and
brass you can send in.

To this point all references have been to
Thomas Leech, Thomas Leech & Company, or

the Memphis Novelty Works. Obviously, Leech
was operating alone and no mention is made of
Charles Rigdon. We can only accept at face
value the directory's listing that he was at his
scale manufactory on Poplar just off Main Street,
three blocks above the Navy Yards. The Memphis Novelty Works was several blocks down
Main Street.

Memphis was, in those days, teeming with
war activity. With Rigdon's background it seems
rather foolish to assume that he was peacefully
engaged in manufacturing druggist's scales
while others with less experience planned to
make the scales that would balance the fate of
the nation. It may be assumed that Rigdon and
Leech became connected long before we can
establish that fact through records. A man who
had been a cotton broker for years would not
be able to open overnight a shop capable of
doing all Leech claimed in his initial advertisement for the Memphis Novelty Works.

It is not too unreasonable to suppose that Rigdon reached Memphis well equipped with machinery—that Leech, who had plenty of money
from the cotton brokerage, hired both Rigdon
and his machinery and opened the Memphis
Novelty Works, but later realized his inability
to operate properly without having the required
technical background and took Rigdon in as a
full partner. This is conjecture only, but unfortunately the lack of records forces us to rely
here upon theory.

The first real evidence we find to link the
names of Leech and Rigdon, comes from the following advertisement in the Memphis *Appeal*
dated May 1, 1862: "Swords! Swords! Swords!
A large lot of fine infantry and field officers'
swords just received from our manufactory in
Columbus, Miss. and for sale at the Memphis
Novelty Works, corner Main and McCall Sts.
Seven or eight brass finishers wanted immediately at the Novelty Works. Leech & Rigdon."
There are several interesting points in this advertisement. First, it is signed Leech and Rigdon, definitely showing the association between

the two; second, it refers at one point to the "Novelty Works" (note it is not "Memphis Novelty Works" just plain Novelty Works); and third, it refers to a manufactory in Columbus, Mississippi. What were the partners doing in Columbus, and why were they there, when Memphis certainly could supply the men and material they needed for their new business?

After the fall of Fort Donelson on February 16, 1862, the Confederates became alarmed for the safety of Tennessee, and on March 4, 1862, General Beauregard made arrangements to have all ordnance property removed to safer places. Grenada, Mississippi, was selected as an ammunition depot and Columbus, Mississippi, as the spot for an arsenal. Orders were issued on March 12, 1862, to move Confederate State Government property to these points and trains were provided soon after. Major William R. Hunt was sent to Columbus to superintend the erection of necessary buildings.[1]

That Leech and Rigdon were not unaware of what was going on is attested by an entry dated March 13, 1862, in Deed Book 33, page 48, Chancery Clerk's Office, Lowndes County, Mississippi, which records a deed between one Thomas B. Bailey and Leech and Rigdon for the purchase of an acre and a quarter of land, right in the heart of Columbus, Mississippi, for the sum of $1,500. Having seen that Leech and Rigdon were actually operating together as far back as March 13, 1862, the question arises as to when their revolver-making activity commenced. It seems almost impossible that they could have made any revolvers while in Memphis.

In the Georgia Room of the Confederate Museum, in Richmond, Virginia, is a finely made sword which was presented to Colonel George W. Raines of the Augusta Arsenal by the firm of Leech and Rigdon. This sword is inscribed on one side *Memphis Novelty Works* and on the other side *Leech & Rigdon*. The presentation of this sword to Colonel Raines may have had some effect on the firm as will be shown later. It was probably given to Raines when he was in Tennessee in 1862, acting under orders from Colonel Gorgas, Chief of Confederate Ordnance.

Leech and Rigdon's previously quoted advertisement of May 1, 1862, indicates that all was calm and serene and that the order of the day was business as usual. However, on May 8, only one week later, there appeared another advertisement in which there is a note of urgency. "Notice! Swords! Swords! A few more infantry and field officers' swords, which will be sold cheap if application be made today at the Novelty Works. All persons who have swords left here for repairs are hereby notified to call for them today, as we are going to start for Columbus, Miss., Friday morning. Leech & Rigdon."

Please note that this also refers to the "Novelty Works" rather than the "Memphis Novelty Works." Another advertisement using this same address appeared on January 11, 1862. It might also be mentioned that the sword which was presented to Colonel Raines is described by him as coming from the "Novelty Works."

COLUMBUS, MISSISSIPPI

The reader will probably wonder why such trouble is taken to make a distinction between the "Memphis Novelty Works" and the "Novelty Works." A number of swords have been found which are marked *Memphis Novelty Works*. Obviously then, these are the products of either Leech or Leech and Rigdon while they were operating in Memphis. After their removal to Columbus, Mississippi, there was no reason to retain the "Memphis" portion of the trade name. As it was, the firm was already better known as the "Novelty Works." This theory would account for a revolver, the barrel of which is stamped *Leech & Rigdon, Novelty Works, CSA*. Aside from the barrel marking, the gun is otherwise a standard Leech and Rigdon. There can be little doubt that it was made while the firm was located at Columbus, Mississippi.

Late 1862 brought a military threat to Columbus, Mississippi, in the persons of General William Tecumseh Sherman, et al., U.S. Army. Acting under instructions from Gorgas, Colonel Hunt prepared to remove his arsenal to Selma, Alabama. Selma was only about 120 miles east, as the crow flies, but the removal was a terrific undertaking. It involved first loading all materials and equipment on the Mobile and Ohio Railway, which took them 175 miles south to Mobile and the mouth of the Alabama River. Everything was then loaded upon river boats and taken northeast up the Alabama River to Selma, an additional 175 miles.

Here Leech and Rigdon left Colonel Hunt and the Arsenal. They traveled 150 miles northeast to Atlanta, and then still another 75 miles almost due east to Greensboro, Georgia, the midway point between Atlanta and Augusta. Here, as the Western novels so aptly put it, "they rested." Their reason for choosing Greensboro, Georgia, or for separating from Hunt and the C.S. Arsenal is not known.

GREENSBORO, GEORGIA

At Greensboro, Georgia, the old Greensboro Steam Factory was purchased from one John Cunningham for the sum of $20,000. This transaction is recorded in Deed Book SS, in the Office of the Clerk of Greene County, Greensboro, Georgia, and is dated February 2, 1863.

The price paid by Leech and Rigdon may seem high in view of the fact that the factory had been sold in 1858 to John Cunningham for $800, but bearing in mind the date of the transaction, it may well have been quite reasonable, as it was no doubt paid in Confederate money. Twenty thousand dollars in Confederate money was then equivalent to about $1,500 to $2,000 in gold.

A letter dated October, 1933, written by T. B. Rice, President of the Bank of Greensboro, Georgia, says in part:

. . . Mr. W. H. M. Weaver, whose address is Cleveland Avenue, Macon, Georgia, is the best posted man on Greene County history that I know. I spent several hours talking with him on Wednesday of this week. He was born in Greensboro in 1857 and spent his early manhood here. He was District Manager for the Southern Bell Telephone & Telegraph Company for many years, and after he was retired he was elected chairman of the Board of County Commissioners of Bibb County. He is a very high type man and what he says can be relied upon. His father was an officer in the Confederate Army and was the source of young Weaver's information on events that had happened before his day. The old pistol factory was very near the house where Weaver was reared and he says it was a favorite playground for the boys of his day. He described the old fill that was thrown up for the side track that went to the factory and says that the boys used to find all manner of waste materials that had been discarded, such as gun-locks, hammers, and defective parts of pistols.

I have also talked with a Mr. C. G. Askew, an old Confederate veteran, who is about 90 years of age. He remembers the old pistol factory well and knew both Leech and Rigdon. He says he was at home (Greensboro) only a few times during the war, but he saw them making pistols there and thinks they made swords and knives as well.

Delia Howell, an old colored woman and former slave of the Nicholson family at Greensboro before the war, says she remembers the old pistol factory well; and that several of the workmen boarded with her "old Miss."

A portion of another letter from Rice dated October 26, 1933, is also interesting:

The old factory was called I think, "Merrill's Factory." It was a brick building as I remember 3 or 4 stories high, and probably 150 by 100 feet in size at the base.

I remember Mr. Rigdon of the firm of Leech and Rigdon, who used the old factory building as a manufacturing plant for pistols, perhaps some guns also. If they made swords or other arms I do not remember about it, or further details of same.

Leech and Rigdon, I think, bought the old factory property including all the small brick cottages adjoining, in which the cotton factory people used to live.

On April 21, 1863, the following advertisement appeared in local papers: "For sale. 200 lbs. choice harness leather, 400 lbs. spelter solder, 200 lbs. sheet steel, 150 lbs. iron wire nos. 12 to 24, 500 lbs. German steel, 10 lbs. brass and copper wire, 50 fine leather belts. Leech & Rigdon, Greensboro, Ga." Thus would appear to have ended the firm's swordmaking, for all these materials were essentials to this industry and would hardly have been disposed of if any future manufacture was anticipated.

The spring of 1863 found the need for firearms in the Confederacy something more than acute. Here in Greensboro the partners' major activity was that of revolver making, although it is probable they did some repairing of guns. At any rate they discontinued making swords—the weapon which had first drawn them together. This was probably due to their having secured a contract from the Confederate Government for revolvers on March 6, 1863.

The original contract is not to be found and hence its exact terms are not known, but later events establish many of its provisions. In late 1862 the firm had submitted two or more revolvers to the government in hopes of a contract. Judging from the date, they must have been made at Columbus, Mississippi. We do not know what the firm proposed, but we do have a report on the pistols from the Superintendent of the Richmond Armory. Superintendent W. S. Downer writes Colonel Gorgas, January 21, 1863, as follows:

I beg respectfully to report in regard to the pistol presented by Messrs. Leech & Rigdon, that I find it a good and serviceable weapon and worthy of the patronage of the Department.

The faults I notice are want of uniformity in the calibre in the chamber and an inferiority of the iron in the barrel. I also note that the parts do not interchange which they should do. In regard to the proposal for a contract which they offer, I would suggest that their terms are only liberal to themselves, but aside from that, the state of the country is such regards supplies, labor, etc., I think we would be impolitic to enter into a contract of such size now. I would recommend however that all pistols which can be made by this firm within a year from this date, or say during the war, be purchased by the Department at the price named, and a small advance made on approved security, they entering into contract to deliver to the Department all the products of their factory.[2]

Fifteen hundred revolvers were made with the firm's name stamped on the top flat of the octagonal barrel housing. On practically all, the *Leech & Rigdon* is followed by *CSA*. We have

LEECH AND RIGDON BARREL MARKING
On serial number 1231.

noted exceptions to this, one being serial number 15, which is marked *Leech & Rigdon, Novelty Works, CSA.* Another exception is noted on at least two revolvers, these being Nos. 328 and 450. They are marked simply *Leech & Rigdon.* Number 328 is stamped to read from breech to foresight, a peculiarity observed on no others. Another slight variance on these two revolvers is that No. 328 is also stamped *72* on the trigger guard, while No. 450 is stamped *5* on the trigger guard. The significance of these extra serials is not known.

All guns bear an inspector's or assembler's stamp on the side of the trigger guard. This most usually takes the form of four square dots so arranged as to form a cross, but sometimes a single capital letter is employed, such as a *J* or *N*. Another stamp occasionally encountered on the butt and strap is *S.C.* or *S. Car.*, which, of course, means "South Carolina." One other mark will be discussed later.

We have no way of knowing how many revolvers were produced at Columbus, Mississippi, but judge the production was small. As the firm's next and last location was Greensboro, Georgia, the natural assumption would be that the balance of the 1,500 revolvers was made there, but such is not the case.

The records of the Augusta Arsenal, under "Ordnance Stores ready for shipment," reveal that as of September 30, 1863, there were at hand "387 Leech & Rigdon Navy Pistols." They issued 300 on October 6 and received an additional 200 on October 30. In November, 101 Leech and Rigdons were received and 262 were issued. In December, only 34 revolvers were received while 100 were issued. On January 4, 1864, the Arsenal accepted 117 revolvers and during the month issued 152. On February 13, 72 revolvers were received and an additional 23 arrived in March. Thus, during a six-month period 547 revolvers were received, or about 100 per month.[3] It is unfortunate that the Arsenal records do not continue beyond March of 1864.

While located at Greensboro, the firm was composed of Thomas Leech and Charles H. Rigdon, each of whom apparently had a 50 per cent interest in the business, but also connected with the firm were Andrew J. Smith, a Virginian, and Jesse A. Ansley. Smith was the traveling agent for the company, while Ansley held the position of bookkeeper.

All did not go well between the principals, for in Deed Book SS, page 156, Office of the Clerk of Greene County, Greensboro, Georgia, is found a dissolution agreement signifying that for the

sum of $10 and other valuable considerations Charles H. Rigdon deeded his entire interest in the property in Greensboro that was recorded in the name of the firm of Leech and Rigdon to Thomas Leech. While this deed is dated in January, 1864, it refers to an agreement of dissolution of partnership made and entered into on December 13, 1863. This was the end of Leech

LEECH AND RIGDON FRAME
Serial number 1231, without channel in recoil shield.

RIGDON AND ANSLEY FRAME
Serial number 1974, showing channeled recoil shield.

and Rigdon's partnership but, strangely enough, it was not the end of the revolvers stamped *Leech & Rigdon, C.S.A.*

The Augusta *Chronicle & Sentinel* of January 15, 1864, contains a notice, "The copartnership hereto pre-existing between the undersigned, is this day dissolved by mutual consent.—Leech &

Rigdon." The same paper, of January 27th, contains a "Copartnership Notice," as follows: "The undersigned have formed a copartnership under the name and style of Rigdon, Ansley & Co. for the purpose of manufacturing pistols (Colt's Navy Repeaters) under contract with the government of the Confederate States. Said partnership to date from January 1, 1864 and continue five years. Office at 300 Broad Street—signed, Charles H. Rigdon, J. A. Ansley, A. J. Smith, Charles R. Keen."

The next definite information about Rigdon is to be found in a waterpower lease between the "Augusta Canal Co., of Augusta, Ga., party of the first part, and Charles H. Rigdon, Jesse A. Ansley, Andrew J. Smith, and Charles R. Keen, partners under the style and name of Rigdon, Ansley & Co., party of the second part." This indenture, dated March 13, 1864, is for the use of waterpower on "the lot, or parcel of land, lying between the second and third levels of the canal, and on the west side of Marbury St."—now 12th Street, Augusta. This site is now occupied by the Georgia Iron Works and their office is where the Rigdon, Ansley and Company factory was located.

Interesting light is shed on the Rigdon-Ansley contract, where in the case of *Ansley vs. Starr*, a reference is made to it as follows: "Charles H. Rigdon testified: That he is a member of the firm of Rigdon, Ansley & Co. carrying on a contract with the government for the manufacture of pistols, known as 'Colt's Repeaters,' engaged to produce a certain number each month, said contract bearing date of January 1, 1864, and binding the said firm to carry out a contract made by Leech & Rigdon with the government dated March 6, 1863." This statement shows conclusively that the company's contract was not a new one, but simply a continuation of the Leech and Rigdon contract.

In separating from Leech, Rigdon must have agreed to carry on the old contract in its original form. Under any such agreement, Rigdon would

certainly have kept the machinery used to manufacture the Leech and Rigdon revolvers, or how else could he have hoped to continue the contract?

That he got not only the machinery, but most of the workmen as well, is shown by another letter from Mr. T. B. Rice, dated November 20, 1933.

The records that you sent me of the Rigdon guards of Augusta, Georgia, prove clearly that the workmen who worked in Greensboro with Leech and Rigdon went with Rigdon to Augusta. The Orderly Sergeant, H. P. Williams, who issued the drill orders to meet at the Pistol Works, was one of the foremen in the Pistol Factory in Greensboro in 1863; and two of the men who were listed among the casualties at Griswoldville were also workers in the Leech and Rigdon organization here. They were W. C. Cartright, and J. D. Andrews. I knew both of these men personally, and H. P. Williams was the father of one of my best friends, James B. Williams of Macon, Georgia.

I talked with Mr. Williams a few days ago about his father's connection with the old Pistol Factory at Greensboro; but he could tell me nothing beyond the fact that he had heard his father tell of him coming here from Tennessee to work in the Pistol Factory with Leech and Rigdon, and that he was married in Greensboro. I got hold of Mr. C. C. Vincent again today; and he gave me the names of some of the workmen in the Pistol Factory that was operated here in 1863 by Leech and Rigdon. And while he was only a boy about 12 years of age, he remembers both Leech and Rigdon well. He does not know where they came from, but he is positive they made pistols of the Colt type and knives. He is not sure about their making guns; however, he is positive that the Confederate Army shipped guns to them for repairs. He says the plant was large and that they worked a good many men. Some of the workmen came here with them. He also recalls that a number of local men got jobs with Leech and Rigdon hoping that it would keep them out of the army, and that most of these men went to

Augusta with Rigdon and worked in his factory here until they were drafted into the service very much against their will.

He claims to have gotten this information from two of the men who worked in the Augusta factory with Rigdon. The names he gave me were John Dunn and Cartright. He says that both of them came back to Greensboro after the war and that he worked with both men for years after the war.

I would take the above as direct testimony in view of my knowledge of Mr. Vincent. He further says that both of the above men told him that Rigdon continued to make pistols in Augusta until the end of the war.

The highest numbered Leech and Rigdon revolver known is serial No. 1461. The lowest numbered "12 stop" Rigdon, Ansley and Company revolver known is serial No. 1546. It is safe to assume that the original Leech and Rigdon contract with the government would have called for a round number, such as 1,500 revolvers, to be delivered. It would hardly have called for an odd number. If this reasoning is correct, then the nearest round number possible in this case would have been 1,500, and this is probably the quantity called for originally.

It has been taken for granted that all revolvers marked *Leech & Rigdon* were made at Greensboro, but a recently discovered order from Colonel Gorgas definitely proves that this is not the case. This order is dated February 22, 1864, over a month after Leech and Rigdon had dissolved partnership, and is addressed to Captain Wescom Hudgins, Assistant Inspector of Small Arms. It says in part:

Sir:—You will please proceed as soon as practicable to Athens, Ga., and take charge of the inspection and improvement of arms manufactured by Cook & Bro.; you will also visit Augusta, Ga., as often as may be necessary for the purpose of inspecting and improving the pistols manufactured by Rigdon, Ansley & Co.

Upon receiving arms from either of the above mentioned parties you will cause them to be turned over to Col. G. W. Raines, Commdg. Augusta Arsenal, at the same time furnishing the contractors with a certificate, in which will be set forth the number of arms received, the price to be paid, the date of contract, and the number

Courtesy Lee Brigham

LEECH AND RIGDON REVOLVER

Serial number 439, with pin and ball loading lever catch.

RIGDON AND ANSLEY SERIAL NUMBER 1974
Showing 12 cylinder stops. Note Colt type loading lever latch.

stamped upon each arm, and these certificates to be presented by the contractors to Col. G. W. Raines, and held by him as vouchers for the settlement of their accounts.

You will forward to me a monthly report showing the number of arms received and rejected; also giving a statement of the principal causes for rejection.

In the event of any changes from the present construction of the arms suggesting themselves you will submit a report in relation thereto.

In the pistols made by Rigdon, Ansley & Co., the use of the safety-pins has been abandoned without introducing a substitute for them; the parties propose the use of another set of check notches in order to prevent the cylinders revolving, when the hammer is not upon the cap.

It is important that some means of securing the soldier from danger should be immediately determined upon; you will therefore urge the parties to hasten to completion the pistol thus altered which they propose to submit.

In the pistol made by Rigdon, Ansley & Co., additional attention is required to prevent ring-boring, and in bringing the cylinder chambers to

the true caliber; and rifling is hardly deep enough; the front sight projects into the bore; the dimensions of the cone to be the same as Colt's; the cylinder must be case hardened, and Colt's lever catch substituted as soon as possible for the pin now used.

All other defects you may observe must be corrected under your instruction.

Proof for the pistol of Rigdon, Ansley & Co., the cylinder chambers to be filled with the best rifle powder until they will just admit of a conical ball being forced even with the face of the cylinder; after this proof the parts to be assembled and the pistol fired with a similar charge.[4]

At exactly what point the firm of Rigdon, Ansley and Company assumed the old Leech and Rigdon contract is not particularly important, but it was probably somewhere over the serial No. 1000. It is noted that serial No. 1055 does not contain the safety-pins referred to by Gorgas, nor is the hammer face grooved, slotted or indented to engage such pins. Guns with lower serial numbers do have these safety-pins or appropriate treatment of hammer faces, so it might be assumed that these features were dropped at the time the partnership was dissolved. However, assumption is not fact and we have no way of really knowing whether serial No. 1055 was made prior to or after the partnership was dissolved.

We can say with assurance, however, that revolver No. 1262, which is marked *Leech & Rigdon C.S.A.*, was not inspected until sometime after Captain Hudgins received his orders to Augusta on February 22, 1864. This we know because many revolvers inspected by this officer bear his inspection stamp on their butts. At first this was a small diamond enclosing the capital

Courtesy Miles W. Standish

DISASSEMBLED LEECH AND RIGDON

Serial number 1231, showing components. The base pin is a replacement.

letters *W.H.* Later the same initials in flowing script appear inside a parallelogram. The first inspection stamp and *S.C.* are to be found on No. 1262.

It is also interesting to note that revolver 1490 is stamped *Address* on the top barrel frame, *C. H. Rigdon* on one side flat and *Augusta, Ga.* on the other.

Still another revolver is known to be stamped *C. H. Rigdon* on the barrel flat. The gun has 12 stops but has only a 5-inch barrel, which is apparently its original length. It is unmarked and has no serial, although the interior of the trigger guard has the letter *R* scratched in with a sharp tool and on the inside of the backstrap appears the same letter fashioned by a series of small "3's."

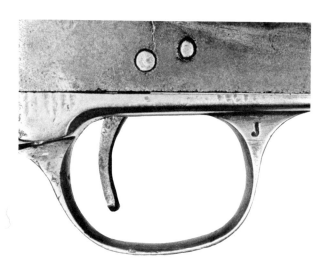

Courtesy Miles W. Standish

LEECH AND RIGDON INSPECTOR'S STAMP

On serial number 1231.

The following is a list of identified and probable Leech and Rigdon revolvers known to the authors, with an occasional description.

8—Not definitely identified as a Leech and Rigdon.

15—Marked *Leech & Rigdon, Novelty Works, C.S.A.* Numbered 15 on all parts except the wedge.

41—Not definitely identified as a Leech and Rigdon.

47—Totally without marks, except for the serial number.

70—Markings, if any, not obtained.

95—Stamped *Leech & Rigdon.*

107—Stamped *Leech & Rigdon, C.S.A.*

109—Same as above.

143—Same as above.

328—Stamping of Leech and Rigdon from a different die and runs from cylinder to barrel with no C.S.A. This gun is also marked 72 on the trigger guard.

346—Standard througout.

439—Stamped *Leech & Rigdon, C.S.A.*

450—Stamped *Leech & Rigdon;* also serial number 5.

496—Barrel only marked. Marked *Leech & Rigdon C.S.A.* The loading lever catch is from a Colt.

497—Barrel not original.

511—Markings not known.

515—Barrel stamped *Leech & Rigdon C.S.A.* This piece is fitted with Rigdon, Ansley cylinder No. 2344, all other parts serial 515.

588—Barrel marked *Leech & Rigdon C.S.A.* cylinder No. 639.

602—Markings not known, but assumed to be the standard *Leech & Rigdon C.S.A.*

605—Stamped *Leech & Rigdon C.S.A.* On the right grip is a small oval disk of silver which is inscribed, "Ensign P. Fred Harington, U.S. Navy, U.S.S. Monongahela, Mobile Bay, Alabama, Friday, August 5, 1864. Captured with the Rebel Ironclad Tennessee."

610—Markings not known, but assumed to be standard.

618—Same as above.

635—Same as above.

647—Cryptic mark *D.* Serial altered to look like No. 1647. No firm name on barrel.

650—Cryptic mark *N.*

662—Listed "poor to fair" on a dealer's catalogue.

686—Markings not known.

691—Markings not known, but assumed to be standard.

693—*Leech & Rigdon C.S.A.*

694—Markings not known, but assumed to be standard.

695—Mixed numbers. Part is Colt and the gun has *36 cal.* stamped on the trigger guard.

786—Marked *Leech & Rigdon.* All original.

823—Markings not known.

845—Markings not known.

856—Standard markings.

894—Stamped *Leech & Rigdon C.S.A.,* but with parts from Rigdon, Ansley No. 2214.

899—Stamped *Leech & Rigdon C.S.A.* Backstrap engraved *Col. Harry Gilmore 2nd Md. Cav. C.S.A.*

903—No information on markings.

916—Standard throughout.

951—*Leech & Rigdon C.S.A.*

959—Barrel stamped *Leech & Rigdon, Novelty Works, C.S.A.*

961—Cryptic mark *N.*

1001—Backstrap and trigger guard marked *1001* and the weapon appears to be larger than the usual Leech and Rigdon. The customary *Leech & Rigdon* stamp does not appear to be correct, *C.S.A.* stamp is O.K. *S. Ca.* on butt. Some parts are stamped *1001* or *1007.*

1010—*Leech & Rigdon, C.S.A.*

1014—Same as above, but believed to have a replaced cylinder.

1019—Markings almost obliterated by age, but *C.S.A.* still apparent.

1050—*Leech & Rigdon C.S.A.*

1052—Markings not known.

1055—*Leech & Rigdon C.S.A.*

1070—No information on markings.

1078—Marked *Leech & Rigdon C.S.A.* No. *157* (or *137*) on the cylinder and the cylinder shows a twist iron grain. Backstrap and

trigger guard are of bronze or red brass and appear to have been made for a Griswold revolver. Grips and mainspring are replacements.

1095—*Leech & Rigdon C.S.A.*

1121—No information on markings.

1123—No information on markings, but believed to be standard.

1138—*Leech & Rigdon C.S.A.*

1156—No information on markings, but believed to be standard.

1175—Same as above.

1195—Marked *Leech & Rigdon,* but has no C.S.A.

1208—*1208* on the barrel, cylinder and loading lever. The balance of the weapon is from an Army fluted .44 caliber Colt, serial number 1212.

1224—Loading lever is the pin and ball type. The face of the hammer is not notched. No safety-pin on the cylinder.

1231—Markings not known.

1262—Marked *Leech & Rigdon C.S.A.* and on the butt *W. H.* in a diamond and *SC.*

1290—*S. Ca.* stamped on the butt.

1380—No information on markings.

1393—No information on markings, but believed to be standard.

1405—Pin and ball type lever, no safety-pins, slotted hammer.

1410—Marked *Leech & Rigdon C.S.A.*

1448—Marked *Leech & Rigdon C.S.A.* The loading lever is a replacement, but the plunger is original. Carved in right stock is "C. H. Milner, Dudlin, Texas." The weapon is in extremely poor condition. Cryptic mark *N.*

1461—No information on markings, but believed to be standard.

1490—Marked on the 3 barrel flats *Address* (top) *C. H. Rigdon* (right side) *Augusta, Ga.* (left side), cryptic mark *J.* This weapon was once chrome-plated!

The revolvers that followed after serial No. 1500 are very similar to the Leech and Rigdons, but with these changes: the cylinder has 12 stops, the recoil shield face on most is channeled, it being flat in the Leech and Rigdon, and the Colt loading lever latch has been adopted. In the 1500 and 1600 series the top barrel flat is stamped *Augusta, Georgia, C.S.A.* Somewhere between No. 1642 and No. 1753 the *Augusta, Ga.,* portion of the die was evidently lost or broken, as markings then continued only as *C.S.A.*

Courtesy Miles W. Standish and Edward N. Simmons

LEECH AND RIGDON, RIGDON AND ANSLEY DIE MARKINGS

Comparison of dies used in production period, Leech and Rigdon serial 1237, Rigdon and Ansley serial 1974.

The same inspector's or assembler's marks appear as previously were to be found on the Leech and Rigdon. Also, the serials are obviously stamped with the same dies. In serial numbers around 2,000 these dies were replaced by ones with considerably larger sized numerals.

This is the 12-stop revolver known to collectors as the Rigdon and Ansley. Only about a thousand were made. Somewhat more scarce than the Leech and Rigdon, a list of those known to the writers is as follows:

1522—Marked *Augusta, Ga. C.S.A.*
1546—Marked *Augusta, Ga.* and *WH* on the butt.
1582—
1584—Marked *Augusta, Ga. C.S.A.* and *WH* on the butt.
1615—
1616—Marked *Augusta, Ga. C.S.A.*
1641—Marked *Augusta, Ga. C.S.A.*
1666—
1723—
1742—
1754—Marked *WH* on butt.
1755—
1757—Barrel cut to 2½ inches. No loading lever.
1768—
1775—Marked *WH* on butt. Has defective cylinder.
1778—
1786—Has a Colt cylinder.
1802—
1849—
1857—
1892—
1934—Marked *WH* on the butt.
1974—
1978—
1990—
2004—Mixed with Colt parts.
2021—
2027—
2091—
2117—Serial on trigger guard only. Marked *Leech & Rigdon C.S.A.* in an unusual stamp.
2146—
2214—
2217—
2221—
2224—
2231—Marked C.S.A. on the flat of the barrel. Marked with an ornate, flowing *W.*
2233—In very good condition.
2258—

2259—Has new grips. Appears to have been in a
      fire.
2281—
2324—Has new grips, backstrap and trigger
      guard.
2330—
2341—
2344—
2359—

The 12 stops on the cylinder of the Rigdon,
Ansley was the application of an improved safety
device brought out by the Manhattan Arms
Company, of Newark, New Jersey, in 1859. The
original Colt safety consisted of an indentation
in the hammer face which engaged a pin projecting from the rear face of the cylinder between
the nipples. These pins were easily damaged,
and the constant strain on the cylinder-bolt stop-
spring in this position (hammer down on pin)
usually resulted in a fracture after a short period.

The extra slots or stops on the periphery of
the cylinder did away with the pins, released
the strain on the spring, and provided a positive
safety by locking the cylinder with the hammer
down between the nipples. Despite the advantages of such a safety, few revolver makers of
that period availed themselves of this principle.
Possibly it would have involved an infringement
of the U.S. patent rights belonging to the Manhattan Arms Company, something that did not
worry the Confederates.

Why Rigdon moved from Greensboro to Augusta is not known. In view of the fact that he
kept control over both machinery and workmen,
it would seem logical that he would have stayed
on in Greensboro while Leech went elsewhere.
The fact remains that he did not. It is possible
that he was influenced by Colonel George W.
Raines, who was in charge of the Confederate
Arsenal in Augusta. The two men must have
been friendly. Why else would the firm of Leech
and Rigdon have presented him with the sword
he wore all through the war?

The Augusta Arsenal was seized from the Federal Government at the time of Georgia's secession and early turned its activities to the benefit
of its new owners, the Confederate States of
America. Under the jurisdiction of the Arsenal
was the "Machine & Foundry Works," where it
is believed 12-stop revolvers were being produced prior to the advent of Rigdon-Ansley's.

On April 19, 1863, Colonel Raines, in charge
of ordnance activities in Augusta, wrote Colonel
J. H. Burton, Superintendent of the Macon
Armory, as follows: "In the first place it is my
desire and Colonel Gorgas' intention to extend
the Arsenal Works or Machine and Foundry
Works, rather, so as to supply a large portion
of all Field Artillery ammunition and equipments, complete which the Army shall require."[5]

From this letter we gather that Colonel Raines
wished to bring to Augusta as many manufacturers of war materials as he could. Possibly it
was he who persuaded Rigdon to come to this
city.

While there is no overestimating the troubles
that beset Rigdon as a Confederate armsmaker,
most of his real difficulties appear to have been
keeping out of the way of the Union Army. His
next trouble came from the Confederate Army.
On April 18, 1864, all was well, but the following day, came a knock at the door, and Captain
Elijah Starr, conscript officer for the Confederate States Army appeared, seeking Jesse Ansley. Captain Starr was of the definite opinion
that Ansley, bookkeeper and financial manager,
should not be making guns in Augusta but
should be carrying one at the front.

After a short delay, Ansley was haled into the
court of the Honorable James S. Hook, Judge of
the Richmond County Superior Court, Middle
District of the State of Georgia. He had been
held in custody incommunicado as a conscript
by Captain Starr. Ansley claimed exemption
from the Army on the following grounds: first,
he had secured a substitute on December 8,

1862; secondly, he was a member in good standing of the Wheeler Dragoons, a local militia company which was guarding hospitals, etc.; and thirdly, he was a member in good standing of the firm of Rigdon, Ansley and Company, said company ". . . carrying on a contract with the Government for the manufacture of pistols known as 'Colt's Repeaters' engaged to produce a certain number each month. . . . The said contract is being carried out faithfully by said firm; that the said Ansley is a member of said firm, its bookkeeper and financial manager; that they now employ some 60 hands, and expect to be able to employ some 250; that the Capital Stock is $160,000 which they expect to increase shortly to $320,000; there are four partners with distinct and important duties, each different from the other, each equally important, that the personal presence of Ansley is indispensable. . . ." This testimony was verified by Captain Wescom Hudgins, whom we have met as an inspector in the Ordnance Department of the C.S. Army.[6]

Despite the pleadings of the plaintiff (or conscript), as well as of the other members of the firm, the Honorable James Hook agreed with Captain Starr that Ansley belonged at the front using arms, rather than making them in Augusta. The case was appealed and in due course reached the Supreme Court of Georgia, at Milledgeville, in the November, 1864, term. The case may be found under *Georgia Reports,* vol. 34, page 85; the decision may be found in the Laws of Georgia, September, 1864, Milledgeville, November Term, 1864, page 21, *Quotations in Support of Conscript Law;* "Contractor to furnish arms for the Confederate States is not exempt by reason thereof from enrollment as a conscript."

The judge of the higher court expressed the opinion that Ansley should be exempted from active duty, and in truth, could have been made exempt, had he made application before the passage of the act of January 5, 1864, which said in effect that armsmakers were not exempt

from military duty although workmen were. How the Confederacy thought the workmen could turn out guns without executives to guide them is not known. At any rate, records do not indicate that Ansley ever saw any active duty beyond that with the Wheeler Dragoons, probably because of Sherman's passage through Georgia and its concomitant confusion and the collapse of the lower south.

There can be little doubt that the long court trial reflected unfavorably on Rigdon, Ansley and Company. It would appear that shortly after his initial arrest, Jesse Ansley withdrew from active interest in the business, as did A. J. Smith.

Augusta newspapers of 1864 carry advertisements for the Rigdon Guards, official militia for Rigdon, Ansley and Company. Why wasn't Ansley a member of this outfit rather than the Wheeler Dragoons? Probably because he joined the Wheeler Dragoons in 1863, prior to the formation of the Rigdon Guards, or perhaps because he owned a horse and preferred to ride to work.

That affairs were not progressing well for the Confederacy is shown by this advertisement of August 26, 1864, in the Augusta *Daily Constitutionalist;* "Rigdon Guards, appear for drill at 5 o'clock this Friday and every Friday evening thereafter until further orders. By order of the Captain. Henry P. Williams, O.S." Affairs were not progressing well for Rigdon, Ansley and Company either. Once again came the threat of Uncle Billy Sherman, U.S.A. The following indicates that all the machinery, machine shops and ordnance materials in Augusta, Georgia, were boxed up and shipped to prevent capture: "Ft. Monroe, Va., 11-30-64. Major Eckert, U.S.A.—Have just received Savannah Daily Morning News. Came to me through the post office from Major Mulford, U.S.A. Following is news: Situated and Prospect. We take the following from the Augusta Chronicle of the 24th (November, 1864) The Grand prize that was to be obtained in case Augusta was captured, has been removed. The Powder works, arsenal, armories, and machine shops, located at this place, have been completely dismantled, and the valuable portion of their machinery has been removed to a location of safety not threatened. The last car-load, we understand left today. The machinery was sent away merely as a matter of precaution. . . ."

The confusion of Augusta at that time must have been something to witness. One wonders how all this equipment left the city, or if it actually did. To have moved by railroad, it would have had to start before November 15, 1864, because Sherman began destroying the Georgia Central Railroad east of Macon on that date. Nothing could have gone direct to Atlanta, as the road had been destroyed part way from Atlanta. The fall of 1864 was a particularly rainy one and the roads must have been indescribably muddy. To have carried heavy machinery by wagon almost seems impossible. As it happens, Sherman did not enter Augusta at that time. It is possible that while all equipment might have been boxed and ready to take to the road, some of it never did, although a portion is known to have reached Athens, Georgia, for safe keeping.

What happened to the government equipment and material is not known, but Rigdon, hardy soul that he was, seems to have kept his machinery and factory intact.

The Rigdon Guards were in the battle of Griswoldville, Georgia, on November 22, 1864, fighting to save the Griswold revolver factory from destruction. The fight at Griswoldville was a very real one, as is evident from one battle report: "Camp near Macon, Ga., Nov. 23, 1864—Casualties in the Augusta Battalion, Co. C, Rigdon Guards, Nov. 22nd, 1864 at Griswoldville. Capt. A. J. Smith, Commanding: Lieut. S. Poor, seriously in head; Serg. W. H. Meriden, in thigh, severe; D. Gaunst, seriously in shoulder; E. Lublin dangerously in head and thigh; W. C. Cartright, in leg; J. D. Andrews, slightly in shoulder; M. H. Woods, in head, slight; Jerry Gleason,

slight in leg; Missing: George Shiver, Jas. Walker, M. P. Scales. . . ."[7]

There was still fight left in Company C, however, for on December 2, 1864, the following appeared in the *Constitutionalist*: "Attention Rigdon Guards—The members of this company who are cut off from their command whether furloughed or detailed will meet at the Pistol Factory on Friday morning at 9 o'clock to be organized for immediate home defence. By order of J. W. Poor, 1st Lieut. Co. C, Augusta Battalion, J. M. Wood, brevet sergeant." On December 4, 1864, the Rigdon Guards had been regrouped sufficiently to take part in the battle at Grahamville. Apparently after this battle they resumed business as usual at the pistol factory.

Excerpts from correspondence already quoted would indicate that at the threat of Sherman's advance, Rigdon closed down his plant permanently. We are fortunate in having at hand the original orders of Captain Wescom Hudgins who was ordered by Colonel Gorgas from Richmond to Macon, Georgia, for the express purpose of acting as Ordnance Inspector for the contract plants of Rigdon, Ansley and Company, at Augusta, and Cook and Brother at Athens, Georgia. His sole purpose for being in Augusta or Athens was to act as the inspector of these plants. Carefully examining these orders we find that Captain Hudgins was in Augusta on the following dates: December 12, 1864, January 8 and January 27, 1865. Had the Rigdon factory not been in operation, there would have been no point to his being in Augusta.

The last date in January, 1865, the 27th, would indicate that this was the end of the manufacture of the Rigdon, Ansley revolver. The handwriting on the wall had been apparent for some time, but the end is probably indicated in the following advertisement from the Augusta *Constitutionalist* of December 20, 1864, which ran for a period of two weeks. "To Manufacturers— A rare opportunity for investment is offered in the purchase of a large factory building, 160 by

40, new with machinery well adapted for all kinds of work in metals, consisting of turning lathes, drill presses, etc. Also a brass foundry of 20 horse (power) which can be increased to fifty. A full quota of shafting, belting and other appliances for adapting it to any kind of manufacturing.

"The attention of Railroad Companies, manufacturers of small arms, cotton and woolen goods is especially directed to these works. Extensive ground for additional buildings and other purposes. For terms, etc. address Key Box No. 49, Augusta Postoffice." There can be little doubt that this advertisement refers to the plant of Rigdon, Ansley and Company and that "Key Box 49" was Charles H. Rigdon.

Augusta was occupied in April, 1865, and the war was over. But before the final shot is fired, let us go back and see what happened to Thomas Leech after his separation from Rigdon, in December, 1863. We can establish that he remained in Greensboro, Georgia, at least for a time, but it has already been noted that the machinery went with Rigdon. What then did Leech do in Greensboro with an empty factory, no machinery and no workmen?

A possible clue may be in the consistent reports in letters examined that Leech and Rigdon, in addition to making revolvers, also repaired guns and made knives, possibly even swords, for the government. It is probable that Leech recruited or kept workmen and part of the machinery and secured a Government contract for the repair of guns and the manufacture of knives.

Evidence points to his having turned out at least 125 revolvers at Greensboro. A revolver has been reported which in appearance is very similar to the Leech and Rigdon, but has no roller or cross hatching on the hammer. This gun is marked *Leech & Co. CSA.* on the flat top of the barrel lug. Its serial number is 125 and this appears on most parts including front of cylinder, barrel wedge, left side of brass trigger guard,

underside of frame in front of trigger guard, hammer and cylinder pin. The number *6* (or *9* depending upon which way the gun is held) is stamped on the left side of the brass backstrap under the wooden grips and just in front of the point where the lower part of the mainspring is attached. The barrel is rifled with a left-hand twist and has seven grooves. The exact caliber is .3825. The barrel is 7½ inches, dragoon-style, part octagon, and the cylinder is 6-shot. The hammer is not a replacement; it has the original serial, No. 125. The gun has an iron frame, post front sight, and a rammer catch of the Colt Navy type.

Where Leech could have obtained the machinery and skilled workmen necessary to make these revolvers is a matter of some conjecture. However, no other Confederate armsmaker named Leech is known. Certainly this gun, if made by our Thomas Leech, could not have been made while he was in Memphis, for at that time he operated consistently either as Thomas Leech and Company or the Memphis Novelty Works. It seems unlikely that he would have changed his company name simply for the manufacture of revolvers, for as has been remarked, a derringer imitation bearing his name is marked *Thomas Leech & Co.*

There can be no question that Leech remained in Greensboro after Rigdon had moved on, or that he had machinery, because in the September 24, 1864, *Constitutionalist*, we find the following: "Lathe for sale. In good order a double-geared screw-cutting lathe; 14 foot shears; will swing 18 inches, for sale by Thos. Leech; Greensboro, Ga."

AFTER THE WAR

Early in 1865 Charles Rigdon left Augusta, Georgia. We have previously quoted from a letter of Joseph Boyce, of St. Louis, Missouri, which threw some light on the operations of Leech and Rigdon. We now quote portions of another letter from this gentleman, dated March 7, 1917:

The mechanical genius of Leech and Rigdon was Charles H. Rigdon, of St. Louis, who left here at the beginning of the Civil War. I knew him intimately. His regular business was scale making, but with this he was an all round master mechanic. The last time I saw him was at Selma, Alabama; this was early in January, 1865. My memory is fairly good for a man of seventy-five, but I may be at fault, yet I hope you will overlook any mistakes for it is over 50 years ago of which I am writing.

Charles H. Rigdon was a St. Louis man, and a most intelligent and popular one with all who knew him. The revolvers were made as I remember at Columbus or Macon, Georgia. We had some of them in my regiment, sent by Rigdon to several of his St. Louis friends. The 1st Missouri Confederate Infantry was composed mostly of St. Louis men (or boys, for the average age was twenty-two years).

Mr. Rigdon did not return to St. Louis. I know he was told that if he came back home he would be prosecuted by the Colts, for using their patents. I believe he feared this, as many of our returning Confederates had a hard time after they reached Missouri, at the hands of the so-called Home Guards.

I have called on the Rigdons listed in our St. Louis Directory, but not one of them was related, or ever heard of my old friend.

Even allowing for the fading of Mr. Boyce's memory after 50 years, it is obvious that he must have seen Rigdon some time in the early spring of 1865 at Selma, Alabama. It seems doubtful that Rigdon could have shipped his machinery there in anticipation of starting operations anew, although it is possible that this was the case. More likely, because of the large Government Arsenal at that point he was there to seek employment in a mechanical or supervisory capacity. At any rate Selma fell in April, 1865, so his activities there, if any, must have been extremely limited and of short duration.

Reluctant to return to St. Louis, finding noth-

ing in Augusta or Greensboro, because he had disposed of his interest there to Leech, Rigdon turned to Memphis, Tennessee. With the exception of St. Louis, he had remained in Memphis longer than in any other place—almost three years—1860, 1861 and part of 1862.

He is listed in the 1866 Memphis Directory as living on Washington Street near Orleans, and his occupation is given as a machinist. Like all Confederate citizens who had been paid for years in Confederate money, his need for cash must have been great. The only asset that he could have had was the property he and Leech had purchased in March, 1862, at Columbus, Mississippi.

In Deed Book No. 36, page 342, Chancery Clerk's Office, Lowndes County, Mississippi, we find a deed dated 28 June, 1866 between Thomas Leech and Charles H. Rigdon and Sarah W. Bailey, for the sale of the Leech and Rigdon property in Columbus, Mississippi, for $550, of which $250 was in cash, the balance being in a note. This is the same property for which they paid $1,500.

This deed, signed by both Leech and Rigdon, is the last record we find linking their names together. Leech, too, must have been hard-pressed for cash, for on September 5, 1865, he conveyed the property he owned in Greensboro, Georgia, to O. C. Jones, as attorney in fact, and authorized him to sell it. This deed was executed in Selby County (Memphis, Tennessee), showing that Leech, too, had returned to that city.

Also executed in Selby County is the deed dated July, 1866, in which Thomas Leech conveyed a house and lot in Greensboro to Mrs. Mary Tunison. There were a number of houses on this mill property in Greensboro and many of them were built of handmade brick. Two of the residences used by the superintendents of the factory are still standing, though they have been remodeled and modernized. Locally it is believed that Thomas Leech lived in one and Rigdon in the other. All of the property that Thomas Leech had acquired in Greensboro was sold as fast as he could find buyers. The old factory building was torn down and some of the bricks were used to build a store. This building, erected by Thomas Scott, was used as a bar-room up until some time in the nineties. The rock foundation was used to build a blacksmith and wagon shop on Broad Street and, paradoxically, was finally remodeled into a service station.

The Greensboro *Argus* of Tuesday, October 9, 1866, contains the following item: "Died: Charles H. Rigdon, on Monday evening at 7½ o'clock, of inflammation of the bowels; age 43 years. Cincinnati, Chicago, St. Louis and Augusta, Ga., papers please copy."

Rigdon was buried on October 9, 1866, in Greensboro's Elmwood Cemetery. Thus exits Charles H. Rigdon, mechanical genius and Confederate revolver maker.

As for Leech, his record trails off into limbo. In the 1866 Memphis directory he is listed as "Cotton Broker, and Comm., 304 Front St." In 1867-68, the listing is the same. In 1869 he is listed as a member of the firm of Leech and Carver, cotton brokers, at the same address. The 1874 directory contains the last record: "Thomas Leech (John B. Leech & Co.) residence—Liverpool, Eng. Leech, John B. & Co. (John B. and Thomas Leech and S. B. Carver) cotton exporters, 266 Front St." Thereafter, his name appears no more.

FOOTNOTE REFERENCES

1. W. L. Lipscomb, *History of Columbus, Mississippi, in the 19th Century* (Birmingham, Alabama, 1909), p. 125. Also O.R., Series I, Vol. XVII, pp. 431, 627, 749, 775.
2. C.R.O.R., Vol. 90, 1-21-63.
3. *Ibid.*, 9-30-63, *et seq.*
4. William A. Albaugh, III, *The Original Confederate Colt* (New York, 1953), pp. 56-58.
5. *Ibid.*, p. 58.
6. *Ibid.*, p. 36.
7. Albaugh, *Original Confederate Colt*, p. 39.

CHAPTER 6

Spiller and Burr

TAKE a commission merchant, an experienced industrialist and a highly trained, energetic ordnance officer; add a contract for 15,000 revolvers; complicate by a total lack of mechanics and machinery, and there you have the firm of Spiller and Burr. Time: the fall of 1861. Place: Richmond, Virginia, the Capitol of the newly fledged Confederate States of America.

This highly unlikely triumvirate bears examination. Concerning Edward N. Spiller, his nephew who served with Mosby had this to say: "... I know nothing of Burr ... but Edward N. Spiller was an uncle of mine. Before the war he ran a commission business in Baltimore, Md., but being a strong Southern man (sympathizer), and overly high-strung, had to leave there and come South. He lived in my father's house in Richmond for some time until he went to Atlanta. On one of his visits back from Atlanta, he brought one of his pistols, and gave it to my father. I remember it perfectly although I was in the Army at the time. Edward N. Spiller lived in Baltimore for years, before and after the war, and there he died."[1]

David J. Burr, a native of Richmond, Virginia, had long been engaged in building steam engines. The company bearing his name was located at 5th and Byrd Streets and in January, 1836, built a locomotive for the Richmond, Fredericksburg and Potomac Railway. In 1842, Burr, Poe and Sampson built the *Governor McDowell*, a 90 by 13 foot steam packet, the first and only one to appear on the James River and Kanawha Canal, the terminus of which was Richmond,

Virginia. In 1852, the Burr and Ettinger Locomotive Works was established, of which Burr was an active member. He was a man of more than a little prominence, and although his connection with Spiller and Burr appears to have been more financial than managerial, there is no doubt that his name added considerable prestige to the firm.

At the time of the Spiller and Burr venture, James Henry Burton was a Lieutenant Colonel in the Confederate Army, assigned to the Bureau of Ordnance, with the official title of Superintendent of Armories, C.S.A. The latter was his full-time job, but at the same time he held others, any of which could well have been called "full-time." Burton's life and innumerable connections would make a most interesting book in its own right, and there is ample material available for some future historian to do him justice.

His obituary appeared in the Baltimore *Sun* on October 19, 1894:

Winchester, Va., Oct. 18, 1894—Col. James Henry Burton, one of the most prominent citizens of this section, died at his home here this evening after a brief illness of pneumonia, having been sick less than a week. Col. Burton was born of English parents, Aug. 17, 1823, at Shennondale Springs, Jefferson Co., Va. After receiving an education at the Westchester Academy, Pennsylvania, he entered at the age of 16 a machine shop in Baltimore to learn the business of practical machinist, and graduated from there four years later.

In 1844 he took employment in the rifle works of the U.S. Armory at Harpers Ferry, and was appointed foreman in 1845. He afterward received the appointment of Master Armorer, which he held until 1854. In 1855 he accepted the appointment of Chief Engineer of the Royal Small Arms Factory at Enfield, near London, England. Five years afterward he returned to Virginia in consequence of failing health. In June, 1861, Mr. Burton was commissioned Lieutenant Colonel in the Ordnance Dept. of Virginia by Gov. John Letcher, and placed in charge of the Virginia State Armory with instructions to arrange for the removal thereto with the utmost dispatch, the machinery, etc., captured at Harpers Ferry, and to place it in position for use. Within 90 days from the date of his commission he had the machinery at work in Richmond, producing rifles of the United States patterns.

The following September he was commissioned (by President Jefferson Davis) Superintendent of Arms, with the rank of Lieutenant Colonel. During the summer of 1863, Col. Burton was ordered to Europe on business for the State Dept. At the close of the war, and after recovering from a severe illness, Col. Burton with his family, spent over three years in England. Upon his return, he located in Loudoun Co., Va., where he resided until 1871, when he again went to England at the instance of a private firm in Leeds, to take direction of a contract entered into with the Russian Govt. for the supply of the entire plant of machinery for a small-arms factory on a large scale at Tula, in Central Russia, for the manufacture of the Berdan rifle, and with the view of ultimately going to Tula as an officer of the Russian Govt. to take the technical direction of the factory. He was constrained to resign his position and returned to Virginia in the fall of 1873, since which time he has been following the peaceful pursuit of a farmer near Winchester.

Add to the foregoing that Colonel Burton found time to beget a family of fourteen, it must be agreed that he was a man who lived a full life. Burton's seventh child, Frank, was Master Mechanic at the Winchester Repeating Arms Company for many years.

The fall of 1861 found Spiller, Burr and Burton in Richmond, Virginia. In this feverish city there were few who had any doubt as to the ultimate success of Confederate arms—these few remained discreetly silent. Hopes were high, patriotism was higher, and while it seems almost unbelievable to realize, the desire to make money was at times above all.

Although definitely not self-sustaining and deficient in many vital necessities, the Confederacy never lacked for those who possessed great ideas and plans for the future—the farther in the future the better. Thus it was that persons whose lives previously had been along peaceful lines, suddenly became certain they would supply the South with 5,000, 10,000 even 15,000 revolvers (or pikes, guns, cannon, or something), provided delivery was not to start until some later date. The sad truth is that during its four-year struggle the South never manufactured 10,000 revolvers or pistols. At any rate, and regardless, Spiller, Burr and Burton felt the manufacture of 15,000 revolvers to be within their capabilities, and November 20, 1861, dated a meeting of the minds of the three. An agreement was then drawn up among them and signed.

Deleting the ponderous "whereas's," etc., this agreement provided: that Burton was to obtain from the C.S. Government a contract for 15,000 Navy size (.36 caliber) revolvers at $40 each for the first 5,000, $27 for the second and $25 for the third. The funds necessary for the starting of this venture were to be advanced by the C.S.A. and no interest would be charged if the enterprise succeeded. Spiller and Burr were to give personal security for double the amount of money so advanced.

Burton was to superintend preparation of the necessary plans, machinery and tools and oversee the erection of a factory. Moreover, he was to "start the machinery" and supervise the manufacture of pistols after the machinery was in operation. Finally, he was to be responsible

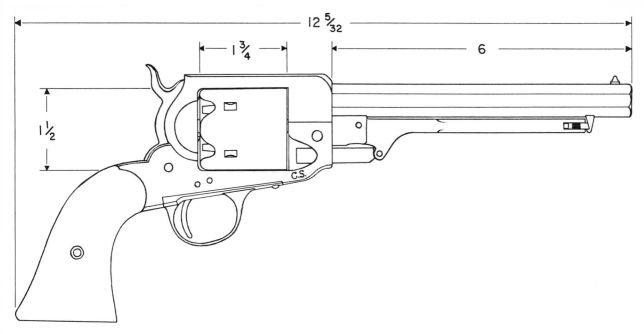

A TYPICAL SPILLER AND BURR REVOLVER   *Line drawing by W. E. Codd*

for the operation of all machinery. He was, however, to give only so much of his time as was not required of him in his work as Superintendent of the C.S. Armory.

Burton was to complete the order for 15,000 pistols in the time specified, which was to be no longer than two years and six months from the date of the contract.

Spiller and Burr were to pay Burton $2,500 as soon as the contract was procured, and a further $2,500 upon the completion of the first 100 pistols. In addition, Burton was to receive one-third of the profits from each year of operation.

Burton was not to be held responsible for any debts or obligations incurred by the firm; he was not a partner and his connection with the business was strictly as specified. The agreement was binding for a period of three years.[2]

One might imagine that such an obvious conflict of interest as this would lead Colonel Burton's superiors to instant and ringing denunciation, followed by a court-martial, but quite the reverse proved to be the case.

Burton was successful in obtaining a contract with the Confederate Government, which in essence provided:

1. The War Department guaranteed an order for 15,000 revolvers of a pattern substantially the same as that known as "Colt's."

2. An advance of $20,000 would be granted by the government to the contractors upon the signing of the contract, followed by $20,000 more at the end of three months, and another $20,000 at the end of six months. In turn, Spiller and Burr were to give satisfactory personal security in the sum of $120,000. The money advanced would be free of immediate interest, but was later to be paid back with interest at 8 per cent per annum. Should the $60,000 be found insufficient, further advances were to be made, provided the entire amount did not exceed $100,000.

3. The Confederate States of America agreed to pay $30 for each of the first 5,000 pistols, $27 for each of the next 5,000 and $25 each for the final 5,000.

4. The Confederate States of America agreed to compensate the contractors for any loss sustained, provided the loss was the result of invasion by the North.

5. Customs duties would be remitted on any material imported for the purposes of the contract.

6. Preference would be given the contractors over all others in case it was desired to increase the orders for pistols. This is a rather strange clause, when one considers the obvious desire the government had to encourage all arms-makers.

7. Inspection by the War Department would take place within two weeks of the date of delivery of pistols.

On their part, Spiller and Burr agreed:

1. To erect and put in operation within the Confederate States of America a factory capable of producing no less than 7,000 revolving pistols per year. Perhaps the government suspected that Spiller and Burr might move to England or France, a not improbable undertaking; after all, they owned nothing whatsoever at the time the contract was signed.

2. To supply the War Department as follows: 4,000 pistols by December 1, 1862, another 7,000 by December 1, 1863, and 4,000 more by June 1, 1864, or at earlier dates if convenient.

3. That only the best obtainable materials were to be used, but in the event steel for the cylinders and barrels could not be obtained it was agreed that iron of suitable good quality could be substituted. The lock frames were to be of good tough brass "properly electro-plated with silver." This is another startling dictate and reflects the impracticality that characterized the early days of the war.

4. That pistols were to conform to the model furnished by the War Department.

5. That all pistols finished were to be submitted to an authorized agent of the War Department, in accordance with special instructions defining the system of inspection and the tests to be applied in their examination.

6. That pistols were to be presented at Richmond in lots of no less than 100 at a time, unless otherwise desired by the War Department.

7. That spare parts for the pistols were to be furnished by the contractor at reasonable prices.

8. That as a means of securing mechanical success, the War Department consented that James H. Burton could give such assistance, etc., as would not interfere with his public duties and obligations.[3]

This remarkable contract is dated November 30, 1861, and shows many things, chiefly the high hopes that could lead Burton, an experienced armorer, and two others totally unacquainted with weapons making, to the signing of a contract for 15,000 revolvers to be delivered within a 27-month period. The contract also shows that even at this early date an impending lack of steel was foreseen. Still further, it revealed the anticipation that considerable material would have to be imported, and knowledge that the Confederacy was not self-sufficient so far as materials of war were concerned. The contract was signed and sealed and a building leased. It is at this point that a gentleman named Samuel C. Robinson enters the picture for a brief moment.

Searching through available records which pertain to Richmond, Virginia, in the early eighteen-sixties, occasional mention is found of a "Robinson Revolver Factory" which "anticipated the manufacture of Whitney-type revolvers." Samuel C. Robinson was the owner of the factory. From a family long-prominent in Richmond, prior to the war he operated the Belvidere Planing Mills, which the 1859 city directory locates at 9th and Arch Streets.

When war with the North appeared possible, and the Virginia Armory was reactivated in 1861, Robinson converted his planing mill into an armory for the purpose of modernizing the state's old Virginia Manufactory muskets, rifles and pistols from their original flint to percussion.

When war with the North became probable,

Robinson, being well aware of the lack of arms within the South, proposed to rectify this deficiency in part by supplying the State of Virginia with revolvers at $18 each. These arms were to have been modeled after the .36 caliber Whitney Navy revolver. Before his offer was acted upon, Robinson changed his price to $20. At this time (April, 1861) war was no longer possible or probable, but all too real, and his offer was finally accepted by the Virginia Legislature. The foregoing is noted in "The Official Records. . . ."

There is not the slightest indication that any of these weapons were ever produced, but Robinson evidently drew up plans and made patterns and machinery for them. In the meantime he became sidetracked in the manufacture of a carbine which closely copied the Sharps model. These guns are known to arms collectors as "Robinson Sharps." They were made until March, 1863, when the plant was taken over by the Confederate Government, who continued manufacture.

Considering that his first carbine was not turned out until December, 1862, and that his plant was purchased by the Confederate States Government the following spring, that Robinson managed to produce some 1,800 arms speaks well of his ability.

Despite the fact that the Spiller and Burr contract called for revolvers "substantially of the Colt's pattern," the guns finally forthcoming were of the Whitney model. Remembering that the Robinson contract called for a "Whitney model revolver," and that none was ever produced, it is not hard to believe that while in Richmond, Spiller and Burr rented a portion of the Robinson factory, and bought his plans, patterns and machinery for revolver making.

To give some strength to this theory, we quote a portion of letter from a George W. Rogers:

During the war, my father was too young to enlist in the regular Confederate Army, but did active service in the Elliott Grays, or Home Guards. He says he is under the impression that the Samuel C. Robinson referred to in your letter was the proprietor of the Robinson Revolver Factory, and a Mr. Lester was superintendent. The factory was on the south bank of the canal, just east of the railroad bridge crossing the James River, and known as the Petersburg Bridge. This would make the location about Eighth St., on the south side of the canal extending to the river. The revolver factory was moved the latter part of 1862 or 1863 to some point south. My father was employed for a while in the Robinson Revolver Factory, which was also called Robinson's Carbine Works, and my mother was employed just a few blocks away at the Confederate Laboratory.[4]

It was the intention of Spiller and Burr to operate as the "Richmond Small-Arms Manufactory," but as their first revolver was not turned out until after leaving that city, they apparently decided to use their own names, *Spiller and Burr*.

Having secured a contract as of November 30, 1861, and shortly thereafter a factory together with plans, patterns and machines for revolver making, the firm went to work to make the 15,000 pistols and deliver them to the government. They were to find the signing of the contract a great deal easier than its fulfillment.

Whatever their setup might have been in Richmond it appears to have been unsatisfactory, and very definitely no revolvers were made at that city.

On May 27, 1862, Burton was relieved of command of the Richmond Armory, and ordered South to establish an extensive armory at or near Atlanta, Georgia. He kept notes and diaries which, though not always continuous, are of great assistance in establishing dates. In Richmond on May 15, 1862, he drew up a memorandum headed "Order of Operations on various parts of the pistol to be manufactured by Spiller and Burr." Note that the future tense is used, indicating that no pistols had yet been made.[5]

Spiller evidently preceded Burton to Atlanta because, in his diary entry of May 31, 1862, Burton comments that upon first reaching that city Mr. Spiller met him and that they walked over the city together. A few days later he wrote Colonel Gorgas, "Messrs. Spiller and Burr have secured premises here (Atlanta) which will answer their purposes, and they now have workmen engaged in refitting the building."

Because Burton's armory was to be a permanent, long range affair, its location was carefully selected. His first plan was to locate in Atlanta, but finding property too expensive there, he settled on Macon, Georgia.[6] A site was offered free of charge by that city to obtain the benefits such a plant offered. There was an earlier large government establishment in Macon, the C.S. Arsenal and Laboratory under the command of Richard Cuyler.

An eyewitness account of what went on there is of interest, so we quote from a letter dated May 6, 1922, of Bridges Smith, formerly Judge of the Bibb County Juvenile Court, Macon, Georgia.

In 1861 when the new Confederate Government saw the necessity of beginning at once the manufacture of army equipment, it depended largely upon patriotism (which wasn't lacking in a town like Macon) for co-operation. D. C. Hodgkins & Sons turned over their gunsmith shop and then began the making of pistols and conversion of old weapons into, at that time, more modern guns. At first these were made of the Colt pattern by Hodgkins, but later were made by the government of the same general Colt model, but by mechanics brought here from Harpers Ferry, and I understand the model was altered in some way. From 1861 to 1865 I was detailed to make ammunition for shotguns, muskets and rifles, but none for small arms and therefore had little opportunity of seeing the manufacture of pistols. . . .

The first cartridges made here, and about the first made in the South, were of the "buck and ball" variety for shotguns, composed of one large (about the size of a boy's marble) leaden ball and three buckshot, a thimble-full of powder, all in a container of brown wrapping paper and tied with small twine, the powder being folded in a way that would hold its position. This is the cartridge that brought the command "chaw cartridge," following after the command "load." The soldier bit off the folded end and poured the powder in the barrel of the gun, and then put the buck and ball with their paper wrapper in, the paper serving as the wadding, and then rammed it down with the ramrod. He then put on his percussion cap and was ready for the command "fire."

You can see how much time was wasted in the earlier stages of the war, when you think of the metal cartridges that came later, especially with the opposing army. Another cartridge was that of the slug for rifles. At first these were moulded, and I think of them when I read about the dum-dum bullet, both being of soft lead. Later, through the ingenuity of a Michigan man, a civil engineer . . . the major of my battalion, these balls or slugs were made as hard as iron. He had lead wire, about the size of your little finger, made in coils, and invented a machine to cut it in proper lengths and made to fall into a recess the shape and size of the slug, where by powerful pressure it was compressed into hardness.

Brown paper was also used for making these rifle cartridges until a vessel loaded with a quality of paper, something of the appearance and texture of what we call "bond-paper" used for stationery, ran the blockade at Wilmington, and then we made decent looking cartridges. After the rifle cartridge was made the slug end was dipped in wax. All cartridges were put in packages of ten, with a small package containing 13 percussion caps.

In 1865, the Confederate Government had just completed large and handsome buildings, one for a laboratory in which to make ammunition and the other for an armory in which to make small arms. Before they would be turned over by the contractors, Gen. Wilson, U.S.A., had the audacity to walk in with his cavalry and demand the surrender of the city, and the people at that time just didn't have the heart to refuse him.

After that, I lost interest in the manufacture of cartridges and weapons.[7]

Although the establishments at Macon were sizeable, the largest south of Richmond was the C.S. Arsenal at Atlanta under the command of Captain M. H. Wright. To it was channeled all supplies from Macon and Augusta for equipping the Army of Tennessee. Bearing this in mind, let us take a look at their supplies on hand as of February, 1863: 1,116 flintlock muskets, 1,132 percussion muskets, 255 rifles, 11 cadet muskets, 117 assorted carbines, 355 double-barreled shotguns, 38 single-barreled shotguns, 202 rifles cut off and bored out, 214 unfinished rifle barrels, 318 sword-bayonets, 1,111 assorted bayonets, and 132 musket barrels.[8] One might say that this was not a large ordnance reserve with which to resupply an actively engaged army. Not a pistol or handgun of any type is listed, a fact which Wright himself acknowledged (the Army of Tennessee had asked for handguns) on March 3, 1863: "I have not a pistol for issue for cavalry. Will send a few carbines when they get the road open."[9]

The pistol factory of Spiller and Burr is believed to have occupied the old Peter's Flour Mill, located near the junction of Peters and Castleberry Streets. It is sometimes referred to as being "where the Georgia Railway Depot now stands" and sometimes as "near the Georgia Railway Depot."

Wallace P. Reed's "History of Atlanta" published in 1889 mentions a frame, three-story, steam flour-mill built in 1848 or 1852, owned by a Richard Peters, L. P. Grant, W. G. Peters, and J. F. Mims. According to Reed, when war broke out the machinery was sold to the Confederate Government and moved to Augusta to make powder, and thereafter the three-story building was used as a pistol factory. As there was only one pistol factory in Atlanta, this must have been the building used by Spiller and Burr.

According to the contract, Spiller and Burr were to deliver 4,000 revolvers by December 1, 1862. Two days before the 4,000 were supposed to have been turned over to authorities in Richmond, Spiller wrote to Burton:

I wrote you sometime ago in which I made a request that you come up (from Macon to Atlanta) this week. As you have failed to do so, I write again as I think it necessary you should see the rifling machine on which all the ingenuity which I have brought to bear has been used without accomplishing what it should do. As it is, I do not think it will do, although it may be changed so as to work. There is too much twist in the grooves for one thing, I think and I am sure that 5 instead of 7 rifles would be better. This machine is the only one in which we are likely to have any delay.[10]

From this, we may conclude that revolver number 1 (let alone 4,000) was still unfinished.

Burton must have fixed the rifling machine, because on December 17, 1862, he wrote Gorgas that the firm was finishing sample revolvers which they would exhibit to authorities in Richmond shortly thereafter, and expressed the opinion that they would be found the best yet produced in the Confederacy. He went on to say that due to a lack of steel, the cylinders of the revolver must be made of iron, but that "by twisting the iron, the fibres can be thrown in a direction around the circumference of the cylinder and the requisite strength thus secured."[11]

On most Spiller and Burr revolvers a close visual examination will reveal a peculiarity in these twisted iron cylinders which also exists in many Griswold and Gunnison revolvers, and this is a point which collectors might bear in mind where faking is suspected. We refer, of course, to the obvious grain resulting from the twisting.

Few people realize how desperate the South was in her need for metals. Possibly an entry in Caroline Jenkin's diary dated March 3, 1864, will show to some extent what the effect of this desperation was on the life of the everyday citizen: "One hears with a sinking heart of the

Courtesy Lee Brigham

SPILLER AND BURR REVOLVER SHOWING TWIST IN CYLINDER
The "fault" lines or twist in the iron of the cylinder shows clearly in this specimen.

dreadful shortage of metal, so much needed for bullets. Another call has come through for lead and steel. With the house already stripped, I can think of nothing to send except kitchenware, of which there is little enough in all conscience. I will send what knives I have that have steel blades, and a coffee grinder which I shall not miss as there is no coffee to grind."[12] New Year's day, 1863, Spiller returned to Atlanta after a visit to Richmond, where he had shown his "samples." Please note that reference is consistently made to them in the plural, so at least two must have been made.[13]

Illustrated is an exceptionally well-made weapon, showing care and precision in all respects. The grips are of good walnut, carefully finished, the frame is well cast, showing no "faults." Instead of the customary brass cone, the foresight is a steel pin carefully fashioned and mounted on a small metal plate set in the barrel. The cylinder is twisted iron. This revolver is wholly without markings, having no name, serial number or inspector's stamp, but comparison with other Spiller and Burr revolvers leaves little

doubt that it is a product of their factory, and possibly is one of their sample revolvers. Upon reaching Atlanta, Spiller wrote of his trip in a letter to Burton, remarking that the revolvers had been very well received, and that on the strength of this, he had requested a new and more liberal contract.

Spiller had every reason to be proud of the official report made by Captain W. S. Downer, Commander of the Richmond Armory, dated December 26, 1862.

I would respectfully report that I have examined the pistol made by Messrs. Spiller and Burr & Co. critically, and find no defects in them which will not remedy themselves as the machinery and tools become adapted to the work required, except such as are incidental to the model. I think the style of the catch to hold up the lever of the ramrod is faulty as the spring is necessarily weak, and after wearing awhile it will become worthless for the purpose for which it is intended. I would recommend a spring and catch like that of Colt's pistol. I would also recommend a slot cut in the base of the cylinder between the cones in which the face of the hammer will fit, holding the cylinder at a half-revolution and making a safeguard from accidental explosion. I would also recommend the adoption of the calibre of Colt's Navy revolver for the sake of uniformity in ammunition. The calibre of this pistol is somewhat smaller than Colt's. The present cylinder and barrel will bear the necessary increase. I think rounding off the muzzle of the pistol is an improvement as well in appearance as in use, as it is less apt to cut the holster or the sharp edges to become bruised. I find the workmanship on the pistol to be of a character in the highest degree creditable to the makers—much of it exceeding in quality that of the model. I would beg to suggest however, that I think a plain brass mounting is superior to plated—as the plating soon rubs off on the parts most handled—giving the work a mottled and unsightly appearance.[14]

On March 3, 1863, a new contract was entered into between the Confederate Government and Spiller and Burr. The old contract was canceled by mutual consent. The new contract called for 600 pistols to be delivered in February, 1863, and 1,000 per month thereafter until 15,000 had been delivered. Payment was to be $43 each for the first 5,000, $37 each for the second, and $35 each for the third lot. These increased prices included reimbursement for the removal of the pistol factory from Richmond, Virginia to Atlanta, Georgia.[15] The new terms were quite explicit except for one thing: with no revolvers produced as of March, 1863, how could they give 600 revolvers to the Confederacy in February of that same year? We can only surmise that the contract was drawn up prior to February when a number of revolvers were near the finished stage.

On April 18, 1863, having been notified by Gorgas of the urgent need for revolving pistols in General Bragg's army, Burton wrote to Colonel Oladowski, Chief of Ordnance, Army of Tennessee:

There is now in Atlanta, a factory with complete machinery capable of producing 1,000 pistols per month, but in consequence of the want of sufficient and competent workmen, but a small portion of that number is turned out. I write at the suggestion of Col. Gorgas to say that if you can manage to detail 10-20 good machinists who are competent to do the finishing work on pistols, and order them to report to Messrs. Spiller & Burr at Atlanta, Ga., you will soon be supplied with pistols of superior description. I am charged with inspection of all pistols made by these parties, who have a large contract with the government, and I am daily in expectation of a small lot—say 100, which doubtless will be sent to you. I shall be glad to know from you that you can detail workmen to the above named contractor as by this means your wants in this particular can be best soon supplied.[16]

Bearing Burton's financial interest in mind, his enthusiasm is understandable, but his attempt to obtain workmen was merely part of the unending struggle all ordnance men waged to keep skilled mechanics at their benches and out of the army.

On May 2, 1863, Burton acknowledged receiving 40 pistols from Spiller and Burr. Only seven passed inspection and these revolvers were by "no means as perfect as they should be. The inspection of the others was not completed because they presented two serious and fatal defects, viz.: the chambers were not in line with the barrels, and too great an allowance between the ends of the barrels and faces of cylinders through which gas can escape. These faults could not be corrected here and 33 pistols are to be returned to you via express. The 7 pistols passed will be retained here."[17] This was May, 1863, and evidently these were the first pistols actually submitted for service use. The contract called for 15,000! Only 14,993 to go.

The manufacturing of pistols, such as it was, continued in the hands of Spiller and Burr until January, 1864. By that time they were so far behind in their deliveries that the plant was bought lock, stock and barrel by the government. The purchase date was January 9, 1864, but payment was not made until February 29th. There seems to be a question whether $125,000 or $190,804 was the purchase price.[18]

Burton was never one to let any grass grow under his feet, and as of January had ordered his Master Mechanic, one Herrington, to "proceed without delay to Atlanta, and superintend the packing and shipping of the machinery, fixtures, tools, etc. of the Spiller & Burr Pistol Factory."[19] Before the end of January all machinery and tools had been safely removed to the Macon Armory and preliminary steps were taken to re-erect them. By February 12, Gorgas was notified that the machinery had been set up and put in operation. For all his energy, however, on April 23, Burton was forced to admit to Gorgas that the "manufacture of pistols does not seem to progress as rapidly as can be desired."

After the sale of his pistol factory, Spiller worked in Augusta, Georgia, for the Endor Iron Works of Chatham, North Carolina, and in August, 1864, advertised in the Augusta *Constitutionalist* for Negro hands and an iron founder wanted by the Endor Iron Works. There is no indication that he had any connection with revolver making after January, 1864. The 1867 Atlanta Directory lists E. N. Spiller as an employee of the foundry of Porter and Butler. Reese Butler, a foreman at the Richmond Armory in 1861, had gone south with Spiller and Burr as their pistol factory manager.

Although Colonel Burton had thought that twisted iron was suitable for revolver cylinders when the pistol works was operated by Spiller and Burr, one of the first things he requested from Colonel Gorgas after he took over the plant was "8,000 pds. of cast steel for pistol cylinders, 1⅝" round," to be secured from Thomas Firth and Sons, Sheffield, England. Burton said that Firth would know what was needed—and well he should, Firth having been one of Samuel Colt's sources of supply.

A year's experience with twisted iron for pistol cylinders had shown Colonel Burton that this substitute was not altogether desirable. On February 2, he again requested Gorgas to expedite the three tons of steel for pistol barrels and cylinders: ". . . am ready to make use of it, if it were here. The machinery is all set up, ready for work again, and yesterday was put in motion. If steel is received the manufactory of pistols can be pushed vigorously. I dislike to make use of iron for cylinders for reasons known to you, but unless the steel arrives soon, I shall be compelled to make use of it to keep the workmen employed."[20]

On March 31, 1864, Burton acknowledged requests for a total of 924 "Revolving Pistols for the Army of Tenn.," approved by Gorgas. Said Burton: "They will be supplied as soon as possible, but I beg to inform you that much delay and loss of time and labor resulted from the use of iron for cylinders. The last powder proof of cylinders resulted in the bursting of 18 out of 32 proved. This proof test is not too great in my opinion, and it is better that the cylinder should burst here than after issuance. Can you hurry on the steel for the cylinders?"[21] Poor Burton— the records fail to show that he ever received this needed material.

Atlanta fell to General William Tecumseh Sherman on November 9, 1864, but long before this the handwriting on the wall was apparent to the nearby Macon Armory. On September 2, Burton ordered his Master Armorer to "take down and pack all machinery for pistol-making," as well as the machinery which supplied the Richmond Armory with gun stocks. On September 5, Colonel Burton notified Gorgas that he was sending his machinery to Savannah for storage, but alas, could find no transportation. He would ship as soon as transportation became available. Upon receipt of this message, Gorgas wired him not to move the pistol machinery.

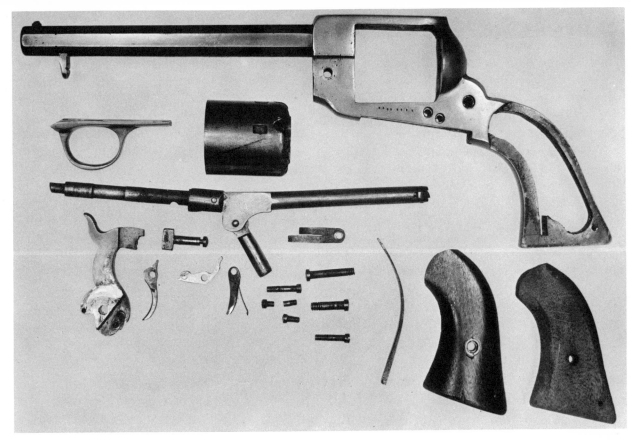

DISASSEMBLED SPILLER AND BURR

Serial number 1140, showing components. Note the markings on the frame.

The gun stocking machinery, Gorgas suggested, should be sent to Columbia, South Carolina.[22]

Only a glance through the correspondence of the Macon Armory for this period is needed to see the real state of affairs within the Confederacy—there was a suggestion to remove the machinery of Louis Haiman's pistol factory from Columbus, Georgia, to Columbia, South Carolina, and to discontinue the making of pistols and utilize the machinery for rifle-making; then the confession on September 23 that no more gun stocks were available, as the entire supply of blanks had been exhausted, and no additional supply was foreseen despite all efforts to secure it.

On the same date in reply to a request from Major F. W. Cook, head of Cook and Brothers Rifle Factory in Athens, Georgia, for a safe place to move his machinery, Burton was forced to write that he knew of no point within the Confederacy which could be called "safe." Four days later, Burton wrote Gorgas that Major Cook's factory had been closed for the past two months because the government had failed to pay anything for the work done since March 1, 1864.[23]

To digress—let us return to the pistols. On October 5, Burton wired Gorgas advising that the Armory was without work and asked whether he should unpack the pistol machinery and put it to work again. The reply to this was in the affirmative, and the following day Burton directed his Master Armorer to set up the machinery and to push the making of pistols "with all vigor possible." By October 13, he was able to advise his chief: "Pistol machinery re-erected here, and manufactury of pistols resumed."[24]

The resumption was of short duration. In mid-November, Sherman's operations near Macon caused Burton to again dismantle his machinery. He wanted to send it to Columbia, South Carolina, but only half got away before the Central Railway was cut by the enemy. When the threat to Macon passed, Burton attempted to resume his pistol-making activities, doing what he could with half of his tools. On December 7, he wrote "I am in hopes to have the pistol machinery back from Columbia in 2 or 3 weeks."[25] Hopes, vain hopes! The rest of his machinery was never recovered, and all work performed after the middle of November, 1864, was done with only half his original machinery and with whatever makeshifts he could devise.

Master Armorer Jeremiah Fuzz suggested on December 7: "If it is intended to resume the making of pistols at this Armory, I would recommend proceeding with the casting of lock frames, as it would always be best to have that branch of the work in advance. Other employment can readily be furnished the founder when it may be desired to suspend casting. No report of operations for November was made because there was no work completed during the month. A few pistols were assembled ready for proving, but as they are unfinished, it was deemed improper to report them."[26] A later report from the Armory on December 31, 1864, indicates that the Master Armorer's suggestion had been followed, because it shows 164 lock frames cast. A January report shows 116 frames and 166 trigger-guards cast, and in addition, 500 triggers filed and 342 main springs completed.[27]

Despite this attempt to do the best they could with what was at hand, there is conclusive proof

that the manufacture of pistols was never actually resumed after November, 1864. This proof comes in the form of a memo from Master Armorer Fuzz to Burton dated March 31, 1865, that one rifling machine would be required before the manufacture of pistols could be resumed. It was never delivered and a month later the war was over.

To summarize, Spiller and Burr, with the assistance of Lieutenant Colonel Burton, contracted to supply the Confederate States of America with 15,000 revolvers. While sample revolvers were forthcoming over a year later, actual production did not start until the spring of 1863, and this was the only year in which pistols were made because in January, 1864, the government bought them out. The factory was then moved from Atlanta to Macon, where manufacture was continued under government ownership, but without a break in serial number sequence.

Reference has already been made to the fact that some of these revolvers are marked *Spiller & Burr* on the top of the barrel and that others are devoid of such markings. "Firearms of the Confederacy"[28] has this theory to offer as to why some are marked and others unmarked. "Of these Confederate 'Whitney's' in museums and private collections, there is no record of a *Spiller & Burr* with a serial above 600. It has been assumed that the unmarked revolvers were made by the government after the purchase of the Spiller & Burr plant, but that is only conjecture." In other words, all revolvers up to serial number 600 were made by the contractors and all over 600 were made by the government. This theory is good only so long as actual serial numbers of known existing specimens are not closely examined. Once this is done, it is seen that the *Spiller & Burr* imprint is likely to appear on almost any weapon.

Let us examine the serial numbers on the guns known to the authors. These have been collected over a period of years, and have been transcribed from one piece of paper to another so often that there is a distinct possibility of error in both the serial number itself and additional markings. However, such errors if they exist should be relatively slight, and will not affect the overall picture.

SPILLER AND BURR REVOLVERS

72–Unmarked except for serial.
75–Serial and firm name.
77–Serial and firm name.
79–Serial on barrel and loading lever. Firm name on barrel. Arbor numbered 17. Some parts not original.

81–Believed to contain only serial.
86–Serial and firm name.
98–Serial and firm name.
101–Markings unknown.
104–Serial and firm name. *CS* on right side of frame.
120–Fitted with a detachable shoulder stock. Barrel, loading lever and cylinder from a Whitney. *CS* on right side of frame. *South Carolina* stamped on barrel top. Roman numeral *VIII* under the barrel and *XI* or *IX* on the stock. *CS* burned in stock.
124–Serial and *CS* on left side of frame.
128–Markings unknown.

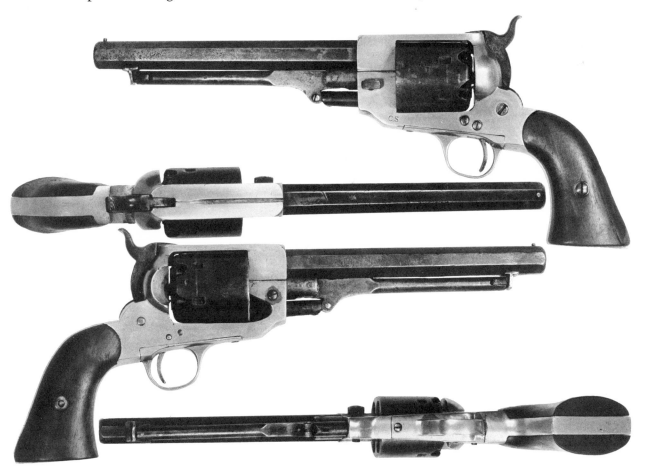

Courtesy Tom Parvin

FOUR VIEWS OF A SPILLER AND BURR REVOLVER

Marked with firm's name, but no serial number. Letter or figure O stamped on loading lever and rear of cylinder.

131—Believed to have only serial.

150—Serial and firm name. *CS* on left side of frame.

160—Serial only.

186—Serial only.

209—Markings unknown.

241—Markings unknown.

268—Serial and firm name.

272—Markings unknown.

319—Serial and firm name.

370—Markings unknown.

379—Serial and firm name. Grips replaced.

421—Markings unknown.

434—Serial only. *CS* on left side of frame.

490—Serial and firm name.

498—Believed to contain only serial.

517—Unmarked except for large *M* under grips. Main spring broken and loading lever lug missing.

518—Markings unknown.

535—Serial and firm name.

540—Markings unknown.

564—Markings unknown.

570—Markings unknown.

585—Believed to contain only serial and *CS* on right side of frame.

616—Markings unknown.

651—Markings unknown. Loading lever replaced.

666—Markings unknown.

703—Serial only.

742—Serial only. *CS* on left side of frame.

752—Markings unknown.

763—Serial only. *CS* on left side of frame.

828—Believed to contain only serial.

855—Serial only.

895—Markings unknown.

903—Serial only.

905—Serial and firm name.

917—Serial only. *CS* on left side of frame.

965—Serial and firm name.

969—Serial and firm name.

983—Serial only. *CS* on right side of frame.

988—Markings unknown.

1028—Serial and firm name.

1031—Markings unknown.

1058—Markings unknown.

1062—Serial only. *CS* on left side of frame.

1086—Serial only. *CS* on left side of frame. Internal parts and trigger-guard missing.

1107—Markings unknown.

1124—Serial only. No *CS* on frame.

1140—Serial only. *CS* on left side of frame.

1182—Markings unknown.

1214—Markings unknown.

1234—Serial only. *CS* on right side of frame.

In addition, two additional Spiller and Burrs should be noted. These bear no serial or firm name. One has already been described as possibly being a sample. The other, not examined, is said to be unmarked except for *CS* on the left side of the frame. It should be noted in the serial listing that in many cases no definite determination has been made as to which guns are stamped *CS* in addition to the serials. Those which are so noted were definitely established, but the statement "unmarked except for serial" does not mean that the gun might not be stamped *CS* in addition.

We have now a list of 62 revolvers of which twelve with serial numbers under 600 are known to carry the firm name. Also to be noted are seven below 600 definitely established as not marked with the name of the firm.

Thus it is seen that the firm name is found both above and below 600, and it is reasonable to believe that whether a gun is marked *Spiller & Burr* or not had nothing to do with whether it was made by Spiller and Burr, or by the Confederate States Government.

A brief note from Burton to Gorgas, dated December 4, 1862, may throw light on the subject. On that date, Burton reported that he had inspected the pistol factory and found it almost ready to turn out the finished weapons, "having on hand 2,650 barrels in the process of manufacture." This one sentence gives us an insight

AN HISTORIC SPILLER AND BURR

The personal weapon of Col. George Raines. Serial number 763.

hitherto lacking. Even before the first revolver was turned out, the firm had more barrels on hand than were ever actually used, in various stages of completion.

Barrels of the Whitney model revolver are not an integral part of the gun. They were merely screwed into the frame. Precision tools are not a recent invention, so the fact that the barrels were octagonal in shape would not prevent them being finished and stamped prior to their assembly. It would appear, and this is substantiated by Burton's report to Gorgas, that the firm first tackled the problem of barrel-making before going on to the frame casting, etc., with a stock pile of barrels accumulating before other components. Trusty old M. T. William, reliable and sober employee, was given the firm's die with *Spiller & Burr* on it—a portion of the final *r* broken—and told to stamp barrels. Hammer in one hand, die in the other, he went about this business with his usual thoroughness. In consequence, those which could be easily reached were marked, those hard to get at are bare.

Now let us return to the question of how many guns were made by Spiller and Burr and how many by the government during their one year of manufacture. Macon Armory records for 1864 reflect the following assembly of pistols: January—0, February—0, March—100, April—150, May—100, June—162, July—80, August—0, September—0, October—50, November—35, December—12. This is a total of 689 revolvers, and as December, 1864, was the last month in which these revolvers were manufactured, this figure must represent the entire output under the Confederate Government.

In the Confederate Museum in Richmond is a Spiller and Burr serial No. 763, not marked with the firm name, formerly the property of General Raines, Commandant of the Augusta Arsenal. This pistol had been presented to him "as a product of the Macon Armory." From this we deduce that the output under Spiller and Burr, in Atlanta, could not possibly have exceeded 762 revolvers, otherwise serial 763 could not have been presented "as a product of the Macon Armory."

General Raines and Colonel Burton had always been closely associated and each was an admirer of the other. It appears natural then that in presenting General Raines with a revolver it would have been one of the first turned out. If this reasoning is correct, then the weapons made by the government started at somewhere near the 763 mark. Having already established that under their manufacture only 689 revolvers were turned out, then the total output of Spiller and Burr (762 revolvers), and the government would be no more than 1,451, or less than this if serial No. 763 was not the first revolver made at Macon.

The *CS* stamping found on most pistols was evidently applied by the C.S. Ordnance Inspector at Macon, after the revolvers had been received there, proved, inspected and accepted. This stamp made them official Confederate property and also showed that they had passed inspection. As far as it can be determined, there is no essential difference between the revolvers made in Atlanta and those made in Macon, considering that all were hand-finished. The later ones, perhaps, have a greater angle between grip and frame.

All barrels are octagon, 6 to 6¼ inches in length, with some stamped *Spiller & Burr*, reading from front to rear. Some are unmarked except for the serial on the underside of the barrel. They were rifled with seven lands and grooves, right gain-twist, and are .36 caliber. The cylinder is 6-shot, made from twisted iron with lateral faults usually visible. Nipples have the English thread rather than the standard Colt's, while as a safety device, the hammer engages a slot between the nipples on the cylinder of the gun. The grips are two-piece walnut, with a brass washer on both sides to hold the screw. The pin which keeps the grips in place is at the far end of the butt. The frame is cast brass, varying in color from yellow to red due to the many sources and mixtures of brass and copper used. Most are stamped *C.S.* on their left or right sides. Several variations of loading lever have been found, but they are similar to the Whitney. On the other hand, the foresight was a distinctive brass "cone," rather than a peg or pin as found on a Whitney. Serial numbers are stamped on the major parts, although some cylinders are found without them. The twisted iron cylinder precludes buffing off the numbers of a Whitney and using it on a Spiller and Burr.

Considering the present value of a Spiller and Burr to be relatively high and rising steadily, it is interesting to note what they cost on September 7, 1864, when Burton wrote Gorgas on "Cost of revolving pistol as manufactured at this Armory at present: Cost of material—$19.59; cost of labor and supervision—$34.62; interest on capital investment at 8% per annum—$8.00. Total cost per pistol, $62.21."[29]

Although Colonel Burton gives $62.21 as the price per revolver, we are inclined to disagree with him. Let someone who is more mathematically inclined figure out the actual cost of these 1,451 revolvers to the Confederacy, remembering the initial outlay advanced, the purchase price paid to Spiller and Burr, the cost of the Macon Armory, etc. We are of the opinion that today's collector who pays $1,000 for one of these weapons is getting it considerably cheaper than did its original owner—the Confederate States of America!

FOOTNOTE REFERENCES

1. Letter from J. P. Smith, Rapine, Virginia, to Richard D. Steuart, February 10, 1920.
2. William A. Albaugh, III, *The Confederate Brass-Framed Colt & Whitney* (Washington, D. C., 1955), p. 28.
3. *Ibid.*, pp. 28-29.
4. Letter to Richard D. Steuart, July 17, 1928.
5. Albaugh, *Brass-Framed Colt*, p. 34.
6. *C.R.O.R.*, Vol. 20, 6-11-22.

7. Letter to Richard D. Steuart, May, 1922.
8. *C.R.O.R.*, Vol. 10, 2-28-62.
9. *Ibid.*, 3-3-63.
10. *C.R.O.R.*, Vol. 20, 11-29-62.
11. *Ibid.*, 12-17-62.
12. Albaugh, *Brass-Framed Colt*, p. 45.
13. *C.R.O.R.*, Vol. 20, 1-1-63.
14. *Ibid.*, 12-26-62.
15. *C.R.O.R.*, Vol. 10, 1-27-63.
16. *C.R.O.R.*, Vol. 20, 4-18-63.
17. *C.R.O.R.*, Vol. 33, 5-2-63.
18. *C.R.O.R.*, Vol. 41, 1-9-64.
19. *C.R.O.R., Ibid.*
20. *C.R.O.R.*, Vol. 41, 2-21-64.
21. *Ibid.*, 3-31-64.
22. *C.R.O.R.*, Vol. 29, September 2, 5, 8, 10, 1864.
23. *Ibid.*, 9-23-64, 9-27-64.
24. *Ibid.*, 10-13-64.
25. *Ibid.*, 12-7-64.
26. *Ibid.*
27. Albaugh, *Brass-Framed Colt*, p. 77.
28. Claud E. Fuller and Richard D. Steuart, *Firearms of the Confederacy* (Huntington, West Virginia, 1944), p. 281.
29. *C.R.O.R.*, Vol. 29, 9-7-64.

NOTES

PART II

CHAPTERS 7 and 8

PRIMARY MARTIAL HANDGUNS
MADE ABROAD

Handguns of foreign manufacture made under contract with the Confederate Government

CHAPTER 7

Le Mat

ONE of the most interesting Civil War revolvers is that made under the Le Mat Patent. Its unusual design has long made it desirable to collectors despite a great lack of information concerning its background. The almost total destruction of Southern records has placed the Le Mat revolver in a controversial class. There has been considerable conjecture as to whether it should be classed as Confederate or simply a revolver of foreign manufacture made for commercial sale. It is usually listed as being "a favorite with Southern officers." While few collectors will disagree with such a classification,

fewer still will list the Le Mat simply as "Confederate." Most have been willing to wait for documentary proof one way or the other.

While what follows does not pretend to answer all questions that might arise concerning these guns, we believe sufficient information is presented to prove that they are Confederate.

DR. JEAN ALEXANDRE FRANÇOIS LE MAT

In July, 1956, the authors had the extreme good fortune and pleasure of locating and interviewing Mrs. Eugenie Le Mat Eggleston,

Courtesy Confederate Museum, Richmond, Virginia

A LE MAT OF NOTABLE ASSOCIATION

A personal weapon of General P. G. T. Beauregard. This specimen is serial number 427. The carefully executed and restrained application of engraving dignifies this arm.

granddaughter of "Colonel" Le Mat, inventor of the "grape-shot" revolver. Although unacquainted with any details of revolver making, Mrs. Eggleston, with the utmost graciousness, granted us access to several photographs and considerable general information as to the Le Mat family.

Mrs. Eggleston stated:

I am the granddaughter of Colonel Le Mat and and the daughter of Maurice Le Mat, eldest son of the Colonel. My father was born in New Orleans in 1850 and he had one sister older than

The name "Le Mat" in accordance with the seagoing background of my family, meant "the mast" or "the good." My grandfather in his early days continued the family seafaring tradition and made many voyages to America. On one such visit he met and fell in love with my grandmother, Justine Sophie Lepretre, daughter of a well-to-do planter near New Orleans. After their marriage in the 1840's my grandfather settled in New Orleans, devoting himself to the practice of medicine.

Always of an inventive nature, about this time he invented a pistol whose manufacture completely absorbed the next few years of his life. He passionately embraced the Confederate States

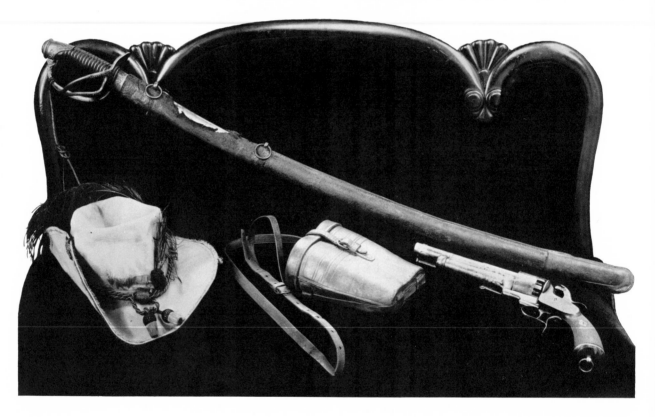

Courtesy Confederate Museum, Richmond, Virginia

MEMENTOS OF THE PLUMED KNIGHT

The immortal Jeb Stuart's sword, field glasses, hat and Le Mat revolver, serial No. 105.

he named Anna. He had two younger sisters named Marie and Jeanne, also a brother Emil who was the baby of the family. My grandfather was born in Paris about 1824, being one of three sons.

when it came into being and forsook the medical profession to supply his beloved South with revolvers in their War of Independence.

I have no idea how he fared in this venture financially but I do know that the family always

Courtesy Mrs. Eugenie Le Mat Eggleston

JEAN ALEXANDRE FRANÇOIS LE MAT, *CIRCA 1860*

maintained a most comfortable establishment in Paris, presided over by an ex-slave who remained with us until her death.

According to my father, during this period of the Colonel's life he was constantly traveling between Paris and the Confederate States and after the war made many trips to America, although always maintaining his home in Paris. During the Franco-Prussian War he served as a surgeon for the French army. I know my grandfather had quite a reputation as an inventor and I wish I could give you more information as to his revolver, but oddly enough the thing I remember best is that he invented some sort of a fire extinguisher. In appearance my grandfather was a very distinguished personage; in character he was noble and generous, in disposition, kind and gentle. I am very proud to be his granddaughter.

Jean Alexandre François Le Mat received his degree as a Doctor of Medicine in 1842; the *Medical Register of New Orleans* carrying this record on page 188: "Porteur d'un diplôme du la faculté du Montpellier, delivré le 15 Juillet 1842." The same source, however, indicates that Le Mat did not secure his license to practice medicine in New Orleans until permission was granted by that city's Medical Committee at their meeting of November 28, 1849. In the meantime he had evidently married Sophie Lepretre, as the 1850 City Directory lists them as man and wife living at 188 Dauphine Street.

The first indication that Le Mat was of an inventive nature appears in 1856, when he was granted a patent by the United States patent office for a revolver which combined the features of the six-shot revolver and the single-barrel shotgun. This was assigned patent number 15925, dated October 21, 1856. It was described later by the New Orleans *Daily Delta* of June 21, 1861, as being ". . . one of the most formidable weapons of the pistol kind ever invented." Formidable was the correct word, for the revolver had a cylinder containing not six, but nine shots of .42 caliber which revolved

upon a central barrel of .63 caliber which contained a buckshot (so-called "grape-shot") cartridge. The revolving cylinder and the buckshot barrel were fired by the same hammer merely by shifting the hammernose up or down. As originally conceived, this hammer had two noses.

Dr. Le Mat appeared before a notary public, Theodore Guyal, on September 14, 1857, and filed a statement concerning his patent of October 15, 1856:

UNITED STATES OF AMERICA
STATE OF LOUISIANA
CITY OF NEW ORLEANS

Be it Known that on this Fourteenth day of September in the year of Our Lord One Thousand Eight Hundred and Fifty-seven and of the Independence of the United States of America the Eighty-second:

Before me, Theodore Guyal, a Notary Public in and for the Parish and City of New Orleans, State of Louisiana, duly commissioned and qualified:

Personally came and appeared ALEXANDRE LE MAT, of the City of New Orleans, aforesaid who produced and exhibited to me said Notary a *Patent* issued by the Patent Office of the United States of America, granting unto him, the said Le Mat, his heirs, administrators or assigns for the Term of Fourteen years from the Twenty-first day of October One Thousand Eight Hundred and Fifty-six, the full and exclusive right and liberty of making, constructing, using and vending to others to be used a new and useful *Improved Fire Arm*, the invention of the said Le Mat as fully described and delineated in the Schedule and drawings attached to said Patent, and in which the invention claimed by him and secured by said Patent consists of First: The substitution of a Shot Barrel to the solid cylinder as a Pin, upon which the revolving cartridge cylinder of revolvers constructed upon Colt's or similar systems revolve, in the manner and for the purposes as described: and Second: The Gun cock No. 11 with a double hammer a & b constructed and operating substantially as described and for the purposes specified.

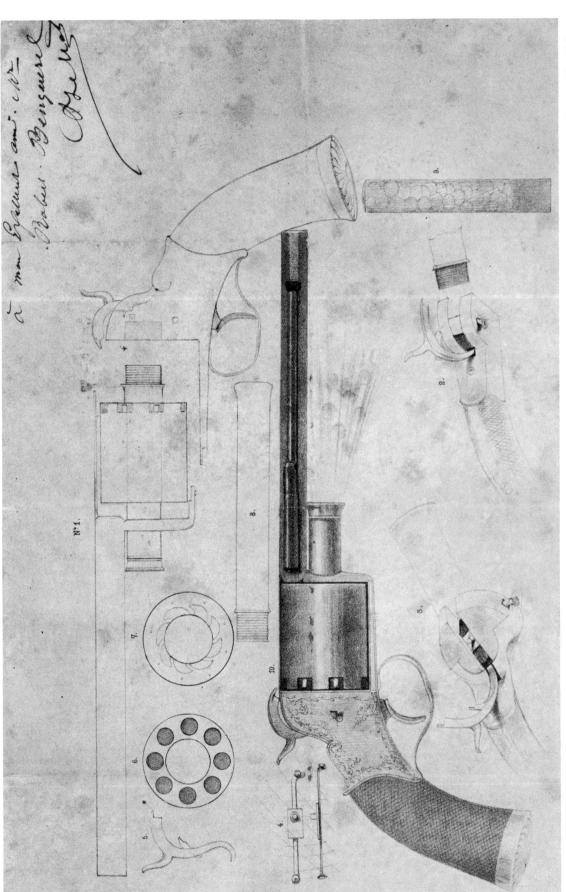

LE MAT'S ORIGINAL SKETCH

A pencil drawing signed by Le Mat and inscribed in French, "to my excellent friend Mr. Robert Benguerel." Robert Benguerel was Le Mat's friend and attorney in the clouded "New Orleans Affair." The reader's attention is invited to detail 6 on the sketch which shows only eight chambers for the revolver loads rather than the nine of all existing specimens. The official patent drawing covering U. S. Patent No. 15925, dated October 21, 1856, was obviously developed from this sketch and it conforms to the detail of the eight chambers as shown.

Courtesy Samuel E. Smith

A FIRST MODEL LE MAT

Serial number 163. The semi-circular inlay behind the silver star is marked *Co. A 18 Ga.* The 18th Georgia regiment was one of the state's most famous.

Which said Patent bears the No. 15925 and dated at the City of Washington on the Twenty-first day of October Eighteen Hundred and Fifty-six.

And the said Alexandre Le Mat having requested me, said Notary, to certify to the existence of the said Letter Patent in his possession. I have granted these presents under my Signature and Seal of Office at New Orleans on this fourteenth day of September in the year of Our Lord One Thousand Eight Hundred and Fifty-seven.

Theo. Guyal

The purpose of such a notarized statement obviously was the future promotion and sale of the revolver so patented. Copies of the statement could be handed out as affirmations of intent.

Two years later a working partnership was formed between Dr. Le Mat and Pierre Gustave Toutant Beauregard, at the time a major in the United States Army Engineers, stationed in New Orleans. Later he was to become one of the foremost Confederate generals.

THE LE MAT-BEAUREGARD PARTNERSHIP

The contract between Le Mat and Beauregard plainly indicates that the two fully intended first to protect themselves from imitations by securing patents in all major countries and, after this had been done, to manufacture and sell the revolver. This contract is dated April 4, 1859, and is entitled "Contract of Sales and Association." It provided that one-quarter of Le Mat's patent rights were to be ceded to Beauregard in exchange for certain favors which Beauregard, as a major in the United States Army, would be in a position to bring about, plus certain financial commitments.

Four days after the signing of the partnership agreement, Major Beauregard signed several notes to enable Dr. Le Mat to raise money to promote the grape-shot revolver. A copy of one of these notes reads as follows:

New Orleans, April 8th, 1859
Being the sole authorized Agent for the United States of Dr. Alexandre Le Mat for the sale and proper disposal of his Grape Shot revolver (a great and superior improvement on Colt's), I herewith promise to pay from his share of the first net proceeds of said sales or disposals—whatever sum or sums may be furnished him (including interest thereon @ 10% per annum) for the purpose of providing him with means to visit Europe for the sale or disposal of his Patents for said arm—

G. T. Beauregard[1]

Beauregard's first attempt to publicize Le Mat's weapon was on March 2, 1859, when a quasi-official board composed of prominent Army, Navy and political personages gave the revolver a public trial. The report by this board was quite favorable.

New Orleans, March 2nd, 1859
We the undersigned have examined and tried the "Grape shot revolving pistol" of Mr. A. Le Mat of this city and feel no hesitation in stating that after a close examination of said arm, we consider it a great and important improvement on Colt's revolver. . . .

We consider this arm far superior to any we have seen for the use of cavalry acting against Indians or when charging on a square of infantry or a battery of field pieces. It is also indispensable for artillerist's in defending their pieces against such a charge, and for infantry defending a breach. . . . Its advantages in the naval service in boarding or repelling boarders is too obvious to require anything but passing notice. . . .

It is more than probable that the introduction and use of this pistol in the cavalry service would give to the latter the preponderance over the infantry, if not armed in like manner, for what would become of a line or square of infantry after its fire should have been drawn by the cavalry when the latter coming up to within a few paces would pour 10 shots into their very faces. . . .

We earnestly recommend that this arm should be introduced in our military and naval services,

so soon as the Government will find it practicable to do so. . . .

Signed by

L. Rousseau	A. C. Myers
Capt. U.S. Navy	Lt. Col. U.S. Army
G. T. Beauregard	R. Smith
B.V. Maj. U.S. Army	Late Capt. U.S. Army
F. E. Prime	G. W. Lay
1st Lieut. U.S. Engr.	Lt. Col. ADC
	to Gen. in Chief

We the undersigned have examined Mr. Le Mat's revolver and fully concur in the above opinions and recommendations.

I think highly of the above weapon
Winfield Scott

Braxton Bragg	P. O. Herbert
Late Lt. Col. U.S. Army	Late Brvt. Col. U.S.A.
N. G. Evans	Late Gov. of Louis.
Capt. U.S. 2nd Cavalry	E. K. Smith
	Capt. U.S. 2nd
	Cavalry[2]

W. H. Stevens

The results of the trial were published May 21, 1859, in *The True Delta, The Bee* and *The Crescent* (all of New Orleans) in the form of paid advertisements. But shortly before their appearance Le Mat submitted this "Report of the Special Board" to Colonel Samuel Cooper, Adjutant General, United States Army, in Washington, D. C., on May 11, going to that city armed with various letters of introduction to the Honorable John B. Floyd, Secretary of War.

A board composed of Lieutenant Colonel Joseph E. Johnston, First Cavalry, Brevet Major George D. Ramsey and Brevet Major Theodore T. S. Laidley, Ordnance, convened at the Washington Arsenal on May 11, 1859, and its report was transmitted as follows:

Washington, D. C.
May 11, 1859

Colonel:
I have the honor, herewith, to transmit the report of the Board of Officers instructed by Special Orders No. 80 of May 9th, 1859 for the pur-

pose of examining a firearm invented by Mr. Alexandre Le Mat.

> Very respectfully, I am,
> Your obt. servnt.
> T. T. S. Laidley
> B. Major, Capt. of Ord.
> Recorder.

Col. S. Cooper
Adjutant General
Washington, D. C.[3]

> Washington, D. C.
> May 11, 1859

Col. S. Cooper
Adj. Gen.
Colonel:

The Board commenced by Special Orders No. 80 dated, War Department, Adjutant General's Office, Washington, May 9th, 1859, "For the purpose of examining a fire-arm invented by Mr. Le Mat," met at Washington Arsenal, agreeably to instructions, and having performed the duty assigned them, have the honor to make the following report:

Description of the Arm

The arm presented by Mr. Alexandre Le Mat for examination is a revolving belt or holster-pistol. In its general features it resembles Colt's revolving pistol, having, like that, a revolving cylinder, containing several chambers, which are brought in turn, in the prolongation of the single barrel. The mechanism by which the cylinder is made to revolve is precisely that used in Colt's pistol.

The distinguishing feature of this pistol is the pin around which the cylinder revolves; This, instead of being solid as in the revolving pistols, is a pistol barrel of large calibre, which can be loaded at the muzzle with ball or buckshot, and fired with the same facility, and by the same means as the revolving cylinder.

The under part of the front end of the hammer is hinged, and revolves through an angle of 90°, and is readily made to strike at pleasure, on the cone of the central barrel, or on those of the cylinder.

The cylinder of the pistol presented has chambers for *nine* separate charges, and each chamber is capable of containing about sixteen grains of powder, and an elongated ball of 0.75 inch. in length.

The lever for ramming the balls of the cylinder is placed on the side of the barrel. It is made hollow to receive the rammer for the central barrel. This latter rammer is not fixed to the pistol but is retained in the hollow lever by the friction on its sides, the hole not being straight. The end of the hammer which strikes the cone is so formed as to prevent the explosion by the caps from bursting it, or scratching its lower end, as it sometimes prevents the cylinder from revolving.

Dimensions of the Arm

Length of the barrel	7.3 inches
" " " cylinder	1.7 "
" " " bore of central barrel.	6.6 "
Diameter of the cylinder	1.95 "
" " " central barrel, ext. ..	.83 "
" " " bore of central barrel	.65 "
" " " bore of cylinder chambers	.41 "
Total length of pistol	14.1 "
Weight of the pistol	3.96 lbs.
Diameter of ball for the revolver ...	0.41 inch
Weight of ball for the revolver .....206 gr.
Weight of charge of powder for revolver	16 gr.
Weight of ball for central barrel ....406 gr.
Number of buckshot in cartridge ..	15 each
Weight of charge of powder for buckshot	40 gr.

Test Firing

The pistol was fired with 16 grains of powder and elongated ball, *twenty-five* times.

The central barrel was fired *three* times with balls and *ten* times with buckshot.

Penetration at 30 Paces

The elongated ball, with 16 gr. of powder, 2½ inches.

The round ball, from central barrel, 2½ inches.

Buckshot, at 15 paces, with 40 gr. of powder, 1 inch.

The board are of the opinion that the arm presented by Mr. Le Mat is an improvement which adds materially to the efficiency of the revolver giving, as it does, a greater number of shots for the same weight of arm and also adding another barrel of large calibre, capable of throwing a heavy ball with a large charge of powder, or, more particularly, a load of buckshot, with great effect at short distance. It is a merit which is not known to be possessed by any other pistol now in use, whilst the additional mechanism for this purpose is practical and simple in its construction.

It is believed that improvements might be made in some of the defects as, for instance, in the lever for ramming, which is large and cumbrous and gives a clumsy appearance to the pistol.

From the nature of the trials which the board could give this arm, its durability (which is the only question with regard to it that requires to be tested) could not be thoroughly tried, and the board respectfully recommends that this arm be subjected to trial in the hands of troops that are in actual service in the field.

Very Respt. your obt. Servt.

J. E. Johnston
Lt. Col. 1st Cavalry
T. T. S. Laidley
B. Major, Capt. Ord.
Recorder.[4]

Although the board recommended the pistol be given a trial by the U.S. Army, there is no indication that this was ever done. However, Le Mat apparently took note of the board's remarks about the "clumsy appearing" loading lever, and it is believed that the Kerr type levers that appeared on some of his weapons were an attempt to overcome this criticism. Unfortunately, the Kerr type lever was not adaptable to the Le Mat pistol as it could not provide for the rod for the shotgun barrel.

While in Washington, Le Mat obtained a patent on a "New and improved hammer for revolving firearms." It was given patent number 24312. This patent is dated June 7, 1859.

If the names of some of the persons who have appeared in the past few pages are familiar, it is not surprising. In the "Report of the Special Board," conducted in New Orleans, Beauregard, Bragg, Evans and Smith became generals in the Confederate Army, while Huger died defending New Orleans as Lieutenant Commander, C.S.N. The "John B. Floyd, Secretary of War" to whom the letters of introduction were addressed was a former governor of the state of Virginia, and later a general, C.S.A. Joseph E. Johnston hardly needs an introduction to those interested in Confederate history, nor does Samuel Cooper who, two years hence, was to be Adjutant and Inspector General for the Confederate States Army. The C. Girard who witnessed patent number 24312 was, in a short time, to become Le Mat's partner and owner of a three-quarter interest in the revolver venture.

For the nine months following the date of the patent for the "Adjustable Hammer," the energetic doctor was in Europe. During this time he accomplished much in keeping with the terms of the partnership with Beauregard. It is noted that one of the letters of introduction written for Le Mat says that "he will visit Washington on his way to Europe." It is to be remembered also, that the patent for the "Adjustable Hammer" was dated June 7, 1859, while the French patent is dated July 20, 1859, so one sees that the busy doctor lost little time in proceeding to Europe. There he took out patents for his grape-shot revolver in Russia, Spain, Belgium, England, Prussia and Saxony.

At this point it might be well to introduce the standard markings that appeared on those pistols made in France. These were in two forms: *Col. Le Mat Bte. s.g.d.g. Paris* or *Syst. Le Mat Bte. s.g.d.g. Paris.* "Bte." is French for patent. The "s.g.d.g." is the abbreviation for "sans garantie du gouvernement" or, in other words, patented, but without guarantee of the government.

It is assumed that while in Paris Le Mat made arrangements for the production of his grape-shot revolvers. Also about this time, unknown to partner Beauregard, Charles Girard was employed by Le Mat as "special agent in Europe."

This last we know because of a letter from Beauregard to Le Mat:

New Orleans   20 March 1860

My dear Colonel,

You tell me that you have received a letter from Dr. Girard, in which he seems to feel hurt by what we wrote directly to Messrs. Newton and [illegible] . . . wyck, concerning the active part I have in the matter of Revolver, etc., etc.

I am truly very sorry, but at the time I did not know that Monsieur Girard was your *special agent* in Europe, and that all correspondence should have passed through his hands, in order not to provoke his extreme sensitivity! In business, however, I know only of one way of procedure and of doing things; it is *in a regular* manner!

Either the thing we have undertaken is serious, or it is pure childishness: in this latter case one can act entirely on confidence—in the other case—it should be done in a regular way, even at the risk of vexing the susceptibilities, not too acute, of certain friends. Anyway, I have not done anything that I would not have done to one of my brothers—no more, no less. And the best proof that I was right is that you've just lost the sale of ¼ of your Patents for $20,000 (which would have helped to eliminate all the difficulties in the manufacturing of the weapon *here* and in Europe), because you did not have the necessary documents *to prove* the purchase of European Patents! That in business your word or mine do not go any farther than the tips of our noses! Anyway, you are not immortal, unfortunately, and, after you, it won't be "the end of the world!"

Without any lack of confidence in your sensitive friend, I recommended to you, as you may well remember, to interest him strongly in our undertaking in order to encourage and to recompense him—and now he is angry at us!

As far as I am concerned, you should know, because I told you quite often—I am ready, whenever you wish, to sell my quarter interest for $10,000, or to transfer it to you, *to you,* for the

amounts that I have invested in this business up to date, all the details of which are at your disposal—without asking anything for my work! I think your friend could not ask for anything more unselfish!

He also seems to think that you have ceded me this quarter interest for "a trifle." Trifle or no trifle, I offer it to him on the same conditions as to you—and I think that in every country of the world, a thing, good or bad, "is not worth more than it produces."

Under present circumstances I would be happy to leave matters in the same condition as they were before your letter of 27 January—if it can help our business, and to retain Dr. Girard as our General and Special Agent for Europe, because he stands high in my opinion, and I have full confidence in him. But shouldn't we at least possess all the necessary documents to prove, if necessary, *to our creditors* that we are not joking, and to our heirs that they can (perhaps) take over our labors where we left them, to lead to success and prosperity—

Yours devotedly

G. T. Beauregard

To Col. A. Le Mat
New Orleans, La.[5]

The partnership of Beauregard and Le Mat came to an end and on April 10, 1860, the former turned over a quantity of papers relating to the grape-shot revolvers. Fortunately, for those of us interested in such things, Beauregard kept duplicate copies and these are still extant. Two are of interest.

The first such paper indicates that all the leading firearms companies in the country had been queried, apparently as to the possibility of their manufacturing the Le Mat revolver. There is no indication that any replied affirmatively.

N. Orleans April 10th 1860

I gave this day the following papers to Col. Le Mat—

1. The Patents of France, U. States, Russia, Spain, Belgian [illegible]

Not yet received—England, Prussia & Saxony—
2. Report of Special Board Wash. May 11th 1859
3.   "   of H. P. Andrews N.Y. Nov. 15th 1859
4. Answer of Manhattan Firearms Co.   ?   1859
5.   "   " Bacon & Co.   Oct. 31   "
6.   "   " Davis & Co.   Nov. 1   "
7.   "   " Chicopee Falls Co.   " 10   "
8.   "   " James T. Warner   "   "
       Springfield Arms Co.
9.   "   " Muzzy & Co.   "   "   "

The second included a listing of expenditures:

April 6, 1859 Paid to make contract
                for Grape shot revolver
                as partner with Le Mat. $500.00
April 16, 1859 Paid to complete con-
                tract.   4,500—
April 19, 1859 S. W. Thuil for copy on
                tracing paper of Grape
                Shot Revolver   15—

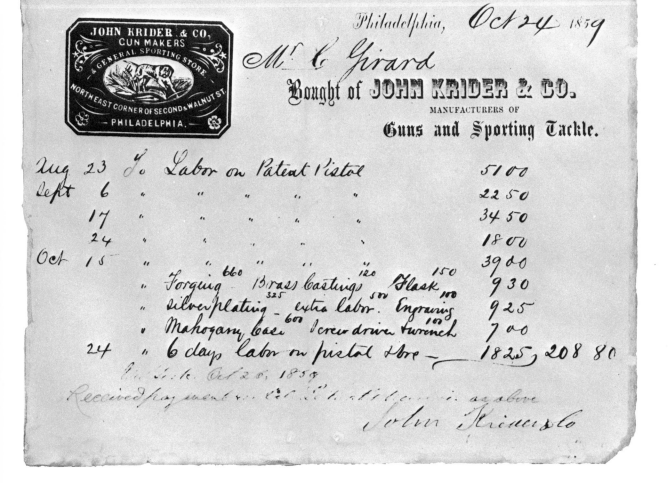

EVIDENCE OF THE FIRST LE MAT

Bill from John Krider & Co., Philadelphia, for "patent pistol," probably for the first working model.

Courtesy Edward N. Simmons

LE MAT PERCUSSION REVOLVER

Marked Serial No. 1

May 25, 1859	To notices in 3 paper of Govt. Trial of Revl.	$9—
[illegible]	Amedee Ducatel for contract	15—
Oct. 26, 1859	John Krider of Phila. for model Revolver	208—
Nov. 15, 1859	H. P. Andrews for expenses to various arms manufacturers	50.00
Nov. 27, 1859	Travelling expenses to & from the North on acc- of Grapeshot Revolver $62½	125.00
Nov. 27, 1859	expenses in Wash. Ph. & N. Y. 1½ months at $150 per mo-	225.00
Nov. 27, 1859	[illegible]	88.00
Nov. 27, 1859	Sundry small expenses in above cities	15.00
		———
		$6,150.00[6]

(It might be interesting to note that the correct total of the above expenditures is $5,750.00, not $6,150.00 as set forth.)

Aside from the "model" pistol made by John Krider of Philadelphia (which was cased with full accessories) there is no indication of his manufacture of pistols. This seems odd as there can be no question that, as of this date, a number of Le Mat revolvers were in existence. How, for example, could the special boards in New Orleans or in Washington have fired and made reports on a nonexistent revolver?

Two early model Le Mat revolvers with serial numbers one and four are extant. They are marked simply "Le Mat's Patent." We assume they were made prior to Le Mat's appointment as Colonel in 1859 and were the ones used by the special board in New Orleans.

On July 2, 1860, Beauregard wrote Le Mat outlining the terms under which he had agreed to sell his one-quarter interest back to the inventor:

Supt's office New Custom house
New Orleans July 2, 1860

Col. Alexandre Le Mat
　New Orleans, La.

Dear Sir,

I herewith authorize you to dispose of or sell your share (¾) of the Patent right or rights (American & European) of your "Grape shot

Revolver" *provided* that the proceeds thus obtained, shall go toward paying the sums advanced by me to you—& expended by me on account of said arm—and those guaranteed by me here on your account.

I will then cede back to you my share (¼) of said Patent right or rights as sold by you—*provided* I am paid also the *pro-rata* of any excess on the sale of said ¾ shares, over the sums due me as above stated—& representing the present value of my share—G. T. B.

Yours very Truly,

G. T. Beauregard[7]

Subsequent events show that Le Mat purchased Beauregard's one-quarter interest in the patent rights and then disposed of a three-quarter interest to Girard, retaining only a one-quarter interest.

Although efforts to obtain national recognition for his grape-shot revolver were unsuccessful, Le Mat was at least accepted in his own state for, on November 15, 1860, the Louisiana Inspector General Maurice Grivot recommended that "The Guard d'Orleans be armed with 400 rifles and sabre bayonets and for the officers—improved revolvers, such as Colonel Le Mat's grape-shot revolver."[8]

THE LE MAT AND GIRARD PARTNERSHIP

Although Dr. Charles Frederic Girard had joined Le Mat in Paris early in 1860, it was not until July of that year that he became a full partner instead of "special agent." That Girard was an accomplished and rather remarkable

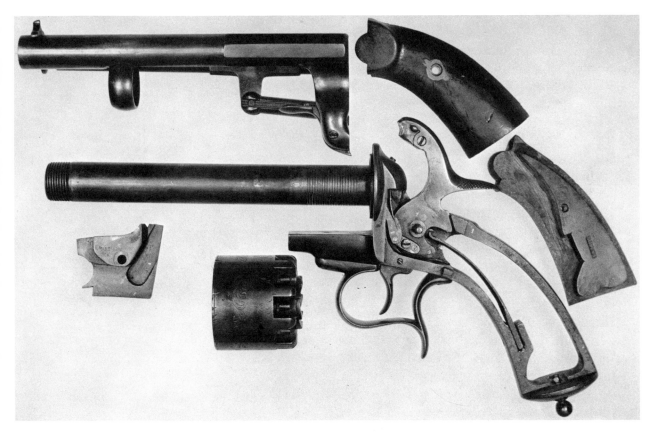

Courtesy Edward N. Simmons

DISASSEMBLED NUMBER ONE LE MAT

Serial number 1, showing components.

person is demonstrated by his biography, as it appears in Smithsonian Institution Bulletin Number 42:

"Born March 9, 1822, he was educated at Neuchâtel, Switzerland, under Louis Agassiz who brought Girard to the United States in 1847. He remained at Cambridge under Agassiz until the fall of 1850, at which time he came to Washington, D. C., and worked under Spencer F. Baird as Assistant Secretary of the Smithsonian Institution in Washington. Baird gave Girard the opportunity to become associated with him in the plan which resulted in the establishment of the United States National Museum in 1857...."[9]

LE MAT CONTRACTS WITH THE CONFEDERATE ARMY AND NAVY

For a number of years it has been thought that perhaps some Le Mat revolvers were actually made in the South during the war years. However, the records simply do not bear this out, although there may have been plans afoot to do so. The New Orleans *Daily Delta* in June, 1861, states: "The firm of Cook and Brother contemplate the manufacture of Dr. Le Mat's grape-shot revolver." So far as the records show, the manufacture by Cook and Brother never got beyond the contemplation stage.

The Confederate Government was formed in the spring of 1861 at Montgomery, Alabama. Undoubtedly, both Beauregard and Le Mat were present during those first hectic weeks when all kinds and types of contracts and positions were being awarded.

Through Beauregard, Josiah Gorgas, previously a captain in the U.S. Army, was offered and on April 8, 1861 accepted, the rank of major in the Confederate States Army with the title of Chief of the Bureau of Ordnance.

On July 27, 1861, the Confederate Congress formally inquired of the Bureau of Ordnance as to arms on hand and as to what steps had been taken to secure additional weapons. This query

Courtesy Edward N. Simmons

LE MAT MARKINGS ON NUMBER ONE

These appear as shown on the barrel and inside of the side plate.

was answered on August 12, 1861, and it is interesting to note at that time the Confederacy had only one contract for the manufacture of revolvers: "Mr. Le Mat of Louisiana has an order to deliver 5,000 of his revolvers."[10]

Courtesty Charles L. Bricker

PACKAGE OF LE MAT CARTRIDGES

Le Mat cartridges contained in square-type packs are quite scarce but this oblong shaped authentic package (4½" long) with original Arsenal label is an extreme rarity and may be unique. It is shown here, in print, for the first time.

While contracting with the War Department for 5,000 revolvers, Le Mat also secured a contract with the Navy Department, although the exact date is unknown, and its first mention does not appear until July, 1862.

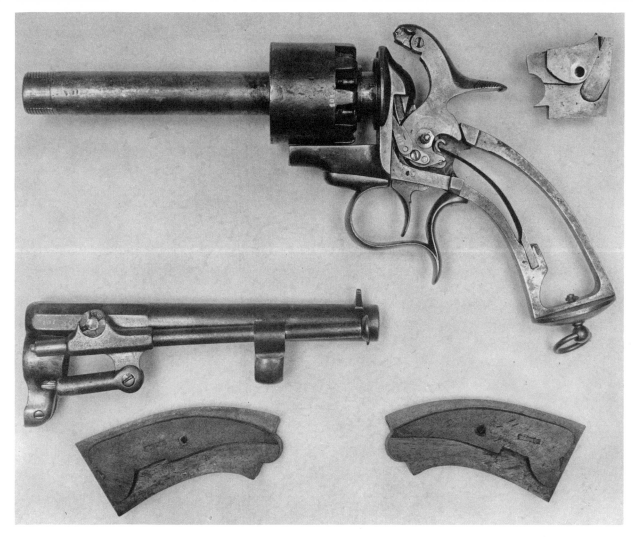

DISASSEMBLED LE MAT

Serial number 101, showing components.

Leaving Montgomery, Alabama, with his contract in his pocket, Colonel Le Mat proceeded to Europe. First, however, he stopped at Milledgeville, the capital of Georgia, long enough to receive a commission to purchase 2,000 English Enfield rifles at $35 each for that state.[11]

Meanwhile, the Confederate Government had chosen James M. Mason of Virginia and John Slidell of Louisiana, to proceed to Europe to establish credit by selling bonds or otherwise

securing loans. The Charleston *Mercury's* account of the sailing of Mason and Slidell notes that they were accompanied by "Colonel Le Mat, the inventor of the grape-shot revolver."

The subsequent capture of the English steamer *Trent* by the U.S.S. *San Jacinto* and the forcible removal of Mason and Slidell is too well known to repeat. Le Mat seems to have escaped attention and to have reached his destination safely.

LE MAT AND THE "NEW ORLEANS AFFAIR"

How long Le Mat remained in Europe is not known, but probably only long enough to deliver the contracts to his partner Girard and to make sure that their Paris manufactory was capable of handling the job. At any rate, early in 1862, we find him in New Orleans, where he remained until that city fell to the Union forces.

Most serious students who have attempted to piece together Le Mat's revolver-making activities have been greatly puzzled by certain cryptic references to him found in Volume 2, Series III, *Official Records of the Union and Confederate Navies*. These involve Le Mat in a highly mysterious "affair" which contains all of the elements necessary for a present-day television spy thriller. Only tantalizing portions of this "affair" are mentioned, insufficient to lead to any logical conclusion as to its true nature, although the possibility that it might have related to the manufacture of pistols in New Orleans could not be dismissed.

On page 771, Volume 2, Series III, of the *Official Records* (Navies) will be found the statement that a lawyer, one Robert Benguerel, was paid to negotiate for Le Mat in this "affair." Benguerel was designated as "my excellent friend" in a signed drawing of Le Mat's revolver patent which we illustrate.

It has been established, however, that Le Mat was merely involved in spiriting more than $400,000 in gold out of New Orleans—right under the nose of U.S. General Benjamin Butler, who is better remembered for his nickname, "Beast."

LE MAT IN CHARLESTON, S. C., IN SEPTEMBER, 1862

Le Mat's whereabouts after the New Orleans "affair" are not known, but in September, 1862, on his way to Paris he stopped in Charleston, South Carolina, at the home of George Tren-

holm. Here he met a youngster named James M. Morgan who was a midshipman in the Confederate States Navy.

Morgan gives us one of the few descriptions we have of our inventor in *The Recollections of a Rebel Reefer:*

> Soon there arrived a Frenchman, a Col. Le Mat, the inventor of the "Grape-shot" revolver, a horrible contraption, the cylinder of which revolved around a section of a gun barrel. The cylinder contained nine bullets, and the grape-shot barrel was loaded with buckshot which when fired would almost tear the arm off a man with its recoil.
>
> Le Mat's English vocabulary was limited, and his only subject of conversation was his invention—so he used me to explain to the young ladies how the infernal machine worked.
>
> Now that sounds all very easy, but one must remember that Le Mat was a highly imaginative Gaul and insisted on posing me to illustrate his lecture. This was embarrassing especially as he considered it polite to begin all over again as each new guest entered the room.[12]

THE CONFEDERATE ARMY CONTRACT AND THE CONTROVERSY WITH CALEB HUSE

While Le Mat had been in New Orleans, the production and delivery of the grape-shot revolver had gone well until July, 1862, when trouble began with the Confederate Ordnance representative in Europe. The first inkling of this controversy is found in a letter to Judah P. Benjamin, then Confederate Secretary of State and an old friend of the inventor:

Paris, September 30, 1862

To:
Hon. J. P. Benjamin,
    Department of State, Richmond,
    Confederate States of America
    The establishment of credit here would save the Government from great embarrassment and

the enormous loss on exchange which it now suffers, as well as relieve the agents abroad from the difficulties of which they complain. I have been requested by Messrs. C. Girard & Co., who are making Le Mat's revolvers for the Government under contracts with the Navy and Army Departments with Colonel Le Mat, a partner in the factory, to forward their correspondence with the agents of those departments in Europe, and to request that effectual steps may be taken to fulfill the Government obligation in that respect. They complain of the loss of both time and money in consequence of the failure of Captain Huse to co-operate with them or carry out his instructions in spirit as well as in letter. I submit this matter without any expression of opinion to the proper departments, with a repetition of my suggestion that additional agents supplied with funds should be sent abroad for the purchase of arms, medicines, and other necessaries.

(signed) Edwin DeLeon[13]

Following DeLeon's letter to Benjamin, Le Mat's partner Girard also wrote the Secretary of State outlining his troubles with Major Caleb Huse, Confederate purchasing agent abroad:

Paris, December 9, 1862
To The Honorable J. P. Benjamin,
　　Minister, Secretary of State of
　　The Confederated States of America,
　　Richmond.

Dear Sir,
　　We take the liberty of sending you a duplicate of the correspondence we had with Major Huse on the subject of "grape-shot-revolvers" for manufacture of which Mr. Le Mat obtained Contracts from the Confederated States.
　　A copy of same correspondence has already been sent by us to Colonel Gorgas, Chief of the Ordnance Bureau.
　　We are not going to make a detailed analysis of this correspondence which is very clear by itself.

Courtesy Chicago Historical Society

AN IMPORTANT LE MAT

This arm, serial number 189, was owned by Captain Henry Wirz, notorious commandant of Andersonville.

We shall only point out to you, Your Honor, that Major Huse has shown, from the very beginning of his mission in Europe, an evident spirit of hostility against us and our revolver, as well as against any commercial business to furnish the South, since in such business too high a premium would not be granted to him. Everything not controlled by him and consequently by the two firms with which he was associated was sure to be refused. It is so, that many contracts brought in Europe by persons desiring to make business with other firms were not concluded, these persons desiring to break the disastrous monopoly for the Confederation, which he was strongly trying to maintain. Nobody ever heard Major Huse being satisfied with the success of the Confederated Army and instead of backing up this Cause as being capable to triumph of all obstacles, he could be heard speaking in a quite opposite way, showing the victory of the North as being a very natural outcome.

This kind of domination he took on everything to be done for the South, stating he was their Sole Agent, with full power, did reduce the capitalists confidence and did restrict the Spirit of Adventure which was only asking to be a little bit more convinced on the intentions of the Confederated Government as well as on the reasons of the fight against the Federal Government.

In the case of our revolvers, Major Huse had the impudence to offer us for payment a sum lower than the actual manufacture price. Moreover, during the conversations with us, regarding our Contract with the Government, the latter was described by him as being of secondary importance because he insisted on the fact that what was capital was to accept or to refuse his own propositions. In other words he acted as if looking for his own interests rather than as a representative of his Government.

With a man considering the interest of his country and acting completely to obtain the best result of his mission, the South would have been purveyed on a far more higher scale and with more advantageous conditions.

During interviews we had with many contractors in England, as well as in France, we very often heard people state how much it was to

regret that the Government of the Confederated States was represented by such a man who was killing his credit. They also stated that the South people were Gentlemen but that this Captain Huse was nothing but a "Yankee" in his way of acting.

We have already said that it was in a spirit of hostility that he refused to help us in the execution of our revolver contracts. When we informed him, on September 5, that we had just obtained a new contract, according to which he was to receive our arms and pay for them in London, he suddenly left England on a pleasure trip to Germany, and during five weeks, he acted as if he was ignorant of this contract so much did he desire to see us in difficulty for the execution of the conditions we had accepted. Finally when he saw that we were ready to comply with our engagements he looked for a bad reason to refuse to inspect and to receive our arms and consequently not to pay. But the correspondence is so clear on this subject that we do not need to give more explanations. However, we consider necessary to point out, which the correspondence does not show, that during a conversation we just had in London with Major Huse, he told us that he received a confidential letter from Colonel Gorgas. In this letter, Colonel Gorgas would have given to Major Huse the confidential instruction that in case we would not deliver the goods within the stipulated terms (before November 1) he was giving him (Huse) the power to break our contract since, it was added, it was too expensive for the Government.

We do not want to continue to argue on that case and do not desire to formulate a complaint against Colonel Gorgas who may not have sent such a letter to Major Huse.

However, we thought necessary to relate this incident due to the fact that the correspondence (herewith included) of Mr. Huse as well as his behavior are demonstrating that he did everything in his power to put us in default: firstly his silence during nearly six weeks on the question we asked him, i.e., if he was able to pay our arms each time we could deliver them and secondly the bad tricks he was using in order to be in a position to date his receipt only of the 8th of November.

We expect, Your Honor, to have your assistance as the Government in order to demonstrate that we did all we could to fulfill the stipulations of our contract: we have delivered on a simple receipt of Major Huse, before the first of November, the number of arms we promised to furnish.

We repeat that we have delivered these arms on a simple receipt of Mr. Huse without having received from him a single piaster to help us for the manufacture of them.

The money we have been obliged to borrow is putting us in such a position that our work regarding the next deliveries is depending only on the payment of the already furnished revolvers. Therefore, we hope that the Confederated Government, considering the attitude of Major Huse as being unfair, will give instructions to another agent of perfect loyalty.

Your Honor, we were plenty satisfied with the conduct towards us of Captain Bulloch, Agent of the Navy Department. We can only regret that Captain Bulloch has not been, up to now, in a position to pay us the arms, we have also delivered on a simple receipt. But, we repeat it, Captain Bulloch is a gentleman in the full sense of the word when Major Huse is only a miserable servant.

The recommendation letter you kindly gave to Mr. Le Mat for Messrs. Fraser & Co., Charleston, gave us the hope that their firm of Liverpool could have helped us. We have been very disappointed. The proposal we made to these gentlemen of Liverpool was not at all disastrous for them, we only asked them to give us the necessary money for the manufacture of our arms; these arms would have been delivered to them for further dispatching to America and the payment would have been made to them, being understood that the difference would only be paid to us when the funds would have reached Europe. We think that we could not offer them any better guarantee than the arms on which their advance of money would have been placed. These gentlemen told us that in spite of the unlimited confidence they had in the Government of the Confederated States, the amount of money they still were to receive from this Government was higher than its credit on the place.

We asked them to indicate us another firm in Liverpool with which we could make an arrangement but their answer was that they did not know anybody. And that is for this reason that we have been put aside. There is evidently an agreement between them and Major Huse, in order to keep the monopoly of the Commerce with the Confederated States.

We just started conversations with Messrs. John and Thomas Johnson of Liverpool, have started the noble enterprise to establish a line of transatlantic boats for the supplying of the South. These gentlemen show more cooperation with us than Messrs. Fraser, Trenholm and Co.

Yours very truly,

C. Girard & Co.[14]

Caleb Huse of the old U.S. Army was early commissioned into the Confederate States service with the rank of Captain. On April 15, 1861, Captain Huse, "Corps of Artillery, C.S.A., on Ordnance duty" was "directed to proceed to Europe, without unnecessary delay, as the agent of this Government, for the purchase of ordnance, arms, equipments, and military stores for its use. . . ."[15] With headquarters in England, Huse remained in that country during the entire war except for occasional buying trips on the Continent.

Huse is still very much of a controversial figure. Without question he had the ability to rub many people the wrong way, and his honesty, integrity and loyalty to the Confederacy were all questioned at one time or another to such an extent that he was the subject of an investigation. During the course of this investigation, Huse freely admitted "kick-backs" or money paid him by the persons from whom he was buying arms. In his defense Huse claimed that the persons with whom he dealt understood no other way of doing business and swore that the money so acquired was never spent in his own behalf, but was turned back to the funds supplied him for ordnance purchases.

Courtesy Edward N. Simmons

LE MAT & GIRARD REVOLVER

The number 9 is shown on the cylinder and "Le Mat & Girard's Patent, London" is engraved on the top flat of the barrel as shown.

The investigation cleared Huse of all charges, and he was passionately defended by his chief, General Gorgas, Chief of Ordnance.

We mention all this not to cast a reflection upon one considered by many as a brave and loyal soldier, but only to supply background for the correspondence that follows. It is suggested that the reader use his own judgment, although we cannot refrain from expressing our opinion that in regard to the Le Mat contract, Huse appears to have been most unreasonable.

The following excerpts from the correspondence between Caleb Huse and C. Girard & Co. are reproduced because they show the many difficulties that arose over the mechanical and financial operations of Le Mat and Girard during 1862 and 1863. These letters are taken from the *Captured Confederate Records*, letters received by the Confederate Secretary of War, file D-70, National Archives, Washington, D. C. These letters have never been published before and do not appear in the official records.

Passage Joinville No. 9
Faubourg du Temple
Paris   10th July 1862

Capt. C. Huse
Dear Sir:

We send you enclosed Copy of a letter handed to us by Mr. DeLeon from the War Department of the Confederate States, authorizing you to receive and pay for at London the revolvers which have been ordered from us by the Government.

We had already forwarded 400 direct to the Confederate States before receiving these new instructions and have now on hand an equal number, with others partially finished and can furnish you at the rate of about 200 every two weeks hereafter with your cooperation. Will you therefore do us the favor to inform us where we shall forward the weapons to you and what deduction you consider sufficient to cover the risk of transportation under these instructions—By this we understand the ordinary expense of transporting the arms to the Confederate States—

An early answer would greatly oblige
                    Your obed. S.
                        (signed) C. Girard & Co.

Capt Huse
58 Jermyn Street, London

The situation deteriorated rapidly from that point on, with Huse "pulling every trick in the book" to avoid receiving any more revolvers from Girard & Co. The prolonged haggling that followed apparently stemmed from the fact that Huse had not sufficient funds with which to make payment for any further shipment from Girard, although of course it would have been unthinkable to admit this. Instead, he raised an interminable series of pettifogging objections having to do with exchange rates, insurance, etc. (alluded to in Girard's letter to Secretary of State Benjamin), finally refusing to accept them on the grounds that their frames were made of cast iron, an unsuitable material for the purpose. They were in fact not cast of ordinary brittle gray iron, but of malleable iron which possessed

ample strength for the use intended. Huse appears to have been trying to stall Girard off until after November 1, 1862, at which time Girard's contract called for the delivery of 500 revolvers. Having accomplished this, he could claim non-fulfillment on Girard's part.

Girard, however, was not to be vanquished so easily. On October 24, he sent to Huse a shipment of 500 revolvers through Perreaux and Co., the English agents for Le Mat and Girard, accompanied by a receipt to be signed by Huse acknowledging delivery. Apparently the letter enclosing the receipt form went astray, and the November 1 deadline passed before another could be sent through Perreaux & Co.

Courtesy H. L. Woodlief
LE MAT CYLINDER

Showing view and proof marks, as well as the mark (M) of the Confederate inspector, Lt. Murdaugh. Serial number 2394.

Huse, now firmly in command of the situation, refused to receive the pistols, claiming that they were not in conformity with the contract. This, of course, was in reference to the "cast iron" frames. As the receipt form, sent by Girard for his signature, made reference to the pistols being in conformity with the contract, he would not sign it. He offered, however, to forward the shipment to the Confederate States War Department together with a report of the facts.

Girard, now desperate, accepted these terms with a final plaintive comment on the slur cast upon his choice of material: ". . . they are made of malleable iron between which and cast iron, there is a very wide difference, as is well known to all metallurgists." Without benefit of knowing what really went on in the mind of the Confederate purchasing agent, we wonder if the pistols would have been much more acceptable to him had they been made of pure gold.

Finally, almost four months to the day from the start of what appears to be a senseless and time-consuming effort, Girard was informed that 500 of the revolvers had been accepted. Thus he had supplied the Confederate Army with 900 pistols.

> 5 Jeffrey's Square   St. Mary Axe
> London 11 November 1862

Messrs. C. Girard & Co.
  Gentlemen:
  We beg to conform our respects of the 7th inst. in accordance with which Mr. Holmes called on

Courtesy Miles W. Standish

A BABY LE MAT WITH "M" MARK

Percussion type, serial number 75, with the star over LM marking on a side flat of the barrel. Also shown are cylinder and top of barrel. The cylinder shows the Murdaugh M. The barrel shows typical engraving. "Systeme Le Mat Bte s.g.d.g. Paris."

Courtesy Edward N. Simmons

ETCHED AND ENGRAVED LE MAT

The leaf inlays are missing from the grips. There is a possibility that the decoration was done in Egypt after the war for a former Confederate officer. Serial number 2475, with the star over LM marking on the barrel.

Major Huse, who informed him that he was willing to receive your 20 cases of revolvers, giving us a simple receipt for the same, which we have the pleasure to enclose you.

Major Huse promised to send us instructions for shipping, but these arrived too late on Saturday. The vessel however, was detained for them, and we now beg to advise having shipped them on board the S. S. *Lustika* bound we understand for Nassau.

We hand you the shipping charges omitting 10 pounds to your debit.

We are
(signed) Perreaux & Co.

Received November 8, 1862, of Messrs. Perreaux & Co. St. Mary Axe London, Agents of Messrs. C. Girard & Co. Paris.

Five Hundred (500) Le Mat's pistols for Confederate States War Department.

(signed) Caleb Huse.

And so ends the controversy between Caleb Huse and Le Mat and Girard. If there is additional correspondence, it does not appear. However, the absence of correspondence did not mean that the troubles besetting the pistol manufactory were over.

The 500 Le Mat revolvers were sent aboard the S. S. *Lustika* on November 8, 1862. From England they went to Nassau, B.W.I., there to run the blockade into Wilmington, North Carolina. All this took time, so much so that by June 1, 1863, they still had not been received by Confederate Ordnance in Richmond, Virginia.

Richmond, Virginia
1st June, 1863

Major Caleb Huse
Sir:

In reference to Le Mat pistols they will of course not be received unless both cylinder & barrel are made of steel (the barrel may be of wrought iron). Malleable iron would not pass inspection & could be of course a sufficient ground for rejection—sending the pistols here alters the case however. The pistols have not yet arrived.

J. Gorgas
Chief of Ordnance.[16]

Without finances, the revolver factory of Le Mat and Girard ground practically to a halt.

Le Mat was in Paris to take care of the business at that end, so Girard decided to come to America to collect for the guns he had sold, evidently believing such a trip to be less expensive than accepting the English equivalent for Confederate dollars from Fraser, Trenholm and Co.

Girard and his pistols seem to have arrived in Richmond, Virginia, at about the same time, as

The foregoing seems like a strange question and just as strange an answer, since Girard & Co. had a contract calling for the payment to be made at the rate of $35 for each pistol. A look at the depreciation of Confederate currency will do much to explain this odd situation. In the year 1862, $2.50 in Confederate currency would have bought $1 in gold. By August of 1863, $21

Courtesy Edward N. Simmons

LE MAT WITH EXTENSION SHOT BARREL

The extension barrel is fitted with the original high folding front sight to permit sighting when attached to the arm.

in July, 1863, he informs Gorgas, "Amongst the five last boxes one of which had been opened on its way hither, eight pistols were found missing, adding the latter to those previously reported as missing we come to the aggregate number of 18, for which we should like a settlement as per agreement."[17]

Colonel Gorgas agreed to pay Girard for the missing guns and asked Girard what price would be agreeable for payment. On August 11, 1863, Girard replied: "In response to your wishes I will state that I have parted with my pistols at the rate of $50 each in Confederate notes and that I am willing to settle all of the 18 missing upon the same terms."[18]

in Confederate currency would have bought only $1 in gold. In 1864 it would have taken $51 to purchase $1 in gold, and on January 1, 1865, the rate was $60 to $1 in gold. Thus it can be seen that if Girard had received $35 each for his revolvers in 1862, he could have bought $14 in gold for each gun, but the $50 each he finally received in 1863 would have bought only $2.83 in gold. The delay had been extremely costly to Girard & Co.

Colonel Gorgas had in the meantime asked his aide, Major E. M. Smith, the Assistant Chief of Ordnance, to inquire into the matter of just how many pistols were missing when they reached the Confederate States Armory in Rich-

Courtesy Edward N. Simmons

LE MAT CARBINE
Serial number 88.

mond. A letter in reply from John W. Krepps dated August 13 stated:

In reply to your note of inquiry respecting the opening of the boxes of Le Mat's pistols sent here by Mr. Girard, I beg to say that I had the boxes opened in my presence and found seventeen pistols missing of the number the boxes were said to contain.

Two of the boxes were broken when received and Mr. Adams had one (one gun) broken up which was not included in the above.[19]

The "Mr. Adams" referred to was Master Armorer Solomon Adams of the Richmond Armory. Although the revolver was broken up for inspection, no record of the results of the test has been found.

A receipt signed by Charles Girard was found in the War Department Record Group 109:

Voucher No. *51*
C. Girard & Co.
14th August 1863
$900.
CONFEDERATE STATES OF AMERICA,
To C. Girard & Co.
1863
August 14 For seventeen Le Mat's Pistols from packages lost in transition from Europe receipted for by Major Huse as per Certified copy attached $850.
C$50   50.
                        ———
                        $900.

For one ditto broken up for inspection by Master Armorer Adams.
Approved
J. Gorgas Col.
  Chf. of Ord.
I certify that the above account is correct and just, and that the property has been received and will be accounted for,

Received, Richmond, Va. August 1863
MAJOR EDWARD B. SMITH,
ASSISTANT TO CHIEF OF ORDNANCE
Nine Hundred Dollars — — — — No cents, in full of the above account
            /s/ C. Girard & Company

It can be seen from the foregoing that on August 14, 1863, C. Girard & Co. was paid in full for the last of the Le Mat revolvers. If Girard had received $35 for the other 482 guns, the amount would have come to $16,870. When we add the $900 received for the 18 guns that had been missing, we find that the total is $17,770 for the entire 500 guns. During the previous nine months the factory had been practically idle. The depreciation of Confederate currency had made the delay especially costly, and as a result, 1863 saw very few grape-shot revolvers reaching the Confederacy.

During this same period the activities of the Confederate agents in Europe were also greatly curtailed. We find on page 30 of *Confederate Purchasing Operations Abroad:*

During several months of 1863, the activity of the agents came to a standstill. One reason was the lack of harmony between the agents. The other was [uncertainty over] the Erlanger Loan [which was then being negotiated]. In the spring of 1863, at a general conference of the agents, Spence, Prioleau, Maury, Bulloch, North, Huse and Ferguson, it was agreed to suspend financial activity until the outcome of the loan could be determined.

As a result of the suspension of activity in Europe, very few records are to be found concerning the production or delivery of Le Mat revolvers, although a dribble continued to reach the Confederacy.

A personal letter from Colonel John M. Payne dated June 8, 1915, states in part: "I was assigned from the infantry to the Ordnance Corps in February, 1863, and was put in charge of Imported Ordnance and Nitre and Mining Stores at Wilmington, N. C., in July 1863. I rarely opened any packages but sent the original cases as directed by telegraph from Richmond; therefore I know but little beyond what I saw myself. . . . I recollect that 150 French made 'Le Mat's' were brought in. These consisted of chambered cylinders revolving around a central barrel, and this central barrel could also be fired. They were not approved. . . ."

Colonel Payne's records as "Collector of the Port of Wilmington, North Carolina, 1864-1865," are still preserved in the Confederate Museum, Richmond, Virginia. They contain many records as to pistols or revolvers which entered the Confederacy at Wilmington. The following excerpts are the only ones pertaining directly to the grapeshot revolvers: The steamer *Pevensey* on May 16, 1864, brought in "five boxes of Le Mat revolvers" as a portion of her cargo. They are noted to have been addressed "To Richmond" and for "W. D." [War Department.] On June 17, 1864, the steamer *Lynx* brought in "four cases Le Mat revolvers," similarly addressed and marked. Again on July 27 the *Lynx* brought in an additional "four cases Le Mat revolvers."

Remembering that these revolvers were packed twenty-five to the case (or box), this would indicate that at least 325 passed through Wilmington, although Colonel Payne "recollects" only 150.

As far as we have been able to determine, these represent the last revolvers supplied on a contract that originally called for 5,000.

LE MAT'S CONTRACT WITH THE C.S. NAVY DEPARTMENT

The details of the Army contract are reasonably clear. For this we can thank the controversy with Huse which resulted in considerable correspondence. On the other hand, the contract or contracts with the C.S. Navy Department are obscure, and in our attempt at reconstruction we have had of necessity to resort in many instances to assumption and deduction. Even the date of the initial Navy contract is not known, nor are its terms. The order, however, was for 3,000 revolvers.

The first reference we find to the contract is dated July, 1862, with a letter from the Confederate Secretary of the Navy, Stephen Mallory, to Commander James D. Bulloch, whose greatest service was the purchase of ships and supplies for the Confederate States Navy. Bulloch was in Europe the greater part of the war and was a highly valuable assistant to the Confederate Secretary of the Navy.

On July 30, 1862, Mallory wrote Bulloch, who was then in Liverpool, saying in part:

You will observe by the term of the contract with Mr. Le Mat that the pistols are to be delivered and inspected in London and you will inspect them or designate an officer of the Navy in England to do so and receive them, after which you will pay for them out of any funds in your hands and forward them to the Confederate States. Two hundred pistols have been delivered and paid for here.[20]

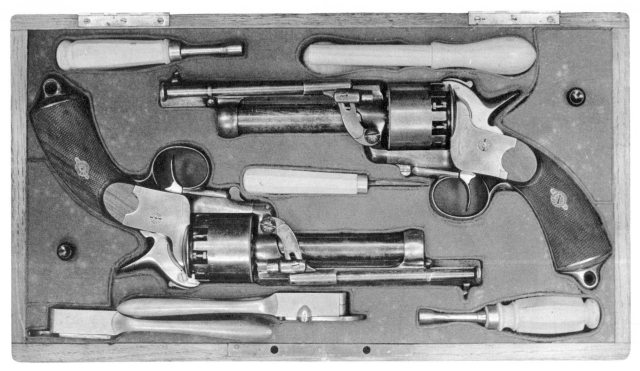

Courtesy Edward N. Simmons

CASED PAIR OF LE MATS

Serial numbers 1078 and 1082, with original and complete accessories. The case is marked Le Jeune/ 18 Passage Choiseul/ à Paris.

From this we can see that as of July, 1862, the Confederate Navy had a contract with Dr. Le Mat for a number of revolvers of which 200 had already been delivered.

Bulloch's answer dated September 24, 1862, is quite clear:

I have the honor to acknowledge the receipt of your letter of the 30th of July, inclosing copy of a contract with Mr. A. Le Mat for 3,000 grape-shot revolvers. . . . About a fortnight since I had a correspondence with the Messrs C. Girard & Co. of Paris, who assumed to be the contractors for the revolvers, and who desired me to fulfill that part of the agreement which devolved upon the agent for the Navy Department in England.

I informed these gentlemen that I was not authorized to act as general agent for the Navy Department, and, as I had no instructions in reference to the particular contract in question, I could not undertake to carry out its provisions.

Immediately upon receipt of your letter of July 30, in which you direct me to carry out the terms of this contract, I wrote to Messrs. C. Girard & Co. informing them of the fact and stating that I would make arrangements for the inspection of the pistols as soon as they could deliver them, at stated periods and in sufficient numbers to make it advisable. I was obliged to inform them at the same time that I had no available funds from which to make the prescribed payments, but to avoid, if possible, any delay in forwarding the arms. I requested them to suggest some means by which I could give them security for ultimate payment, and am now awaiting their reply.[21]

On October 25, Bulloch again wrote the Secretary of the Navy as follows:

Messrs. C. Girard & Co. have agreed to deliver the revolvers without payment being made here. No sample of the pistol furnished the War Department has been sent me, and it is therefore impossible to judge of the relative character of those the Contractors are making for the Navy.[22]

From this there seems little question that at this time the revolvers furnished the Navy were identical to those being supplied to the Army, otherwise Bulloch would not have needed a sample from the War Department. On November 7, 1862, Bulloch again wrote his superior:

First, contract for revolvers. This contract, whether regularly made over by Colonel Le Mat or not, is in the hands of Messrs. C. Girard & Co. of Paris. When these gentlemen, after some correspondence, declared their willingness to deliver the revolvers upon a simple receipt with or without payment, I directed the inspecting officer, Lieutenant Chapman, since relieved in this duty by Lieutenant Evans, to ask for a sample of the pistols already delivered to the War Department and to get a written certificate from the manufacturer that the one furnished him was identical with those previously accepted. He was then to see that the revolvers offered for the Navy came fully up to the sample. One hundred have been accepted by Lieutenant Wilkinson. Lieutenant Evans reports that these hundred are quite as well finished in every way as the sample, but adds that the barrels, lock frames, and hammers are of cast iron; that the contact between the barrels and cylinders is so loose as to permit much escape of gas; and that the cylinders, not being provided with springs, as in other repeating arms, are apt to revolve too far when the pistols are rapidly cocked, so that the hammers are likely to fall upon the divisions between the nipples when the firing is quick. These are such serious defects that I shall decline receiving any more of the revolvers under this contract unconditionally, but will write Lieutenant Evans to say to Messrs. Girard & Co. that he will forward the balance (of 400) subject to inspection upon arrival in the Confederate States. I presume you have not seen any of the pistols already sent forward, but beg that you will have them inspected and instruct me what to do in the matter as soon as possible. The ordi-

nary revolver costs in England about 63s, and the grape-shot revolver Messrs. C. Girard & Co. are now supplying can be manufactured by the London Armory Co. for something less than 5 pounds each.[23]

Bulloch appears somewhat perplexed that, although the contract in question is drawn up in the name of Le Mat, it is actually being fulfilled by Charles Girard. He may not have been aware that Dr. Le Mat was in America at the time, and he had no reason to know that Girard was three-quarter owner of the revolver factory and was in fact its real manager.

Bulloch has considerable fault to find with the pistols, which as we have already seen, were to be identical to those furnished the War Department. Nevertheless, his inspecting officer accepted 100 of the 400 that were ready for delivery. The remaining 300 were to be sent directly to the Confederate States subject to inspection prior to acceptance.

Some slight additional information on the Navy contract is contained in a letter from Mallory to Bulloch dated January 7, 1863, in which Bulloch is informed that: "Should any serious defect develop, this contract shall terminate with the delivery of the first 1,000." Mallory further advised: "If you shall determine to limit the delivery to 1,000, only 800 remain to be received, and these 800 you will please decline to receive and advise the contractors that they will be received and inspected."[24]

It is quite obvious that at the time of this writing the 100 accepted by Evans and the 300 additional revolvers had not yet reached the Confederacy. Apparently, then, a total of 600 guns had been shipped or delivered toward the Navy contract in 1862, of which 400 were still unreceived by January, 1863.

During the time Secretary of the Navy Mallory was carrying on this correspondence, he was also organizing his department for efficient work in providing for the needs of all the Confederate States Navy forces:

"He organized bureaus consisting of Orders and Details, Ordnance and Hydrography, Provisions and Clothing, which had charge of the paying of the naval forces, and a bureau of Medicine and Surgery. The detailed works of the C.S. Navy were soon being carried on by competent men, and the bureau of Ordnance and Hydrography was put under the able direction of Commander John M. Brooke."[25]

In regard to the guns made for the War Department, we again refer to a letter written to Caleb Huse by Gorgas on June 3, 1863, in which he advised: "In reference to the Le Mat pistols they will of course not be received unless both cylinder and barrel are made of steel (the barrel may be of wrought iron). Malleable iron would not pass inspection and would be of course a sufficient ground for rejection—sending the pistols here (to the Confederacy) alters the case however."[26]

Now both the War and Navy Departments had adopted practically the same policy of rejecting the guns in Paris, demanding they be

sent directly to the Confederacy, where they would be inspected and accepted or rejected. Evidently some of the guns were rejected and subsequently put up for private sale. For example, in the Richmond *Whig*, December 4, 1862, Kent, Paine and Co., military outfitters of Richmond, advertise the sale of Le Mat revolvers.

It was about this time that production of the revolvers was at its low ebb. More than likely Le Mat was engaged in designing the improved cylinder and the "Baby" model revolver. He must have spent considerable time and effort in endeavoring to overcome the mechanical faults of his guns, as is reflected in their innumerable variations, both major and minute.

Evidently in 1863 there was a modification of the order that all guns be sent to the Confederate States of America. We are unable to find record of this modification, but a look at the revolvers themselves will prove our point.

Here a brief recapitulation is necessary. An undetermined number of revolvers were made prior to the war, but as of 1863, 900 had been

Courtesy Edward N. Simmons

A GROUP OF 8 LE MAT PERCUSSION CYLINDERS

Top row, left to right, cylinders from arms numbered 21, 101, 309, 314. Bottom row, left to right, from arms numbered 663, 850, 2448; and from Le Mat and Girard Number 9.

delivered to the War Department and 600 to the Navy Department, a total of 1,500. Assuming that some 300 were made prior to the war and that the serial numbers on all guns are consecutive, let us look at a few specimens with serial numbers around 1800.

We find that the guns with serial numbers up to 1809 are marked: *Col. Le Mat Bte. s.g.d.g. Paris.* On guns after 1809 the markings change to: *Syst. Le Mat Bte. s.g.d.g. Paris.* This change in itself is not startling, although it might point to a further selling by Le Mat of his patent rights to Girard, whereby the pistols were made only under "Le Mat's system" and without the direct supervision of the Colonel himself. Indications are that if the partnership was not completely broken, they certainly were not working very closely together at this time. All this is not particularly soul-stirring, but it is of great interest to us that many of the known guns in the serial number range of 1810 through 2499 also bear London proof marks despite the Paris address on the barrel.

It appears that, in order to save time and money, the revolvers for the Confederacy were being made in France, then sent to London for proving. If they stood the tests they were there subjected to, they were then accepted by the Confederacy. Proof of having passed inspection lies in their bearing London proof marks.

A description of the method of proving gun barrels, applicable for use at this date and later, is thoroughly detailed in W. W. Greener's *The Gun and Its Development; with Notes on Shooting*, first edition, published in 1881 at London, Paris, and New York. The history, acts, rules, regulations, marks of proof, scale for proof of rifles and small arms of every description—together with mode of proving at London and Birmingham, with a brief paragraph on Belgian gun barrel proof—is included on pages 274-290 of Greener's book.

While in America collecting for the revolvers that had been delivered to the Confederacy prior

to his arrival in July, 1863, Girard somehow found time to write a book entitled *Les Etats Confédérés d'Amerique Visités en 1863.*

It is possible that he received some form of remuneration from the Confederate Government for this work, for despite his thus far unfortunate dealings with this government, the book is heavily biased in favor of the South in its conflict with the United States. It undoubtedly was an able bit of propaganda for French consumption. Lord knows, at this point, the Confederacy could use all she could get of favorable comment. The New York *Army Navy Journal,* January 16, 1864, mentions the book as a "form of memoir to Napoleon III, written by Dr. Charles Girard, former secretary of the Smithsonian Institution, Washington. An entire chapter is taken up with Captain Brooke's (C.S.N.) celebrated gun (rifled cannon), and accounts of its performance. Captain Brooke favored the author with a description of the sea duel of the *Monitor* and *Merrimac* which so startled Europe and inaugurated a new system of Naval warfare."

Identified as "Captain" by the *Army Navy Journal,* John Brooke was actually Commander in Charge, Office of Ordnance and Hydrography, Confederate States Navy Department. Not only did he favor the author with a description of the *Monitor* and *Merrimac,* but he also favored him with another Navy contract for an additional 2,000 Le Mat revolvers. On April 7, 1864, Brooke wrote to Commander Bulloch:

Sir:
    Herewith, you will receive a copy of a contract with Messrs. C. Girard & Co. for 2,000 "grapeshot revolvers," for the use of the Navy, to be delivered and inspected in England.
    Commodore Barron has been requested by this office to select an officer to inspect and receive the pistols, and upon presentation of bills properly certified by such officer, you will please direct Messrs. Fraser, Trenholm & Co. to pay them according to the terms of the contract, chargeable to the appropriation for the ordnance for the Navy.

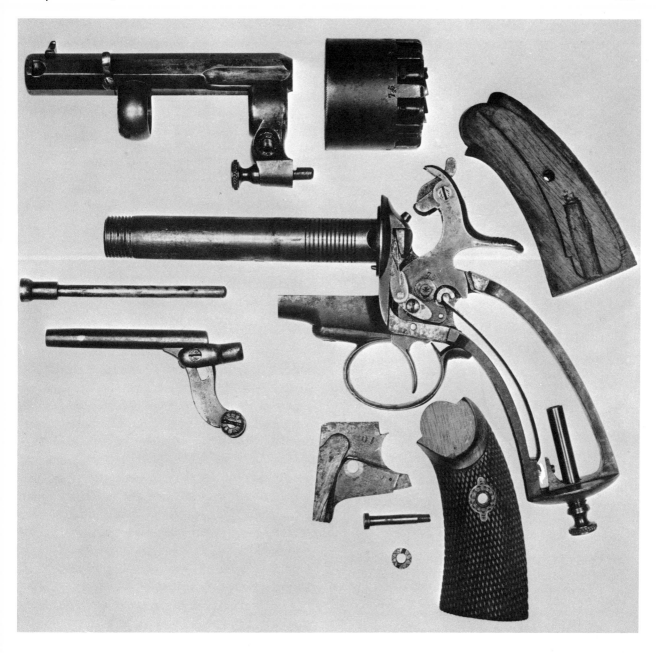

DISASSEMBLED BABY LE MAT

Serial number 75, showing components.

When the pistols are received for service with 10 rounds of ammunition for each (percussion caps to be included) please have them shipped by first favorable opportunity to Nassau, New Providence, consigned to L. Heyliger, Esq., agent, Navy Department, with instructions to him to ship them to a Confederate port in lots of 250 each marked *OH, ND* (Ordnance and Hydrography, Navy Department), accompanied by invoices and letters of advice, or they may be shipped in lots of 500, if favorable opportunities offer, direct.[27]

Looking closely through available records, we find no mention, Army or Navy, of a canceled contract. In fact, there is much to show that they were neither filled nor terminated. Be this so, why then the new contract for 2,000 revolvers? We believe it was because the new contract referred to what are now known as "Baby" Le Mats. It has been observed that the Baby Le Mats have a container screwed into the butt cap in lieu of a lanyard ring—a container with capacity for exactly ten percussion caps. This might fit in with the statement of being received "with ten rounds of ammunition for each (percussion caps to be included)." Ensuing correspondence from Commodore Barron also indicates that the second Navy contract was for the small caliber Le Mats rather than the regular size.

In sending a copy of the contract to Bulloch, Brooke mentions that it was with "C. Girard & Co." Possibly this also includes Colonel Le Mat, but we have no way of knowing what interest the Colonel had left at this time. We note, for example, that on April 15, 1862, provisional specifications had been filed by Le Mat and Girard on an English patent on the grape-shot revolver. We also note that the final specifications on this particular patent were furnished and signed by Girard and E. Gautherin on October 10, 1862. One of the provisions of the first filing is that the final papers must be delivered not later than six months from the first filing. The fact that Girard delivered the final specifications within the time limit indicates their intention of shifting operations and having the guns made in their entirety in England rather than in Paris, France. That Le Mat did not sign the final papers on the Le Mat and Girard's Patent, London, might mean only that Le Mat was in America at the time, or it might mean that he had ceded his entire interest to Girard. We believe it means only that he was not at hand to sign.

However, as the war proceeded, Gautherin and Girard became more closely connected, and Le Mat moved farther toward the sidelines. It seems that Le Mat was content to devise improvements and to make the many changes reflected by the numerous variations in the guns. As Le Mat designed and developed the guns, the rights to manufacture were bought either partially or entirely by C. Girard, the financier; and when the financial difficulties of 1863 developed, Girard in turn received capital from Edward Gautherin and Co., which resulted in the partnership of Gautherin and Girard. Even this financial aid from Gautherin was not without its limitations, as we can see by a letter written to Mallory by John De Bree, paymaster for the C.S. Navy, who advises on April 28, 1864, that: "Messrs. Gautherin & Girard (the only ones upon whom past transactions give us cause to rely) have been greatly cramped and delayed by failure of the government to reimburse them for very heavy deliveries made in Texas."[28]

The matter of finance was the determining factor in the branching out of the Le Mat and Girard partnership. The defects in the guns contributed to this lack of money, and the endeavor to overcome the defects led to other designs and modifications such as the improved cylinder lock for reliability and the contracts with the London and Birmingham proof houses for quality. These methods of operations led to further splitting of the partnership. The breach of the Le Mat and Girard partnership was widened to the extent that the revolvers produced during this period of operations resemble the products of two firms more than the efforts of one.

The revolvers delivered to the Confederate States Navy during 1864 must have been relatively few for several reasons, foremost of which was the manufacture of the new locking device which was time-consuming and delayed the delivery of guns for several months.

On January 11, 1864, Brooke had called to Commodore Barron's attention one Lieutenant William H. Murdaugh, stating:

Sir:

The rapid progress being made in England and France in the construction of ordnance, and in all that relates to the armaments of war, renders it extremely important that one of the naval officers abroad should be directed to procure for this office such information on these points as may be required. A supply of standard works embracing all branches of the art and manufacture of guns, projectiles, fuses, powder, etc., is needed. Lt. Murdaugh who is familiar with this subject and peculiarly well qualified for the work has expressed his willingness to undertake it. I therefore request he be assigned this duty.[29]

On June 13, 1864, Flag-Officer Barron wrote Lieutenant Murdaugh as follows:

Under a contract by the Confederate States Navy Department with Messrs. C. Girard & Co., for 2,000 grape-shot revolvers, for use of Confederate States Navy, you are hereby appointed

the officer to attend to the inspection and reception of the pistols. You will certify bills for all that may pass a satisfactory inspection, and direct the payment according to the terms of the contract.[30]

On June 23, 1864, the newly-appointed inspector reported to Barron on his assignment:

In obedience to your order of the 13th instance I have inspected the pistols made by C. Girard & Co. under contract with the Navy Department and have the honor to report that from the general bad character of the workmanship I have declined to receive those which they had on hand ready for delivery. As a specimen of the workmanship, I would state that of the first seven examined six had defects, as follows: viz., In one the grape-shot barrel went off at the fourth or fifth fire of the revolving cylinder from a defect in the hammer. In the next the cylinder would not revolve from defect in the spring of revolving apparatus. In the next the hammer at times would

Courtesy M. Clifford Young

BABY LE MAT

Serial number 35 with the star over LM marking on the side of the barrel.

miss striking the nipple altogether, seriously damaging it. In the other three the fixed and revolving barrels were not true with one another when in position for firing, and in one of these the hammer did not strike square.

Of all examined, none appeared reliable, and almost all of them had serious defects, such as enumerated. In all, the metal of which the faces of the hammers were made was too soft.[31]

The Le Mat revolvers that were inspected and passed on by Lieutenant Murdaugh bear his stamp, which is the letter *M* in relief inside a square cartouche. This is to be found on the cylinders of the guns inspected.

Another factor involved in the delivery of guns to the Confederate Navy Department was that once the mechanical faults were corrected and passed, the guns had to be proved for actual firing. This final step was left to the London proof house. The steps involved were identical to those employed at the Birmingham proof house, with the exception that the provisional proof mark was not required on arms made outside of England. It has been observed that those revolvers bearing a Paris address, but which were proved in London, bear no provisional proofs, thus the absence of a bore number on the shot barrel is because they received both proofs at the same time.

Having the revolvers made in France but proved in London was unsatisfactory from the standpoint of time and money. This difficulty was readily overcome by having the revolvers actually made in England under the Le Mat and Girard patent. We know that they were made in Birmingham, England, and we assume that they were made by the Birmingham Small Arms Company.

Manufacture of the Baby Le Mats continued in Paris and apparently this was the only product there.

For Le Mat and Girard 1865 held promise of becoming the best year of all, and they must

have had high expectations for the production of the grape-shot revolver. On the other side of the Atlantic, the outlook for the Confederate States of America was exceedingly grim. The hopes of a victory were destined to be dashed by "overwhelming numbers and resources" as General Robert E. Lee so aptly put it in April of that year.

Seemingly, the difficulties of the past years had been overcome by the two contractors. The guns that were being made in Birmingham caused some confusion in serial numbers, inasmuch as the first ones produced were numbered with serials of 1 to 128 (and possibly higher) before there was enough coordination between Birmingham and Paris to stop the duplication of numbers. In order to avoid further duplication, numbers were jumped to the 5000's. If serial numbers are an indication of the number produced, 208 revolvers were made in this range before it was realized that it would be necessary to start at the 8000 level to avoid duplication. This is another indication that the first contract with the War Department for 5,000 guns and the first contract with the Navy for 3,000 guns were still in effect. The second contract with the Navy for 2,000 revolvers would present no problem, for they were of different sizes.

During the month of January, 1865, Commodore Barron annulled the Girard & Co. contract for the small caliber Le Mats, and Girard wrote to him on February 5, 1865, asking "for a copy of the order from the Navy Department of the Confederate States giving you authority to send such notice." On the following day Barron answered:

In reply to your request I have to state that the contract made by you with the Navy Department has been sent to me for my guidance, and in it you agree that 500 of said revolvers are to be delivered per month, the first delivery of 500 to be made before the 1st of November 1863. The terms stipulated in this agreement have by no

LE MAT PIN-FIRE REVOLVERS

Upper, serial number 165, with percussion shot barrel. Lower, serial number 20, is a "Baby" Le Mat.

means been complied with by you up to this day.[32]

On February 7, Barron wrote to Commander John M. Brooke:

According to the terms of the contract made by Messrs. Girard & Co. with the Ordnance Bureau, the first 500 pistols were to have been delivered on the 1st of November, 1863. They have not been delivered up to this date, but 100 are now reported ready for inspection. I have directed these to be inspected, and such as are reported worthy

of being received, to be paid for, and have notified Messrs. Girard & Co. that I do not feel myself authorized to continue the inspection and receiving under the present condition of affairs until I learn the views of the department. The closing up of our ports by the blockade and the fall of Fort Fisher, thus rendering it quite impossible to get arms into the Confederacy and cotton out, together with a report from Commander Bulloch, financial agent of the department, of the shortness of money to meet all the engagements made under bona fide contracts and faithfully complied up, and the noncompliance of these contractors with their agreement, have induced me to notify these gentlemen in order that they may not run into any further expense on account of this contract. They shall lose nothing by what they have already manufactured so far as they are reported favorably on. I do not think these gentlemen will have any just grounds of complaint after the indulgence that has been shown to them. They complain of my decision and are about to make a formal protest, which I shall forward to the bureau when it is received by me.[33]

Girard had planned to send the Baby Le Mats to the Birmingham house with whom he held a contract for proof testing; but, of the 100 guns reported ready for inspection, little is known as to how many passed Murdaugh's inspection and were sent there. The last entry in Barron's diary is dated Paris, France, February 16, 1865, and confides, "Wrote to Bulloch today and directed him to pay for the pistols that may pass under the Girard & Co. contract with the Birmingham house." The highest serial number of a Baby Le Mat known to the authors is 75. It bears the Birmingham proof marks and has the Navy inspector's stamp of *M* on the cylinder with the Paris address on the barrel, as do all the Baby Le Mats.

April 9, 1865, marked an end to the war and to the possibility of Le Mat or Girard delivering any more grape-shot revolvers to the Confederacy. A summary of serial numbers indicates that they made revolvers with serial numbers up to 2500 with the Paris address on the barrels. In addition they made 100 Baby Le Mats in Paris. The number of guns made by the Birmingham house which are marked "Le Mat & Girard's Patent London" is not accurately known at this time, due to the lack of specimens available for study. There are about one dozen guns in this series of markings known to the authors, and they range in serials from 1 to 128 and then jump to 5208. One gun is known in this range. The next jump is to the 8000's, and there has been one gun reported with a serial number of

9009. These serial numbers do not reflect the true number of guns produced, for they would indicate a production of several thousand, which seems unrealistic at this time. We would guess that only about 500 revolvers were made in Birmingham. The partners who started out with hopes so high actually produced less than 3,000 percussion grape-shot revolvers.

THE TWO MODELS OF LE MAT REVOLVERS

Despite innumerable small variations, there were only two basic models of the Civil War Le Mat revolvers. These variations will be described, but first, the two basic models.

The outstanding features of the first model Le Mat percussion revolvers are: the part octagon and part round barrels; the loading lever on the right side; the spur on the trigger-guard; the full swivel lanyard ring in the butt; and the Le Mat trademark of script letters *L* and *M* enclosed by a circle. These features are found on revolvers with serial numbers from 1 to 450.

The distinguishing features of the second model Le Mat revolvers are: the full octagon barrels; the loading lever on the left side; the round trigger-guard; the fixed butt-ring for the lanyard; and the Le Mat trademark of block letters *L M* surmounted by a five-pointed star. The earlier second model revolvers retained one of the features of the first model: the spur type trigger-guards which were used until the supply was exhausted. Gun number 941 is the highest serial noted to retain the spur-guard. The full swivel lanyard rings were retained up to serial number 800.

THE VARIOUS BARREL MARKINGS OF LE MAT REVOLVERS

Dr. Le Mat patented his grape-shot revolver in the United States on October 21, 1856. For this he would have needed a "patent model" pistol. This has never been found.

Although there is no question that some revolvers had been made by 1859, the first documentary evidence does not appear until the fall of this year, when the Beauregard papers show a receipt for a cased grape-shot pistol made for the partners by John Krider of Philadelphia, with its cost of $208.80 itemized in detail. It was paid for by C. Girard, acting for Le Mat and Beauregard. The receipt dated October 24, 1859, shows it as a "patent pistol," but in a statement of expenditures made out by Beauregard and delivered to Le Mat the following year it is referred to as a "Model Revolver." The purpose of this gun is not known, but possibly it was to have been used for advertising or patent purposes abroad.

As Le Mat was appointed a "Colonel and Aide-de-Camp" on the staff of the Governor of Louisiana in 1859, we assume that those revolvers that do not bear "Colonel" as a portion of the barrel marking were made prior to 1859. An undetermined number of these were made, but numbers 1 and 4 are still extant. Possibly these were the revolvers used by the testing boards in New Orleans and Washington.

Upon Le Mat's appointment as Colonel, all revolvers made were numbered from 1 and continued to number 450, being marked *Col. Le Mat's Patent*. There are a few exceptions to this: namely, numbers 5, 309 and 346, which are marked *Col. Le Mat Bte. s.g.d.g. Paris*. These exceptions we regard as duplicated serials due to confusion in setting up manufacture at a new location. Setting aside these exceptions, we conclude that the guns bearing simply *Col. Le Mat's Patent* were made between 1859 and 1861. Of these 450, we believe approximately 300 to have been made before the outbreak of hostilities between North and South and during the time when Le Mat still had a three-quarter interest in the patents.

Where these first revolvers were made is not known, but the Beauregard papers indicate that several of the large American gun makers were contacted in 1859, relative to the manufacture of the pistols. There is no indication that any of these firms consented to make them.

However, the fact that these revolvers are marked with the English (or American) word "Patent" leads us to the conclusion that they must have been made in England or America. As Le Mat had no English patents at the time but did have American patents, we can discount the possibility of English manufacture and conclude that they were made in America.

Placing ourselves in Le Mat's position in 1856, when he first wished a gun made for an American patent model, we believe we would have approached a local gunsmith to do the job. Had this workman done a creditable job, he would also have been engaged to have made the guns for the Army boards.

Probably the workman's shop would have been small and his potential output limited. As we began to envision the manufacture of thousands of our guns, we would have written persons capable of producing such amounts— namely, the large gun manufacturers—but in the meantime would have had the small production continue.

Meanwhile, we have obtained a French patent and a new partner, Charles Girard of Paris, France. Suppose this new partner had access to a plant in Paris where guns could be turned out in quantity and not by the hundreds as previously? We believe we would be tempted to move to France, particularly if the new partner owned a three-quarter interest in the business and insisted on it.

Still theorizing, if we did decide on a move to France and could not go ourselves, who would be the next best person to send? Why, the man who had been making the guns, of course! After all, he had the plans, specifications, tools and, best of all, the experience.

We believe that the first revolvers were made in New Orleans by an unidentified gunsmith. Although we are unable to locate such a name in the New Orleans City Directories, it is possible that this gunsmith's name was Baguet.

THE FIRST SERIES OF MARKINGS

Revolvers with serial numbers 1 and 4 and with the simple barrel markings *Le Mat Patent* in engraved block letters are noted to have the name or word "BAGUET" stamped on the inside of their wooden grips and also on the inside of their metal side-plates. The same "BAGUET" is also to be found on the inside grips of revolver number 101, which has the barrel marking *Col. Le Mat's Patent.*

Thus we link a common denominator in the manufacture of the first series to the second series.

THE SECOND SERIES OF MARKINGS

The second series of barrel markings are *Col. Le Mat's Patent* engraved in script on the barrel top. Some are marked "COL. LE MAT'S PATENT" with engraved block letters.

To continue the theory of manufacture by the same person and/or tools, upon examining the serial number 101 microscopically, we find a fault or flaw in the "O." We are gratified to find this same break or fault also appearing in the later guns bearing the Paris address, showing that the same die was used.

Courtesy Edward N. Simmons
FIRST TYPE OF LE MAT MARKINGS

Serial number 25, showing LM in a circle. The marking "104 CS" was probably added when the arm reached C. S. Ordnance Department. The only CS marking on a Le Mat known to the authors.

Courtesy Edward N. Simmons
MARKING ON LATER LE MAT ARMS

The star/LM marking as found on the side of the barrel of serial number 2448.

Upon moving to Paris it was first decided to begin with serial number 1; but, upon reflection, and after at least five had been made, such plans were discarded in favor of continuing the existing serials which, by this time, were around 300. This series continued to approximately 350, when once again—for what reason is not apparent—it was evident that another false start had been made, and the "Col. Le Mat's Patent was continued to serial number 450.

THE THIRD SERIES OF MARKINGS

Thereafter the barrel markings changed to reflect the change of address and French patent.

Courtesy Edward N. Simmons
LE MAT BARREL MARKING

The Paris address appears on top of the barrel of serial number 2448.

Henceforth, from serial 451 to a little over 1800, the barrel markings are consistent in showing *Col. Le Mat Bte. s.g.d.g. Paris.* It is our belief that guns with these barrel markings were made between 1861 and 1863, and were supplied to both the Confederate States War and Navy Departments.

Courtesy Miles W. Standish

SECOND AND THIRD LE MAT MARKINGS

The second barrel marking, on serial number 314, is shown at the top. The third marking, on serial number 1666, is shown below, together with the first Paris address.

THE FOURTH SERIES OF MARKINGS

In late 1863 or 1864, at serial number 1812, the barrel markings were changed—possibly to reflect an internal change in relationship between Le Mat and Girard—to *Syst. Le Mat Bte. s.g.d.g. Paris*, this being engraved with script letters on the barrel top. Others are found stamped, *SYSTme LEMAT Bte S.G.D.G. Paris*. The highest serial in this range known is number 2469. As we have stated, many guns in this series, although bearing the Paris address, also contain the London proof marks, showing that they were inspected and received by the Confederacy in London, England. Some also contain the *M* stamp of Lieutenant Murdaugh, the inspecting officer of the Confederate States Navy.

The *other series* of barrel markings found on the revolvers made in England are "LE MAT & GIRARD'S PATENT LONDON." These markings are engraved in block style letters. Upon comparison of these revolvers with the ones bearing the Paris address, it can be demonstrated that the former were made in England. The Le Mat and Girard revolvers resemble the Paris-made guns, but there are several points of variance which materially aid in establishing the fact of English manufacture.

The most important point of difference, of course, is that the London address is included in the barrel markings. One purpose of the address, among others, is to gain protection of the patent under which the gun was manufactured. The English patent number 1081 of April 15, 1862, for the grape-shot revolver has been noted to have received full protection. Had the guns not been manufactured in England, the patent would have received only provisional protection. Another factor to be considered is the drawings accompanying the English patent papers. These illustrate distinguishing features of construction and design which are found only in the Le Mat and Girard revolvers. Some of these features which are most noticeable and easily observed are: the small type serial numbers; the flat, dark-grained grips of wood; the quality of checkering on these grips; the rifling in the barrels; the type and pattern of checkering on the hammer; and numerous other items which add up to evidence of English manufacture. The most tangible evidence of English origin of the Le Mat and Girard's patent revolvers is found in the proof marks on the barrels of these guns. A brief review of the method of proving guns at the Birmingham proof house reminds us that a preliminary proof test (provisional) was made on the barrels in order to eliminate those which were faulty or unable to withstand the pressures of firing. This method saved time, labor and money, as no time or labor was expended on barrels which would be lost later during testing. The provisional proof marks found on all the Le Mat and Girard revolvers consist of the bore number "18" and the crossed scepters. Later, after the gun was completed and assembled, it was given the final proof test and stamped with the *definitive* proof marks found on the Le Mat and Girard guns. These marks consist of the letter "v" surmounted by a crown for "viewed" and the letter "p" surmounted by a crown for "proved." The presence of the provisional proof marks on the Le Mat and Girard revolvers show that these guns were made in England, for neither time, labor or money would have been saved by shipping the guns "in the bright" for testing and finishing in England as heretofore assumed. We believe all guns in this range to have been for the Confederate States Navy.

SERIAL NUMBERS KNOWN TO THE AUTHORS

Le Mat percussion revolvers with the first series of barrel markings which were recorded by the authors are as follows:
1—Has "Baguet" stamped on inner side of grips. 4—Has engraved cylinder, the design of which is similar to No. 1. Has "Baguet" stamped on inner side of grips.

Le Mat revolvers with the second series of markings recorded are as follows:
1—Serial number only, in the Winchester Museum. 10—In Milwaukee Museum. 21—Carried by Private William F. Ruger, Company E, "Eutaw" Regiment, S. C. 25—Has "CS" and station number 104 on cylinder, indicating shipboard use. 28, 34, 37, 39, 47, 69, 71. 73—National Museum, Washington, D. C. 74, 90, 97. 101—Has "Baguet" stamped on inner side of grips. 107. 115—Carried by General J. E. B. Stuart, in Confederate Museum, Richmond, Va. 146, 156, 158. 163—Grip has silver inlay engraved, "Co A 18 Ga." 165, 167. 189—Carried by Major Henry Wirz, Commander of Andersonville Prison, Ga., now in Chicago Historical Society. 210, 212, 227, 240, 246, 269, 277, 282. 303—Carried by the Colonel of the Chesterfield Dragoons, Virginia. 314, 343. 354—In Fort McHenry Museum, Baltimore, Md. 390, 396, 402, 408. 427—Engraved "To Gen. P. T. Beauregard, CSA," now in Confederate Museum, Richmond, Va. 444.

Le Mat revolvers with the third series of markings are as follows: 5—The first octagon barrel Le Mat recorded. 309, 346, 459. 475—Carried by General Patton Anderson, CSA, now in Confederate Museum, Richmond, Va. 476, 496, 516, 518, 525, 536, 559. 576—Has Kerr-type loading lever. 578, 579. 586—In Jefferson Memorial, St. Louis, Mo. 608, 622, 626, 645, 648, 663, 667, 679, 690, 700, 737, 755, 780, 807, 825. 826—Said to have been carried by a Virginia scout. 830, 847, 850. 852—Carried by Col. John Lamb, CSA, North Carolina (supposedly one of a pair). 853, 861, 877, 912, 920, 937, 941, 944, 947,

964, 1002, 1078, 1082, 1094, 1097, 1121, 1125, 1131, 1222. 1273—Carried by General Braxton Bragg, CSA. 1303, 1312, 1375, 1405, 1495, 1506, 1511, 1552, 1573, 1608, 1626, 1645, 1666, 1672, 1694, 1703, 1739, 1757, 1774, 1809.

Le Mat revolvers with the fourth series of markings are as follows (the revolvers with the Murdaugh stamping also have London proof marks):
1812—At West Point Museum. 1824, 1849, 1876, 1888, 1891, 1914, 1916, 1918, 1929, 1937, 1952, 1978, 2003, 2143. 2145—Has London proof marks. 2162—In National Rifle Association Museum, Washington, D. C. 2239—Has CSN Inspector Lt. William H. Murdaugh's stamp "M" on cylinder. 2263—Has London proof marks. 2289—Has London proof marks. 2339—Has CSN Inspector Lt. William H. Murdaugh's stamp of "M" on cylinder. 2360—Inlaid with silver and has crescent and star motif. 2389—Has London proof marks. 2393—Has CSN Inspector Lt. William H. Murdaugh's stamp of "M" on cylinder. 2443—Has London proof marks. 2448—Has CSN Inspector Lt. William H. Murdaugh's stamp of "M" on cylinder. 2469—Has CSN Inspector Lt. William H. Murdaugh's stamp of "M" on cylinder.

The Baby Model Le Mat revolvers are marked with the fourth series of markings, and those recorded by the authors are: 18—Engraved frame and cylinder. 35. 72—No address or barrel markings. 75—Has CSN Inspector Lt. William H. Murdaugh's stamp of "M" on cylinder, also Birmingham proof marks.

There are two other percussion Baby Model Le Mats known to the authors, the serial numbers of which are not known.

Le Mat percussion revolvers with the "LE MAT & GIRARD'S PATENT LONDON" markings on the barrel which are known to the authors are as follows:
3—Has no external markings, the number 3 is found on inner parts. 9—Has barrel markings but no external serial number and the number 9 is found on the inner parts. Both Nos. 3 and 9 have

Birmingham proof marks. 128, 5208, 8074, 8084, 8177, 8448, 8483—Have Birmingham proof marks. 8490, 8626, 8917, 8948, 9009.

PERTINENT LE MAT PATENTS AND THEIR DATES

Number	Date	Subject
UNITED STATES		
15925	Oct. 21, 1856	Grape-shot revolver
24312	June 7, 1859	Adjustable hammer
24313	June 7, 1859	Automatic finger for closing cannon vents
97780	Dec. 14, 1869	Breech-loading revolver
FRANCE		
2408	July 20, 1859	Grape-shot revolver
	July 17, 1861	Improvements in cylinder locking
	April 27, 1865	"Baby" model revolver
BELGIUM		
6208	Oct. 30, 1857	Revolver
	July 20, 1858	Addition to revolver
7810	July 28, 1859	Finger for cannon vents
7812	July 28, 1859	Revolver [improvement on No. 6208]
ENGLAND		
1622	July 8, 1859	Grape-shot revolver
1081	April 15, 1862	Le Mat & Girard patent revolver
3131	Oct. 13, 1868	Breech-loading revolver
3218	Nov. 28, 1871	Safety lock for gun hammer [provisional protection only]

As before noted, in quoting from the Beauregard papers, patents were also taken out in Spain, Prussia and Saxony.

The English patent 1081 is of special importance because it positively identifies Girard as the Charles Frederic Girard of Washington, D. C., as the partner of Le Mat, and also as the partner of Gautherin, in the firm of Gautherin and Girard.

One question which remains unresolved at this time is the matter of just when and where the pinfire model Le Mats fit into the series of revolvers. The first United States patent and the Belgian patent of 1857 contain drawings showing pinfire revolvers. It is reasonable to expect that at least a few guns were made under one or both of these patents. The serial numbers of the pinfire revolvers examined by the authors reflect

very little production of these guns, as no serial numbers above 200 have been recorded. It would be very easy to assume that the pinfire revolvers were made either before the war between the States or in the very first part of it, were it not for the physical construction of the guns, which points toward post-war production. Until documentary proof can be found, the establishment of the date of production of these revolvers must remain a question.

The above applies to the large pinfire Le Mat revolvers, as the construction of the Baby pinfire revolvers contains several features which iden-

Courtesy Edward N. Simmons

A POST-WAR LE MAT

This is a nine shot, 9 mm. center-fire weapon with a .50 caliber shot barrel. The weapon is serial number 30, and the top of the barrel is engraved "Colonel Le Mat." A bullet and a "grape-shot" are shown resting on the frame.

tify them as being made from parts left over after the Baby percussion Le Mat revolvers were discontinued.

Except for his patents, little is known of Colonel Le Mat's activities after the war. The New Orleans *Bee* of July 13, 1879, carried this notice: "Died in Paris the 24th of June, 1879, Sophie Justine Lepretre, wife of Dr. Le Mat." The Le Mats maintained their "establishment" in Paris. According to his granddaughter, Mrs. Eggleston, Le Mat—the inventor, the doctor, the Colonel—passed away quietly at this home a few years after the death of his wife.

The last trace found of Charles Girard after the war ended is to be found in the *Dictionary of American Biography* in which is related: "After the close of the Civil War, Girard no longer found life in America attractive, and he entered a career in medicine in Paris, to which he devoted the next 20 years of his life. In 1870 he was chief physician to one of the military ambulances during the siege of Paris. The last recorded publication by Girard was an etiology of typhoid fever titled, *L'Ambulance Militaire de La Rue Violet*. This was published in Paris in the year 1895."

Thus the final curtain falls some 30 years after the Civil War, but we have the grape-shot revolvers of Le Mat and Girard as reminders of the part they played in this war.

FOOTNOTE REFERENCES

1. *Beauregard Papers,* Louisiana State University Archives: the P. G. T. Beauregard Papers list 106 volumes and 815 items, in The Manuscript and Archival Collection, Dept. of Archives, Louisiana State University, Baton Rouge, Louisiana. Hereinafter: *Beauregard Papers, L.S.U.*
2. *Ibid.*
3. *National Archives.*
4. *Ibid.*
5. *Beauregard Papers, L.S.U.*
6. *Ibid.*
7. *Ibid.*
8. *Inventory of Arms,* State of Louisiana.
9. *U.S. National Museum Bulletin,* Number 42, 1891.
10. *O.R.,* Series 4, Vol. I, p. 211.
11. *Confederate Military Records,* State of Georgia, p. 137.
12. *Recollections of a Rebel Reefer,* Col. James M. Morgan, p. 94.
13. *O.R. Navies,* Series 4, Vol. II, p. 105.
14. *War Department Collection of Confederate Records,* Group 109, "Citizens Files," C. Girard voucher number 51, National Archives, Washington, D. C.
15. *O.R. Navies,* Series 3, Vol. I, p. 220.
16. *National Archives,* Record Group 109, War Department Letters Received.
17. *Ibid.*
18. *Ibid.*
19. *Ibid.*
20. *O.R. Navies,* Series 2, Vol. II, p. 230.
21. *Ibid.,* Series 2, Vol. II, p. 275.
22. *Ibid.,* Series 2, Vol. II, p. 282.
23. *Ibid.,* Series 2, Vol. II, pp. 291-292.
24. *Ibid.,* Series 2, Vol. II, p. 332.
25. *Miller's Photographic History of the Civil War,* Vol. 6, p. 88.
26. *National Archives,* War Department Letters Received, G-773, 1862.
27. *O.R. Navies,* Series 2, Vol. II, p. 620.
28. *Ibid.,* Series 2, Vol. II, p. 644.
29. *Ibid.,* Series 2, Vol. II, p. 572.
30. *Ibid.,* Series 2, Vol. II, p. 670.
31. *Ibid.,* Series 2, Vol. II, p. 676.
32. *Ibid.,* Series 2, Vol. II, pp. 795-796.
33. *Ibid.,* Series 2, Vol. II, p. 821.

NOTES

CHAPTER 8

The London Armoury and the Kerr Revolvers

INTEREST in arms collecting has become so great in the past twenty-five to thirty years that within this period nearly every type of weapon has had a serious study made of its background and ancestry. However, one great unexplored field still remains: foreign arms in relation to their use in the American Civil War. The surface of this subject has barely been scratched and many more years of research will be necessary before a significant degree of perception is forthcoming.

Few persons realize the quantities of weapons required to keep the armies of the North and the South in the field for four years, and the extent to which foreign arms were used.

At the start of the war it is understandable that the Federal Government and the Confederate States both sent agents abroad to purchase arms. Less understandable is the fact that most of the individual states, North and South, also had their agents in Europe for the same purpose, each competing with the other. One can imagine the effect this had on prices. To get some concept of the vastness of the enterprise, let us look at a few figures.

Colonel George L. Schuyler, U.S. Army, was sent to Europe in 1861 to buy arms for the Union Army. On September 5, 1861, he wrote Secretary of War Cameron from Paris that he had made contracts for 45,000 to 48,000 French army rifles, caliber .701, Model 1853. He also contracted for 10,000 Lefaucheaux revolvers and added "General Fremont has already sent out a

quantity of these pistols."[1] Colonel Schuyler subsequently bought 10,000 carbines, 10,000 English Enfields, and 27,000 Enfields "from Dresden."[2]

By June 30, 1862, General James W. Ripley, U.S. Chief of Ordnance, reported that up to that date he had purchased the following weapons abroad:

8,999 English Tower muskets
116,740 English Enfield rifles
6,409 Prussian rifles
105,140 Prussian muskets
135,755 Austrian rifles
34,755 Austrian muskets
23,994 Belgian rifles
33,200 Belgian muskets
48,108 French rifles
4,850 French muskets
5,179 Minie rifles
203,831 Other rifles
10,000 Bohemian carbines
1,113 Other foreign carbines
11,940 Lefaucheaux revolvers
3,350 Other foreign revolvers[3]

Supplementing this listing, Volume IV of *Ordnance Reports & Other Important Papers 1860-1889*, page 903, reveals that the U.S. Ordnance Department from January 1, 1861 to December 31, 1866, purchased the following during the course of the Civil War: 10,251 carbines, 428,292 Enfield rifles, 736,049 muskets and rifles (all other kinds), and 12,374 revolving pistols.

The last item is of interest to us in view of

General Ripley's statement of June 30, 1862, that he had purchased 11,940 Lefaucheaux revolvers and 3,350 other foreign revolvers, or a total of 15,290. It is difficult to reconcile this statement with that of the Ordnance Department that only 12,374 foreign revolvers had been purchased during the entire war. Possibly 15,290 had been bought (as reported by Ripley), but only 12,374 actually delivered. During the same period the Ordnance Report shows that 359,449 revolving pistols had been purchased in America. Thus it appears that foreign purchase of revolvers was confined mainly to the first year or so of the war and that the largest single maker was Lefaucheaux.

It is hoped that this data relating to the purchases by the United States will tend to dispel the persistent myth that all Enfields are of the "type used by the Confederates." The number of English Enfield rifles and carbines used in both armies was second only to the Springfield of which 801,997 were manufactured during the war.[4]

We have not intentionally slighted the South's efforts in arms-buying abroad. They had by no means been inactive, and according to a report from General Gorgas to the Secretary of War on February 3, 1863, the following had been bought and shipped from Europe:

> 70,980 Long Enfields
> 9,715 Short Enfields
> 354 Enfield carbines
> 27,000 Austrian rifles
> 21,040 British muskets
> 20 Small-bore Enfields
> 2,020 Brunswick rifles

Awaiting shipment at the time of the report were 23,000 Enfield rifles at London and 30,000 Austrian rifles at Vienna.[5]

All foreign weapons of the Civil War period fall into four categories so far as the present-day collector is concerned. They are as follows: One, those purchased by the Confederacy; two, those purchased by the U.S. Government; three, those purchased by the various states, both North and South; and four, those that did not come to this country until sometime after the war, or from 1866 to the present. To be able to positively identify any of these classifications would be of considerable assistance to the collector and continuing attempts should be made to do so.

Anyone who has ever examined an Enfield rifle must be impressed by the number or marks, numerals and names stamped upon it. Such stampings are to be found on the lock, stock, barrel and mountings—even under the ramrod. Their significance is only partially known. We do know that the finished rifle was stamped 22 times with the mark of the assembler who was held responsible for the gun, and that the English proof and viewer's mark is to be found on the left side of the barrel near the breech along with the numbers which denote the caliber. The names found in such profusion are assumed to be those of the persons making the particular part on which the name is stamped, because in the Birmingham Gun Trade many manufacturers figured in the making of only certain parts. To give some idea of the vastness of this enterprise in Birmingham, the 1866 directory for that city indicates 599 names of manufacturers engaged in different branches of the trade. Of these 599 manufacturers, 174 are listed as "gunmakers," 32 are "barrel makers," 23 "furniture makers," etc.

Obviously, there was no basic difference between arms made for the North and those made for the South. The only hope of establishing any difference rests upon the correct interpretation of the stampings found upon them. With such a profusion of marks on each gun, how can this be done? To one Confederate purchasing agent, Edward C. Anderson, Major of Artillery, C.S.A., this appeared as no problem. On August 14, 1861, he wrote the Confederate Secretary of War from London that arrangements were in progress to purchase a large number of Enfield rifles, he having recently received $100,000 from the Governor of Georgia to purchase arms for that state. "This," writes the major, "will enable me to take up many muskets that are at this time being offered, a large portion of which, I am inclined to believe, were ordered for the U.S. Government, but which, for the want of funds in hand, they [the Yankees] were unable to obtain from the mfgrs. Some of these guns now in our possession have *their viewer's mark upon them* [italics ours, Ed.], indicating that they have been inspected and accepted by their agents. Of course we subject them to the ordeal of our own standard of perfection."[6]

This clearly indicates that Major Anderson was able to pick up an Enfield rifle and (probably without disassembling it) tell by looking at it that Yankee buyers had already set their seal of approval on it. Obviously, if we knew what the "viewer's marks" were, we could come to the same determination. Further, when Major Anderson concluded, "Of course we will subject them to the ordeal of our own standard of excellence" it appears that the Confederates also had their own viewers and undoubtedly their marks would have been equally apparent to Major Anderson's counterpart in the Yankee army—Colonel Schuyler.

In addition to *US* and *CS* marks, state stampings may also appear, for in 1861 James L. Peyton, agent in England for North Carolina, wrote to Governor Clark advising that he had purchased Enfield rifles for the state and had ordered them stamped *N.C.* on the barrel.[7] In April, 1862, the steamer *Nashville* arrived at Wilmington, North Carolina, with a cargo of 2,000 Enfields for the state of North Carolina which must have been those referred to by Peyton.[8]

Before the start of actual hostilities between the North and the South, it was a favorite boast of Southern politicians that "We can whip them with cornstalks!" In 1860 the fact became pretty apparent to the South that armed conflict was somewhat more than probable and following this came a realization of the resources necessary to wage war. It was soon discovered that the politicians must have been right, for to beat the North, the war would have to be fought with cornstalks, these being about all the South could muster in the way of weapons.

A frantic attempt to rectify this deficiency was promptly made by the individual states not yet bonded together by the ties of the Confederacy. Agents were sent through the states to collect anything that would kill, wound or maim. Others were sent North in various guises to purchase arms and were amazingly successful, perhaps we should say shockingly successful, in their ability to purchase munitions of war from manufacturers and dealers who were well aware of the intended use of such purchases. Perhaps it wasn't Socrates who first said: "Under the opiate of a fast buck patriotism is put to sleep." Such a saying might well explain Eli Whitney's contract of June 6, 1860, with the state of Mississippi for 1,500 rifles[9] or North Carolina's purchase of 500 Colt revolvers from Colt in March, 1861, for $8,454,[10] Horstmann and Brothers' offer to furnish sabers, cartridge boxes and bayonet scabbards to the South, the seizure of 38 cases of muskets in New York City on the S.S. *Monticello* which were headed for Montgomery, Alabama, on January 23, 1861,[11] and many other similar acts. Apparently human nature and its insatiable lust for money was no better (or worse) then than now. We could go on and on, but we believe that we have made our point.

It was not until about May, 1861, when Northern markets were closed to Southern buyers, that Colonel James Cameron of the U.S. Army was ordered to visit Baltimore, Philadelphia, New York, Providence, Boston and Hartford to collect evidence relating to the manufacture and/or sale of arms, ordnance and ammunition on contract with persons in the Southern States.[12]

Before this time, however, the Southern States had joined together to form the Confederate States of America and the new government was well aware of the need for arms. One of the first acts of President Jefferson Davis was to send Captain Raphael Semmes to the North to make purchases and place contracts for machinery and munitions, or for the manufacture of arms. Davis suggested that the proprietors of the Hazzard Powder Works be contacted as he was sure they would be cooperative.[13] Semmes is better known as Captain of the C.S.S. *Alabama*.

April 15, 1861, Captain (later Major) Caleb Huse was ordered by Samuel Cooper, Adjutant and Inspector-General, C.S.A. to proceed to Europe to purchase ordnance, arms, etc. For more information concerning him, refer to the chapter on Le Mat.

Evidently one of the first contracts, if not the first, made by Huse upon reaching England was with the London Armoury Company of London, because on May 21, 1861, he wrote Gorgas that since its organization the London Armoury Company had been under contract to the British Government and that an additional 18 months would be required before this contract could be completed. Nevertheless, the firm was willing to accept a contract with him for 10,000 rifles (no less), which proposition Huse accepted, each to cost three pounds, sixteen shillings and sixpence. Huse went on to say that the Yankee agent was buying everything he could lay hands on and would have contracted with the London Armoury Company for all they could furnish for a year to come, but "his instructions were to obtain the whole number within two months. The next steamer will without doubt, as I learn from a reliable source, bring orders for him to close with that company." Huse figured the company's production at 1,300 rifles per month of which 100 per week were already under contract to be supplied the North for three months, but that the contract could be canceled with one week's notice. "If the company accepts my proposition, this notice will be given, and at least 1,200 Enfield rifles that would go North will be secured for the Confederate Government. The company will accept my proposition if they can obtain a release from their contract with the [British] Government." Having made application along this line, he expected an answer in a day or so.

"If I could have offered to take 20,000 they would have broken with the government." Huse next commented that the agent sent by the U.S. to purchase arms was the best who could have been selected for the job, a Mr. McFarland, who was the superintending engineer for the London Armoury Company during its erection and until it was in complete working order. "His instructions to make a similar contract with that company for the U.S. Government will come too late. In my contract I stated that I shall be the preferred purchaser for from 6,000 to 10,000 in addition to the number now ordered."[14]

The London Armoury Company to which Caleb Huse referred so often was a private enterprise which had been founded only a short time prior to the American Civil War as a supplement to the Enfield Works and to supply the British Government with arms. Apparently at the time of its formation that was its only contract. The "Mr. McFarland" mentioned by Huse was Corey McFarland, formerly employed in Chicopee, Massachusetts. It was he who arranged the transfer and erection of machinery from the Ames Manufacturing Company from Chicopee to London, and personally supervised the erection of the London Armoury Company Plant. This same gentleman also organized the Birmingham (England) Small Arms factory.

The *Official Records of the War of the Rebellion* contain ample documentation that the London Armoury Company was the unofficial London headquarters for Confederate Army and Navy officers during the war. After the first month or so of the war, there is no indication whatsoever that any of their products went to supply the North. As a matter of fact, the United States purchasing agent, Colonel Schuyler, reported on August 16, 1861, "No Enfield rifles can be procured in England. All private plants in London and Birmingham are working for Ohio, Connecticut, and Massachusetts, except the London Armoury Co. whose product is supposed to be for the South."[15]

Caleb Huse's plans to contract for all of the London Armoury's output fell through because the British Government declined to consent to an extension of time for fulfillment of their own contract, but according to a letter from Huse to Gorgas, August 11, 1861, "The principal manager of that company (LAC), Mr. Hamilton, of the firm of Sinclair, Hamilton & Co., is a merchant of the highest respectability and is acquainted with every gunmaker in England and would, for a commission of 2½%, obtain guns for the Confederacy." Huse originally placed $100,000 at the disposal of Sinclair, Hamilton and Company, which at the time of writing had been almost exhausted. An additional $125,000 was placed to the firm's credit. Huse was quite pleased with the arrangement and entirely satisfied with Mr. Hamilton and his results.[16]

The Confederate Navy in the meantime had sent Captain James D. Bulloch to Europe to purchase arms and was supplied with funds amounting to $600,000. On August 13, 1861, Captain Bulloch wrote Secretary of the Navy, S. R. Mallory, that he had arrived in Liverpool on June 3 and soon found "There were already in England agents for the Federal Government as well as for several of the Northern States, each with large orders and abundance of ready money, and these persons, in their zeal, were actually bidding against each other, thus running up the prices of arms . . . Captain Huse, C.S. Army, had felt the effect of this rivalship among the Northern agents to a very serious extent." Bulloch went on to say "None of the leading gun factories were in condition to take contracts except upon a very long time, and I was forced to adopt the plan Captain Huse fell into of employing a commission house here familiar with the gun trade and directors in the London Armoury Co., to contract for the sea service rifles my orders called for, with the small makers in Birmingham and elsewhere . . . The 100 sea service rifles and cutlasses could not be had already made, but will be in about three

weeks. The cutlasses are identical with those used in the British Navy and can be shipped upon the end of the rifle as a bayonet . . . Revolvers were not to be had on any terms. I therefore contracted with a large factory for 1,000 as per order; these I hope will be ready for shipment as soon as the great guns."[17]

By March, 1862, Captain Huse could report that the contract between the London Armoury Company and the British Government was about to expire and that he had requested the managing director of the company not to apply for a renewal so the Confederacy would be able to make a contract for all arms produced in the coming three years. Huse stated that he had done this because the products of the company were so far superior to all others.[18]

In April, 1862, Huse continued his praise of the London Armoury Company: "I have previously informed you that I have reason to be entirely satisfied with the London Armoury Co. in all transactions that I have had with them." Huse continued by stating that their rifles were far superior, the component parts being all interchangeable. "I have requested the chairman to hand to me a tender for supplying 40,000 rifles from their manufactory. Enclosed I have the honor to submit a copy of their proposition. In case the Department should desire me to make this contract, I beg to be informed at the earliest moment, as otherwise I may find it impossible to arrange the matter."[19]

If we are correct in assuming that the products of the London Armoury Company went only to the British Government and to the Confederacy, and none to the North, then for our particular purposes they can be divided into two categories: those that were exported to the Confederacy and those that remained in England for the British Government. The problem is to distinguish one from the other.

The London Armoury Company was engaged largely in the manufacture of rifles, a prime example of which is in the Smithsonian Institution,

KERR'S PATENT REVOLVER

Serial number 19, patent number 5801, by the London Armoury Company. This arm shows much holster wear and it will be noted that the front sight has either been worn down or filed down to facilitate holster use.

Washington, D. C., stamped with the firm name and the date *1862*. This particular gun was taken from Confederate President Jefferson Davis at the time of his capture after the war. In addition to the rifles, however, the firm was also engaged in the manufacture of revolvers under the Kerr (and Adams) patent.

J. Kerr (pronounced "Carr") of Southwark, England, was granted a patent for his single-action five-shot revolver on April 14, 1857, and on his five-shot double-action revolver on August 4, 1863. They were made in both 54 and 80 bore (approximately .44 and .384 calibers). Whether any were produced by Kerr personally is not known to the authors. Apparently he assigned his patent rights to the London Armoury Company who turned them out in large quantities. They were well-made and excellently finished and were looked upon with great favor by Confederate soldiers.

These pistols are marked as follows: All are engraved (not stamped) *London Armoury* on the lock and engraved (not stamped) on the right side of the frame *Kerr's Patent No.—.* The same number is also engraved, not stamped, on the cylinder. The left side of the frame is die-stamped in an oval *London Armoury*. The barrel is die-stamped *LAC*. Barrel and cylinder bear English proof marks.

In addition to the above markings, the major parts of each gun are die-stamped with a number which we assume applies to the total number made and which is in fact the true serial. This serial is most evident on the face of the cylinder and on the inside bow of the trigger-guard. This stamped number is so inconspicuous as to escape any but very close notice and because of this, the large engraved number on frame and cylinder is mistaken by many as the serial number of the gun.

This method of marking is a peculiarity which extends to several other English revolvers, and the reason for it may well be common knowledge in that country but the authors have been unable to determine any logical answer on this side of the Atlantic. A review of the known serials that follow, compared with the engraved numbers, indicates no apparent pattern or relationship of one to the other. Possibly the connection will be obvious to others, and if so, we would appreciate such information.

Still one more stamping appears on the weapons of the London Armoury Company, and is to be found on some in the wood of the stock just below the strap of the trigger-guard. This is a small anchor surmounted by the letters *J.S.* Because of the checkered stock, the marking has been mistaken by several as being *U.S.* but a sufficient number of revolvers in excellent condition have been examined to determine that it is really *J.S.* For those that insist that the letters are *U.S.*, we can only suggest that somewhere along the line the piece has been tampered with by someone, who believing *U.S.* correct, changed the tail of the *J* into a *U*.

It is recorded in Executive Document Number 99-18681 that from November 11, 1861, to April 23, 1862, 16 Kerr patent revolvers were purchased by the United States from Schuyler, Hartley and Graham of New York. This is the only recorded purchase of Kerr revolvers by the United States yet to be discovered. The document in question does not say where or exactly when Schuyler, Hartley and Graham bought the 16 revolvers they sold to the United States, but it would be our guess they were secured by that firm prior to the war.

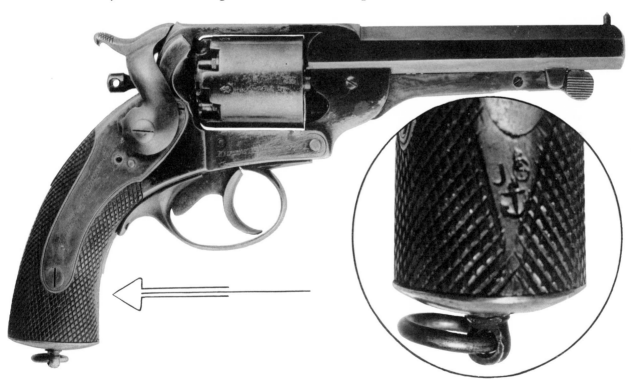

Courtesy Hugh Benet, Jr.

CAPTAIN J. D. SMITH'S KERR

This Kerr revolver, serial number S461, patent number 726, was carried by Captain John Donnel Smith of Battery A, Alexander's Artillery Battalion, Army of Northern Virginia. It shows the typical sharp front sight. An arrow indicates the location of the distinctive JS over anchor mark as shown in the detail.

While we make no pretense of knowing the meaning of the *J.S./anchor* stamp we do feel sure that it was not applied on guns meant for domestic use. In other words, at the very least we think that it was an export stamp, and if all exported Civil War Kerr revolvers are Confederate, then those bearing this stamp are Confederate. The mark has also been noted on two London Armoury Enfield rifles, one of which was also marked *C.S.A.*

We have been able to document the use of many of the Kerr revolvers listed hereafter on the Confederate side during the war. It is of interest that none claim Yankee usage.

It would further be our assumption that the absence of the *J.S./anchor* stamp on a pistol would not preclude its Confederate use. Possibly only one of each lot (of undetermined number) was so stamped rather than each individual gun.

We report the following shipments of revolvers to the Confederacy, believing many of them relate to the London Armoury Kerrs:

500 revolvers on Steamer *Fingal*, November 1861.[20]

On April 11, 1862, in writing Confederate Secretary of the Navy, Bulloch mentioned that he had enclosed a memorandum of "The Navy revolvers already shipped and will send 100 more next week."[21]

By S.S. *Melita*, Bulloch shipped 380 revolvers with cartridges, caps and spare parts, April 19, 1862.[22]

900 Kerr revolvers with extra parts and 900 Kerr powder flasks received at Wilmington, N. C., October 31, 1864, on Steamer *Hope*.[23]

According to General Gorgas in a statement to the Honorable James A. Seddon, Secretary of War, on December 3, 1864, 1,716 "pistols" had been imported during the year 1864.[24]

According to *Confederate Blockade Running Through Bermuda 1861-65*, by Frank E. Vandiver, the following passed through that port on their way to the Confederacy: May 7, 1864, 33 cases of pistols; July 8, 1864, four cases of

pistols and March 8, 1865, eight cases of revolvers.

Better made and infinitely better finished than any revolver made in the North or South, the Kerr revolver was undoubtedly imported and issued by the South in large numbers. It is not considered a rare or scarce arm, but is nevertheless most desirable in a Confederate collection.

LIST OF LONDON ARMOURY KERR REVOLVERS KNOWN TO THE AUTHORS

Serial Number (Stamped)	Patent Number (Engraved)	J.S. and Anchor stamp
19	5801	?
46	9708	?
53	9722	?
250-E	S394	yes
300	8865	yes
346	6959	?
430	9567	yes
492	4549	?
535	11027	?
604	9932	yes
642	10110	?
726	S461	yes
758-D	3351	yes
775	10203	?
815-E	4791	?
852	11319	?
966	4395	yes
979-AB	3712	yes
1057	1301	?
1193	1453	?
1199	1440	yes
1292	1505	?
1669-Y	1730	yes
1675	1726	yes
1917	1861	yes
2314	2368	yes
2439	2469	yes
not known	10181	?
not known	2807	?
not known	3801	?

In the preceding pages much mention has been made of Caleb Huse, purchasing agent for the Confederate War Department in Europe. After the war Huse wrote a booklet entitled *The Supplies of The Confederate Army and How They Were Obtained in Europe and How Paid For.* This was published in Boston in 1904, and the following is extracted from it.

My resignation was accepted by the United States Army February 25th, 1861. In April—I think it was April 1st—I received a telegram from the Confederate States Secretary of the Navy Mallory, to come to Montgomery and take a commission for active service. I started without delay, and on arriving in Montgomery was introduced to Secretary of War Walker, who soon said to me: The President has designated you to go to Europe for the purchase of arms and military supplies; when can you go? I replied I could go immediately. I was then introduced to Col. Gorgas, Chief of Ordnance, to whom I was to report.

Huse proceeded by way of Charleston, South Carolina, where he viewed the scene of Beauregard's firing on Fort Sumter. He went to New York City and from there to Portland, Canada, where he boarded a ship to London. There he lodged at Morley's Hotel in Trafalgar Square.

My orders were to purchase 12,000 rifles and a battery of field artillery, and to produce one or two guns of larger calibre as models. A short time before the beginning of the war, the London Armoury Company had purchased a plant of gun-stocking machinery from the Ames Manufacturing Company of Chicopee, Mass. Knowing this, I went to the office of the Armoury Company the day after my arrival in London, with the intention of securing, if possible, their entire output.

On entering the Superintendent's office, I found there the American engineer who superintended the erection of the plant. I had known him in Chicopee. Suspecting he might be an agent for the purchase of arms for the United States Government, I asked him, bluntly, if he was, and

added, "I am buying for the Confederate Government." Such a disclosure of my business may seem to have been indiscreet, but at that time I thought it my best plan, and the result proved that I was right. He made no reply to my inquiry, but I was satisfied my suspicion was correct and resolved on the spot, to flank his movement if possible.

As he had entered the office first, it was in order for me to outstay him, which I did. On his leaving, I asked for a price for all the small arms the Company could manufacture.

The Superintendent said he could not answer me, but would refer me to the Chairman of the Company—president, we should call him—and would accompany me to his office. There I repeated my inquiry for a price for all the arms the Company could make for a year, with the privilege of renewing the order. The president was not prepared to give me a price, but would do so the next day. On calling at his office the following day, he told me that the Company was under contract for all the arms it could turn out, and considering all the circumstances, the Directors felt they ought to give their present customer the preference over all others.

Huse was aware that the "present customer" was the agent for the United States Ordnance Department. He was also aware that this person had not such freedom of action as had he (Huse), and to top any large offer made by Huse would first have to secure permission from Washington. Thus, in making his proposal to the London Armoury Company, Huse stipulated that his offer either be accepted or rejected immediately.

Confirmed in my belief that my competitor was no other than the man whom I had encountered the day before [he continues], I was now more determined than ever to secure the London Armoury as a Confederate States arms factory.

The Atlantic cable was not then laid and correspondence by mail required a month—an unreasonable time for a commercial company to hold in abeyance a desirable opportunity for profit.

Within a few days I succeeded in closing a contract under which I was to have all the arms the Company could manufacture, after filling a comparatively small order for the United States agent. This Company, during the remainder of the war, turned all its output of arms over to me for the Confederate Army.

It remains for an English collector to do the research necessary to complete the story of the London Armoury Company's Kerr revolvers in the Confederacy.

FOOTNOTE REFERENCES

1. *O.R.*, Series 3, Vol. I, p. 484.
2. *Ibid.*, p. 485.
3. *O.R.*, Series 3, Vol. II, p. 855.
4. *Ordnance Reports and Other Important Papers,* 1860-1889, Vol. IV, p. 903.
5. *O.R.*, Series 4, Vol. II, p. 382.
6. *O.R.*, Series 4, Vol. I, p. 559.
7. *MSS.* in North Carolina State Archives, Greensboro, North Carolina.
8. Confederate Military History, North Carolina.
9. *O.R.*, Series 4, Vol. I, p. 62.
10. *Southern Historical Papers,* Vol. XXIX, p. 150.
11. *O.R.*, Series 3, Vol. I, p. 53.
12. *O.R.*, Series 3, Vol. I, p. 167.
13. *O.R.*, Series 4, Vol. I, p. 106.
14. *O.R.*, Series 4, Vol. I, p. 343.
15. *O.R.*, Series 3, Vol. I, p. 418.
16. *O.R.*, Series 4, Vol. I, pp. 538-542.
17. *O.R. Navies,* Series 2, Vol. II, pp. 83-87.
18. *O.R.*, Series 4, Vol. I, pp. 1003-1005.
19. *O.R. Navies,* Series 2, Vol. II, pp. 177-180.
20. *Secret Service of the Confederate States in Europe,* James D. Bulloch, p. 112.
21. *O.R. Navies,* Series 2, Vol. II, p. 185.
22. *Ibid.*
23. Records Book of Colonel J. M. Payne, collector, Port of Wilmington, N. C., C.S.A. MS., Confederate Museum, Richmond, Virginia.
24. *O.R.*, Series 4, Vol. III, p. 986.

PART III

CHAPTERS 9 through 17

SECONDARY MARTIAL HANDGUNS

Handguns made by or for the various
Confederate States

CHAPTER 9

Thomas W. Cofer

T HERE comes a time in every aspiring historian's career when he pushes back from his typewriter and utters the academic equivalent of "to hell with it." The frustrations and uncertainties which lead to such imprecations are legion and none are more exasperating than those which beset the foolhardy amateur who attempts research on a secondary source of Confederate arms. This is particularly true when one digs into the record of one Thomas W. Cofer, of Portsmouth, Viriginia, who invented and patented a process for loading certain types of firearms. The weapons he manufactured in 1861 and part of 1862 represent one of the few types of revolving pistols that can truly be called *secondary* Confederate martial weapons. Such arms were uniformly made for military use during the war in sufficient quantities to be recognized as a type, and were used by troops in the field as a sidearm even though they were not official "issue" weapons. At this writing, at least seven Cofer revolvers are known to have survived the years.

The story of Cofer and his revolvers is a challenge to the collector-historian. Unfortunately, most of us lack the three essential prerequisites for a really definitive study—time, money, and patience. Through tolerant, kindly, and extremely cooperative friends, we have checked almost every source we could think of for data, but doubtless more exists. It now remains for local collectors in Virginia, Washington, D. C., and adjacent areas, to pick up the trail and see what they can do. The trail may lead to still another revolver and patience like virtue, hath its reward, although it is doubtful that the successful seeker will receive what he deserves. With this glum observation, we proceed to Thomas W. Cofer and his works.

TIDEWATER GUNSMITH

According to family genealogical notes, the ancestors of Thomas W. Cofer settled in Tidewater Virginia around the middle of the 17th century, in the vicinity of what is now Smithfield, Isle of Wight County. Concerning the name, it is pertinent to know that it was spelled *Coffer* in various records until the end of the 18th century. Then, for a short period, *Copfer* alternated with *Cofer*, and the latter has been the preferred spelling since the first decade of the eighteen hundreds. This sort of evolution in American names is by no means unusual, but presents certain difficulties to the historian.

Thomas Wrenn Cofer[1] was born March 22, 1828, near Smithfield. If his ability as a grammarian and orthographer is any criterion, he was not given too lengthy an education, but this does not mean that he was unintelligent, backward, or neglected. He appears to have received about as much formal education as any farm lad did in those days, and if anyone cavils at Tom's phonetic spelling, let him but view the efforts of many a latter-day scholar. His penmanship was excellent and he could write a clear, direct, forceful letter, as will be seen.

A bit of information furnished by a descendant was that Cofer had been "in business" with a cousin, one P. D. Gwaltney. This seemingly unimportant tie is actually the reverse, because Pembroke Decatur Gwaltney was a gunsmith. What's more, in 1859, when Cofer was 31, Gwaltney was doing business as P. D. Gwaltney & Company. It is quite logical to assume that young Cofer had been apprenticed to his cousin at a fairly early age and had later gone into business with him, particularly in view of the close-knit family society of the Tidewater. Ironically enough, the firm's address was 8 Union Street, Norfolk. Norfolk, incidentally, is just

tion of city directories, because Cofer seems to have gone into business for himself sometime before 1861. The proof of this lies on the locks and barrels of two shotguns, both of which leave no doubt of their being from T. W. Cofer & Co., Portsmouth, Va., and both being of pre-war manufacture. These weapons are discussed in detail later on.

A summary of gunsmiths and their addresses from the Norfolk-Portsmouth City Directories, and comparison with a contemporary map, shows that Norfolk, like most cities, once had its Gunsmith's Row, and 8 Union Street was in the heart of both it and the business district. We also

LISTINGS FROM THE NORFOLK-PORTSMOUTH DIRECTORIES

Gunsmith	*Address*	*Year or Years at Location*
BELL, LLOYD C.	5 Union Street	1860
CARR, JOHN J.	Crawford near High	1872–73
CARR, JOHN J.	20 High Street	1874–75
COFER, THOMAS W.	Market Square	1869, 1870
COFER, THOMAS W.	13 Union Street	1872, 1872–73, 1874–75
DEY, DAVID, JR.	8 Union Street	1867, 1869, 1870
DEY, DAVID, JR.	15 Union Street	1872, 1872–73, 1874–75
FOSTER, W. E.	23 Bank Street	1866
FOSTER AND SPAULDING	23 Bank Street	1867
FREEMAN, JAMES	75 S. Church Street	1860
GWALTNEY, P. D., AND CO.	8 Union Street	1859, 1860
GWALTNEY, B. L. W. [*sic*]	8 Union Street	1860
HUDGINS, W. R.	35 Market [*sic*]	1874–75
MORRIS, DAVITON [*sic*]	5 Union Street	1859, 1860, 1866, 1867
MORRIS, DAVID	5 Union Street	1869, 1870, 1872, 1872–73
MORRIS, DAVIDTON [*sic*]	8 Union Street	1874–75
REED, JAMES H.	8 Union Street	1866, 1867, 1869, 1870
ROBERTS, THOMAS	106 Crawford Street	1872–73
SOREY AND DEY	15 Union Street	1872, 1872–73, 1874–75
SOREY, P. A.	15 Union Street	1874–75
SPRATLEY, W. S.	14 Union Street	1851–52, 1859, 1860, 1866, 1867

across the Elizabeth River from Portsmouth, a distance of less than a mile.

It is unfortunate and rather maddening that there were gaps of many years between publica-

find that Cofer was active as a gunsmith after the war, but without Gwaltney.

Cousin Gwaltney is well remembered, but not because of his activities before the war, or for

Courtesy Hugh Benet, Jr.

A VIEW OF NORFOLK AND PORTSMOUTH, VA.

Published by Chas. Magnus, Circa 1850

his service as a field ordnance repairman in T. J. "Stonewall" Jackson's 2nd Corps of the Army of Northern Virginia.[2] Rather, he was Virginia's postwar "Peanut King," the man who put Smithfield back on its feet and was responsible for the name "Smithfield" now being synonymous with ham (at least to most Virginians, and to many Marylanders). He who has not enjoyed the gastronomical delights of real Smithfield ham has my sympathy. The connection between peanuts and hams, for the benefit of the uninitiate, is hogs, who eat the one and are made into the other, and it was Gwaltney who founded a business of national scope and reputation to capitalize on the felicitous result. Forsaking his former trade as a gunsmith at the war's end, he returned to his family's farm and shortly built an enterprise which, under the capable direction of his grandson and great-grandson, upholds a glorious tradition today.

Cofer, who was quite capable of producing small numbers of serviceable revolving handguns, apparently never sought a government contract to furnish them, nor private or governmental financial backing to manufacture them in quantity. This is puzzling, because his invention received a fair amount of publicity at a time when no other revolver manufacturer had appeared on the scene, and he was actually making and selling his revolving pistols when there was a desperate need for weapons. However, as far as it is known, the Chief of the Confederate Ordnance Corps, General Gorgas, never mentioned Cofer in any of his letters, orders, or personal papers,[3] and no trace of him has been found in any other official records.

One may only surmise that Cofer was satisfied with the income he received from making, repairing and selling arms in Norfolk early in the war, and made no real attempt to enlarge his operations. It is further surmised that our Tidewater entrepreneur was somewhat outclassed by the big operators who had gathered in Richmond by the time he moved there, and that this and the loss of his home, shop, tools and everything else he possessed when Federal forces captured Norfolk and Portsmouth proved too much for him.

However, from conjecture we now move to reality. On July 19, 1861, only 49 days after the

COFER'S CONFEDERATE PATENT

Patent number 9, given 12 August, 1861, for an improvement in firearms.

Confederate Patent Office was established,[4] Cofer filed the specifications for his patent.

In so doing, the services of a certain James S. French, late of Washington, D. C., were obtained. Upon the secession of Virginia, Mr. French (perhaps scenting profit and undoubtedly for patriotic motives as well) emigrated to Richmond, where he proclaimed in a handbill: "Having for many years been connected with the United States Patent Office, as one of the principal examiners, I am familiar with the special knowledge and experience which this long service is calculated to give, and after a careful examination and comparison of the respective laws of the United States, and Southern Confederacy (the latter had simply copied those of the former) in relation to this most important public interest, am prepared to transact all business connected in any way with the Confederate Patent Office, Richmond, Virginia."

Mr. French did indeed know his way around and Cofer had his patent—the ninth granted by the Confederate Patent Office—in jigtime. It was issued on August 12, only 25 days after filing, a bureaucratic record of some sort, even then. Cofer's invention seems to be a successful evasion of Smith & Wesson's Rollin White Patent (U.S.) for a bored-through cylinder, but this was probably of no particular consequence to Tom, French or the Confederate Patent Office.

Whatever French's other professional qualifications may have been, he or an employee was an excellent draftsman, and the patent drawing is crystal clear.

The working model, required by the Confederate patent law, must have been a revolver (probably imported from England) made under the Adams patent, and altered to the Cofer system, inasmuch as one such is shown in the patent drawing. The weapon is referred to in the patent specifications as no longer needing its rammer lever, once having been converted to the Cofer system.

This brings us to a consideration of just exactly what Cofer patented. Was it a new type of pistol, or was it a means of loading a revolving pistol, or what? A look at the patent will answer these questions, which have intrigued collectors for years.

THE CONFEDERATE STATES OF AMERICA

To all to whom these Letters Patent shall come:

Whereas Thomas W. Cofer, of Portsmouth, Virginia, has alleged that he has invented a new and useful Improvement in Revolving Fire Arms which he states has not been known or used before his application has made oath that he is a Citizen of the Confederate States, that he does verily believe that he is the original and first inventor or discoverer of the said Improvement and that the same hath not, to the best of his knowledge and belief, been previously known or used; has paid into the treasury of the Confederate States, the sum of Forty dollars, and presented a petition to the Commissioner of Patents, signifying a desire of obtaining an exclusive property in the said Improvement and praying that a patent may be granted for that purpose.

These are therefore to grant according to law, to the said Thomas W. Cofer, his heirs, administrators or assigns, for the term of fourteen years from the twelfth day of August one thousand eight hundred and sixty-one the full and exclusive right and liberty of making, constructing, using, and vending to others to be used, the said Improvement a description whereof is given in the words of the said Thos. W. Cofer in the schedule hereunto annexed, and is made a part of these presents.

In Testimony Whereof, I have caused these Letters to be made Patent, and the Seal of the Patent Office has been hereunto affixed.

Given under my hand at the City of Richmond this Twelfth day of August in the year of Our Lord one thousand eight hundred and sixty-one Specifications annexed to Patent No. 9, granted to Thomas W. Cofer, August 12, 1861.

To all whom it may concern:

Be it known that I, Thomas W. Cofer of Portsmouth, in the County of Norfolk, and State of Virginia have invented a new and improved mode of making many chambered revolving pistols, which may also be applied to firearms and to cannon, and I do hereby declare the following is a full and exact description thereof reference being had to the accompanying drawings and to the letters of reference marked thereon.

The nature of my invention consists in so arranging the chambered cylinder of breech loading pistols, firearms, so that the chambers in the revolving cylinder shall be charged with cartridges or ammunition contained in thimbles, in place of the chambers being loaded with powder and ball as usual, and that the nipples for the reception of percussion caps shall be inserted in a circular plate distinct and separate from the revolving cylinder, yet corresponding with it in diameter and fitting close to its rear end, so that when fitted to, and placed in conjunction with the revolving cylinder, the added plate and cylinder revolve together on the same pivot causing the cylinder to present no changes in appearance, other than that it is lengthened by the thickening of the plate.

The drawing Fig. 1, shows the rammer marked A, attached as usual, but this arrangement entirely dispenses with it, and increases greatly the facility of loading.

To enable others skilled in the art to make and use my invention, I will proceed to describe its construction and operation.—I take the common revolving chambered cylinder as used by Colt and others, and in the rear end of this cylinder I insert in each chamber a thimble fitting closely and flanged around its outer end to prevent its being driven into the chamber as shown in B, Fig. 2.

These thimbles are charged with powder and ball and constitute the cartridge, and have a small hole in their flanged end, by which fire is communicated to the powder. I then take a circular iron plate about one fourth of an inch thick and fit it closely against the chambered cylinder, and mark out recesses in it corresponding exactly with the chambers in the cylinder— these recesses I turn out, or cut down, so that they shall receive and hold the rear end of each flanged thimble as shown in Fig. 3, and the plate marked C, yet fit close against the cylinder D, as shown in Figs. 1 and 2, fitting close, yet separate from it.

From the outside of this plate C, communicating with these recesses I screw into the plate nipples for holding percussion caps, so inserted that the hole through the nipple shall be in a line with, and correspond with the hole in the thimble, so as to form a direct communication between the percussion cap and the powder, which is best done by making the vent hole in the thimble in the center of its flanged end.

The cartridges being placed in the cylinder and the percussion caps on the nipples, the recessed end of the plate C is fitted over the flanged thimbles, and the whole cylinder formed of the two parts; the plate, with its nipples and recesses and the chambered cylinder, are then placed in position, and the pivot rod run through them, and the pistol is ready for use.

Or the nipples, in place of being screwed into the plate, may be screwed into the thimble, or the thimble, still reserving the flange on it, may terminate in a nipple, as shown in Fig. 4, so that the cylinder may be capped at the same time it is loaded, and the plate will then be fitted on with the ends of the thimbles terminating in nipples, and projecting outwardly as in plate C, Fig. 1.

While I have described this invention as applicable to a pistol, it is obvious that the same principle may be applied to firearms generally and even to a cannon, the mode of communicating fire to the powder in the cannon being adapted to the cannon in any known way—Figs.

5 and 6 represent it as applied to a cannon. In such, even the pivot rod for holding the revolving cylinder would pass in through the rear end of the frame, and a small platform placed in a horizontal plane with the bottom of the cylinder would have to be placed on each side of the frame, so that the cylinder, or the pivot rod being withdrawn from it, can be rolled out on the platform in order to be charged; these platforms are represented in the figures last mentioned by the letters M & N.

Having described my invention, what I claim and desire to secure by letters patent, "is the divided cylinder D-C, formed of the chambered portion D and plate C in combination with thimbles for holding the ammunition when constructed and used substantially as herein described."

/s/ Thos. W. Cofer

Witness
/s/ Robt. D. Ward
/s/ James S. French

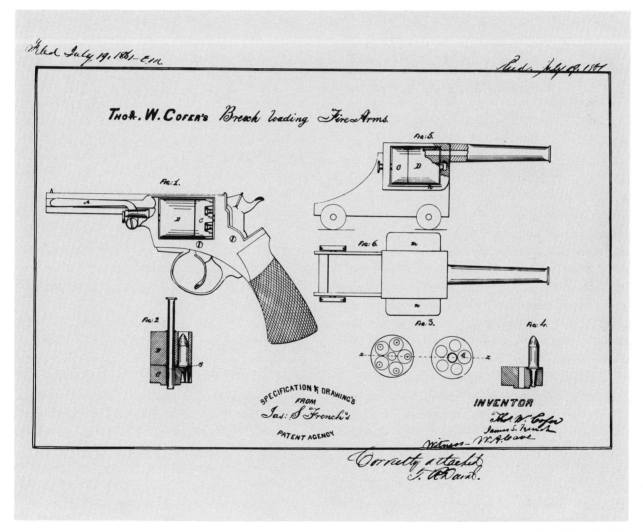

Courtesy Mrs. Richard S. Cofer

PATENT DRAWING FOR COFER'S BREECH-LOADING ARMS

Received July 19, 1861, and letters patent given 12 August, 1861. The elapsed time would indicate alacrity on the part of the young Confederate States Patent Office.

Boiled down and wrung out, the specifications call for "a new and improved way of making many chambered revolving pistols, which may also be applied to firearms and to cannon," which upon analysis, means two systems by means of which any percussion weapon with a revolving cylinder could be equipped with either variation of Cofer's two cylinders and loaded with fixed ammunition. Cofer did not invent a pistol or a cased cartridge (although he designed two types) but a means of bringing the two together.

In retrospect, one might well regard the invention is impractical; it was practical for the times—if we except its application to cannon and consider it in relation to the many other ignition systems then in use. It is true that formed metal rimfire cartridge cases were even then being manufactured for .32 caliber Smith & Wesson revolvers, and that the end of the war would see full-scale production of heavier rimfire loads for Yankee military rifles and carbines, but in 1861 Cofer's second system made sense.

It is important to make a distinction between the two cylinders Cofer designed. The first described in the patent specifications (Fig. 2, Patent drawing) was not particularly original, having been tried before with matchlock weapons and always discarded because of ignition difficulty. No examples of this cartridge or cylinder are known, however, so whether or not Tom ever made either is a matter for conjecture.

Four cartridges like Cofer's second type (Fig. 4, Patent drawing) were found with an unmistakable Cofer revolver, and another has been identified in a midwest collection after puzzling cartridge collectors as to its origin and identity for many years. They are remarkably like those used in northern "Coffee Mill" machine guns and early model Gatlings with some degree of success.

The relatively crude Cofer system is remarkably similar to the various conversion systems designed shortly after the war by Rider, Thuer,

Richards and Mason, and applied to Colt's percussion pistols prior to the expiration of the Rollin White patent. The unknown gunsmith who altered a .36 caliber percussion Manhattan to cartridge (perhaps Tom Cofer) certainly used the same principle.

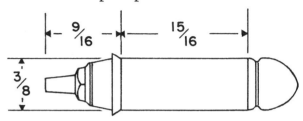

A COFER CARTRIDGE

Drawn by W. E. Codd from one of four found in a Patent Cylinder Cofer revolver. The case is brass and the nipple is steel.

There is more to be said about the patent, but let's look at what was going on in Norfolk and Portsmouth in the spring of 1861, and get back to the patent later.

Although the notice Cofer's patent received was scanty by today's standards, there was some publicity, and four surviving newspaper accounts of Tom's activities, although the mainstay of all previously published articles on Cofer, must be recounted (at least in part) for the sake of continuity.

In the Richmond *Examiner*, July 17, 1861: "Mr. T. W. Cofer of Portsmouth, Va., has just completed an improvement in a revolving firearm whereby the process of loading is so much facilitated over that of a colt [sic] or other revolver that it may be loaded and discharged with fourfold rapidity. Mr. Cofer has just left for Richmond to secure a patent for his invention." The last sentence we know is fact, because of an existing letter from Cofer which mentions that he and Gwaltney made the trip together.

A week later, the *Examiner* mentions that a "pistol factory" had been established at Portsmouth, Virginia, and it is assumed that this casual and perhaps inaccurate statement might

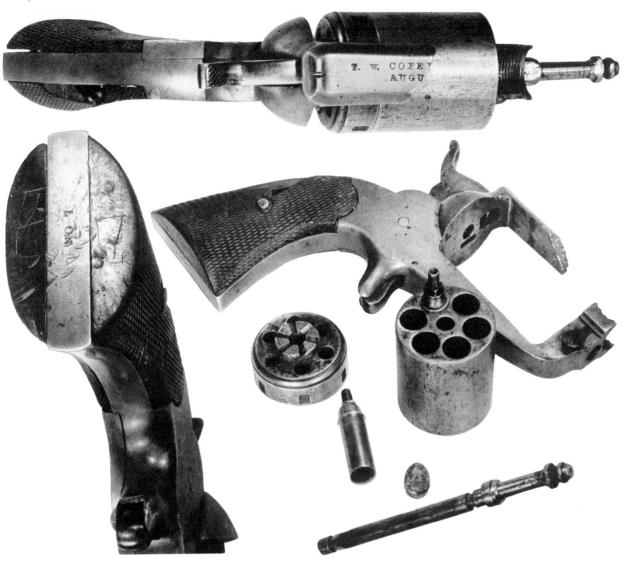

Courtesy National Rifle Association

THE FIRST, OR PATENT CYLINDER MODEL COFER

Marked with serial number 7 on the bottom of the grip frame, this arm was made expressly for the divided cylinder. The complete marking on the top strap of the frame was probably T. W. COFER'S PATENT/ AUGUST 12, 1861. The trigger and hammer screws are blind in this model. It is said to be the only known specimen. The thinness of the metal in the top strap of the frame is readily apparent. The failure of this part was in great measure responsible for the damage to the arm.

refer to Cofer's activities. What this had to do with the aforesaid trip to Richmond leads to much interesting speculation. Had Cofer tried for a government contract and failed? Had he sought financial backing and failed? Did he decide to go ahead on his own at home after an official rebuff?

On October 17, 1861, the *Examiner* again refers to Cofer and his pistol, "which seems to possess very many advantages over Colt's. . . . It is fired with a prepared minie cartridge. . . ." True enough, except that a prepared minie cartridge was *paper*, whereas Cofer's was *brass*.

DeBow's *Review*, March-April issue, 1862,

page 327, manages to confuse matters by allowing that "Mr. Thomas W. Cofer of this city, has, since the commencement of the War, invented and patented a revolving pistol, pronounced by judges to be superior to the celebrated Colt pistol. He is engaged at present in manufacturing them on a small scale, as his means are limited."

DeBow uses the dateline *Portsmouth*, but does not say the pistols are being produced there, while the *Examiner* does. Cofer's use of a die to mark not only his pistols but his longarms, *PORTSMOUTH, VA.*, leads one to think that his shop was there, but members of the family state otherwise and certainly it is logical to assume that he would use the facilities on Union Street and not go to all the trouble of moving and setting up across the river. The reader may draw his own conclusions as to the actual site of Cofer's "pistol factory," but the writer leans toward Norfolk and 8 Union Street.

One may imagine how fast Cofer's product was snapped up, limited production or no. In 1861, from Norfolk County alone, no less than 32 Virginia militia units were mustered for the defense of the Norfolk area.[5] Confederate troops were sent in also, until many thousands manned the forts hastily thrown up outside the ports, and during off-duty hours the men thronged the streets of both Norfolk and Portsmouth, a great many anxious to purchase revolvers. The war was young, sidearms were scarce, greatly in demand. Every soldier felt that he absolutely must have a pistol and a bowie knife, no matter what other weapons he carried or was issued. Countless warriors had their fierce-visaged daguerreotypes made, their right hands clutching a "Navy" revolver of some sort, while their belts were stuffed with at least one, sometimes two, bowie knives. In many cases, these stark images are the sole records these pleasant young men left for posterity and their families. The demand changed later, when experience and Army orders put a quietus to the desire for other than service issue weapons.

In March 1862, at Norfolk, a unit of the Confederate Signal Corps, 127 strong was formed.[6] Many years later, there appeared for sale a Cofer in a holster marked: "21 July 1864. This revolver and holster was [sic] captured from a rebel signal officer by Capt. S. H. Merrill, 11th Maine Reg't." Coincidence? Hardly. Very likely the unknown rebel purchased his weapon from Cofer in 1862. If so, it must have given good service, to have withstood over two years of use in the field.

In 1956 the writer had the pleasure and privilege of discussing Cofer with his kinsmen in Norfolk, and learned that many papers had been destroyed by the recent hurricanes that had successively inundated a family home in Ocean View, where they had been stored. Among them were Cofer's account books. Without them, and owing to the peculiar system, if system it was, he used to number his weapons, we can only guess at the total production of his shop.

Cofer did not furnish a pistol of his own design and manufacture when he filed for his patent on July 19, 1861, hence we may assume that he did not have one to file. Norfolk and Portsmouth were captured by Butler's Yankees on May 9, 1862, and Cofer's shop and home with them. Between these dates, there were roughly 42 weeks of production. Let us further assume that a survival rate of 5 per cent would be about right. (Sam E. Smith estimates 10 per cent for single-shot U.S. martial pistols and 6 per cent for the relatively scarce Dance Brothers revolvers,[7] while James E. Serven estimates the survival rate of Colt's famous Walkers at 5 per cent.) Seven pedigreed Cofers of all types exist today so, if seven equals 5 per cent, then perhaps 140 were made. Certainly, an average output of around three a week is not unlikely, considering that Cofer must also have repaired arms and probably took a day off now and then to look at the troops or go fishing.

It may be that the survival rate would have been higher, were it not for two peculiarities seen in all existing pistols, regardless of model. We refer first to an error in design that becomes obvious when pictures of all specimens are examined: a weak frame. The top strap and the front end of the frame that hold the barrel simply do not contain enough metal, particularly the soft brass Cofer used. The cartridge pistol appears to have blown apart at this point. Also, the top straps of the frames of most other Cofers seem to be ever so slightly bent downward, or humped. This is usually noticed in an otherwise perfect specimen when one attempts to aim the piece and finds that the front sight is invisible, even though its pin seems to be about the right height.

Also, the rammer lever is poorly case-hardened and, like its Whitney prototype, tends to stick, so that considerable pressure on the lever is necessary to force it home. As a result, most levers are bent to some degree. On one revolver, the front of the lug in which the rammer pivots was actually sheared off by someone with more strength than brains.

Finally, the absence of ordnance reports, government contracts or other official records, together with the other reasons mentioned previously, indicates that the Cofer revolver was not a government issue weapon, but found its way into service through private purchase. As such, no spare parts were available from the Ordnance Department, and field repair would depend necessarily upon availability of parts from other weapons which just happened to fit, or needed only a minimum of alteration. An example might be the Whitney rammer assembly found on the Steuart Battle Abbey Cofer. This lever is numbered *21177A*, and so is its base pin. The cylinder is not numbered, but it is not like other Cofer cylinders and appears to be Whitney also. With the hard use a weapon, even a sidearm, normally receives in the field, the low survival rate estimated makes sense—it may even be a bit optimistic.

Now let's take a good look at Tom Cofer's

pistols—the ones that remain, that is. It was impossible to gather them all together and take them apart and study them privately and seriatim, but by means of reports from several critical and knowledgeable collectors and through examination of excellent photographs we believe that we have the data we need.

There exist today seven revolving pistols, undoubtedly made by Cofer. There can be no doubt that these weapons are genuine. It may be that others will turn up, and we hope they will—just as long as they were made in 1861 or 1862.

Courtesy Harry C. Knode

COFER MARKINGS

Frame and barrel markings on a Third Model Cofer. It is interesting to note that a dot or period was used in Cofer's name, possibly because an apostrophe stamp was not available.

At one time we intended to supply the minutiae of each known Cofer in tabular form, down to the last .001 of an inch, but decided against it. There should always be at least one unknown point to confuse those among us who are possessed of great mechanical skill but few scruples. All known Cofers are .36 caliber, brass-framed, octagon-barreled, 6-shot "Navy" revolvers, with sheath triggers and two-piece walnut grips. Why Cofer didn't put a trigger-guard on his pistols, we'll probably never know. The rear sight is cast into the frame and a pin front sight of brass was used.

Contrary to popular belief, the most numerous variety of Cofer bears many marks which appear to be serial numbers but may be assembly marks. With the exception of the Patent Cylinder model, surviving Cofers are uniformly and painstakingly marked *T. W. COFER'S/PATENT* in two lines on the top of the frame. The

TRANSITION MODEL COFER

This example embodies Cofer's original patent cylinder frame, but uses a conventional cylinder. The barrel had to be run back to accommodate the shorter cylinder. The base pin and rammer are definitely replacements. The cylinder also appears to be a replacement. This might be called the "Transition" or "Second Model."

stamping was done letter by letter, and guide lines were scribed in the brass. On the tops of the barrels, he stamped with a die, *PORTS-MOUTH, VA.* In general, all screw heads are marked with a numeral or a letter, and the same number or letter will appear on most of the parts. We are inclined to believe these are assembly marks and were not intended as serial numbers, although numbers do appear on three pistols. Whatever they were intended to be, today's Cofers are marked as follows: *1, 13* (*3* on screws), *M, L, T* (*8* scratched inside grips), *No. 7, V.*

A none too careful examination of the photographs and specifications of all known Cofers led to a conclusion that is, in a way, absurd, but is borne out by subsequent careful evaluation. This is that Cofer produced three definite types of pistol, each easily recognizable, and quite logical from a standpoint of practical evolution.

The first type is, of course, typified by the cartridge pistol. This is, quite obviously, made expressly for the patented divided cylinder and is designed after a Whitney Navy, without

trigger-guard. Perhaps it should be called the *Patent Cylinder* model.

The second type, or *Transition* model, followed the Patent Cylinder model as inevitably as night follows day. It is a simple adaptation of the Patent Cylinder model so as to make use of a common percussion cylinder, and was undoubtedly the result of buyer demand for a conventional loading system as well as the need for a simplified weapon that could be produced more rapidly. However, certain aspects of the construction of the only known example (now in the Battle Abbey, Richmond, Virginia) are puzzling. The removable side plate is carefully made up of two pieces of brass. Why did Cofer laminate the side plate of this weapon? Was it to use up parts? Or was it a repair made at the time the Whitney parts were added? It is unfortunate that this pistol has, in addition to a replaced rammer assembly, what appears to be a replaced cylinder. Comparison with all other Cofers immediately reveals the difference in the shape of the nipple slots, and the cylinder looks

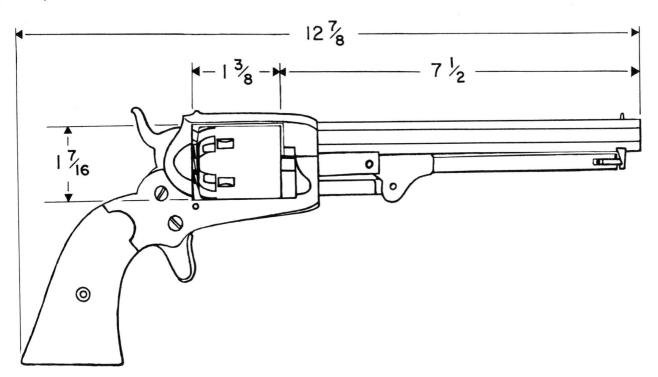

A TYPICAL PRODUCTION MODEL COFER REVOLVER

Line drawing by W. E. Codd. While dimensions will vary slightly from piece to piece, due to wear and hand assembly, these measurements are representative of the Production Model Cofer.

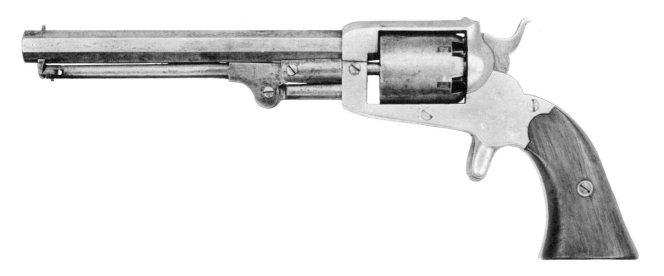

Courtesy M. Clifford Young

COFER WITH SHOULDERED FRAME

This example of the most numerous of existing Cofers shows the abandonment of the patent cylinder and resulting frame modification to fill the space between barrel and cylinder. Possibly a pattern alteration made after the patent cylinder frames were used up. This could be called the "Production" or "Third Model" Cofer.

as though it too came out of a Whitney. However, the frame and barrel are Cofer.

The most numerous of the Cofers is typified by a shoulder between frame and cylinder. One imagines that Tom Cofer used up the frames cast for his Patent Cylinder model and converted his pattern for continued production by inserting the shoulder to position a conventional percussion cylinder. This also had the effect of strengthening the weapon, and may account for

wise, he did a pretty good job, all things considered.

Longarms by Cofer are even more uncommon than his pistols. A pre-war punt gun, typical of the type used in market hunting on the Chesapeake Bay in happier times, has been reported. This percussion monster is about 9½ feet overall, with a bore of ⅞ inch or slightly larger. The lock is marked *T. W. Cofer*, and the barrel, *COFER, PORTSMOUTH, VA.* The general im-

Courtesy Waldo E. Nutter

ENGLISH SHOTGUN IMPORTED BY COFER

This piece, of excellent quality, is inlaid in gold, on the rib between the barrels, with Cofer's name and address as shown in the enlarged detail. This illustration is included to show that Cofer was also interested in imports for the sporting field and to present one of the best examples of this sort that has come to the attention of the authors.

the greater number (5) of this, now extant, and known as the third type or *Production* model.

From a rather elaborate start, Cofer seems to have refined and simplified his weapons and their production. Checkered grips are found on the Patent Cylinder model, as are blind screws, but they are not to be found on either the Transition or Production models. However, his craftsmanship is to be seen throughout the series in such things as the escutcheons for the two-piece walnut grips of all models and in the butt pins for them. Cofer went to great pains to produce his pistols, but some of his castings are typically "Confederate," replete with sand pits. Other-

pression one derives from its description is that Tom made this weapon himself.

Another weapon, an imported English 16-gauge double-barreled shotgun, serial number 2122, must be described as being of excellent quality. It bears a full set of Birmingham proofs and was probably made in the 1850's.

Said to be a Maine soldier's trophy of war is another 16-gauge shotgun, considerably cruder than the first mentioned, whose locks are marked *T. W. COFER & CO.* and *PORTSMOUTH, VA.*, respectively. The piece is 52 inches overall, is well-made and is certainly prewar. It too is an import, with Birmingham proof marks.

ON TO RICHMOND!

On to Richmond! was the Yankee war cry in the winter of 1862, and as Major General George B. McClellan planned it, the seizure of Norfolk and Portsmouth was a necessary preliminary to the big push which was to roll up the Peninsula to the Rebel Capital. Plenty of notice was given the South of Little Mac's intentions, but there was a general attitude of indifference and disbelief in Northern capabilities. After First Manassas it was popularly held that Southern armies could whip anybody, and no one seems to have paid much attention to the lessons taught by joint U.S. Army-Navy operations in both the East and West. There was incredible disorganization, which made it next to impossible to meet the logistics requirement of armies in the field, let alone move to safety the fledgling war industries which dangled, defenseless, within reach of the encircling land and naval forces of the United States.

In March of 1862, Cofer paid a visit to Richmond, in company with cousin Gwaltney. One would like to imagine that they were thinking of setting up shop there, looking for a government contract, or both. Whatever happened, Cofer's shop remained in the Norfolk-Portsmouth area.

On May 9, 1862, a contingent of Federal troops left Fortress Monroe, landed unopposed near what is now called Willoughby Spit, then Willoughby's Point and received the surrender of Norfolk. Portsmouth was no problem to them. A corporal's guard in a rowboat could have taken it, and probably did, because the Rebels had pulled out, regarding the ports as indefensible. Cofer, under no illusions as to what the Yankees were likely to do with a captured rebel gunsmith, prudently hied himself to Richmond, sending his wife and children to live with her parents in the hamlet of Somerton, Gates County, North Carolina.[8] The U.S. Marshal took over the pistol factory, if it may be called that.

The *Old Dominion,* a newspaper of Portsmouth, carried the following notice for one month, starting December 18, 1863.

CONDEMNATION NOTICE

January 1, 1864, Portsmouth, Virginia

District Court of the United States, for the Eastern District of Virginia.

To Thomas W. Cofer and all whom it may concern, Greeting: Notice is hereby given, that on the second day of December, 1863, all the right, title, interest and estate of Thomas W. Cofer in and to all that certain lot of land situated at the intersection of Court and Clifford Streets in the City of Portsmouth, in the Eastern District of Virginia, beginning at said intersection and running north on Court Street, thirty feet, thence west one hundred twenty feet, thence south thirty feet to Clifford Street, thence east one hundred twenty feet to the beginning. Together with the furniture, goods, wares, chattels and other property and in and upon said premises belonging to the said Thomas W. Cofer, was seized by the Marshal of the United States for said District as forfeited to the use of the United States and the same is libeled and prosecuted in this Court in the name of the United States, for condemnation for the causes in the said libel set forth and that said cause will stand for trial at the Court-room in the City Hall of Norfolk, on the third Monday of January next, when and where all persons are warned to appear to show cause why condemnation should not be decreed and to intervene for their interests.

December 18, 1863   William H. Barry, Clerk

In due course, on February 18, 1864, in United States District Court, Portsmouth, Virginia, Judge J. C. Underwood presiding, testimony was elicited proving the disloyalty of, among others, Thomas W. Cofer, and a decree of condemnation was ordered against his property.[9]

Unfortunately, the court records are lost or misplaced, and we will perhaps never know if Tom's account books were used as evidence, or what they contained. Shortly after the condemnation of Cofer's property, it went under the hammer at a U.S. Marshal's auction, to be purchased by a speculator from Philadelphia, Pennsylvania. This worthy, one Samuel Freedley, obtained Tom's Court Street house for $500.[10]

THE WAR YEARS

After the capture of Norfolk, barring at least one interval when his name came up in the draft (known, in those days as "The Conscription") and he reported to the Richmond Camp of Instruction, Cofer seems to have been employed by the Confederate Government at the Artillery Work Shops in Richmond. This assumption is borne out by Special Orders No. 316, issued to Cofer at the Richmond, Virginia, Camp of Instruction. In no uncertain terms, these orders ordered conscript Cofer of Richmond to report to Brigadier General Gorgas for duty with James D. Brown, Superintendent of the Artillery Work Shops, Richmond Arsenal. It is safe to suppose that Tom had rather powerful influence exerted to get him back whence he had departed in the first place. For some unaccountable reason, despite the havoc wreaked upon the struggling Southern arms industry (and others, equally vital) by the conscription, and a general recognition of this lamentable state of affairs which had resulted in a system of exemptions supposed to prevent it, mechanic after mechanic was inducted. No matter what his superiors said or did thereafter, usually the hapless artisan was never seen by his erstwhile employer again. It is thought by his family that Cofer was a foreman, was well connected, and a key man. It is certain that he was lucky.

Only two of Cofer's letters are known to have survived the war years. One, mentioned before, contained but a scrap of information. The other,

transcribed here, is the sort of material one dreams of finding, but seldom does. If ever an unwitting capsule description of a nation's economic and military agony was written, Tom Cofer wrote it. Never mind the spelling, just read it.

Richmond Va. May 3rd, 1864

Dear Mag

I have though of writing to you for the last thre or four day thinking you would be anctious to heare frome me. I wrote in my last letter I thought we would have to go out in a few days but it past oft and we have not yet ben cald out but can not say how soon. Mag, I would like to come to see you but I can not say when I will come. I think not untile we have the big fight that every one is expection to come oft soon so you must not look for me soon but write as often as you can and I will do the same. I wish it was so you could come to Richmond and spend a week or so with me but I do not see much chance of that as you could not well leave the children so I will get along the best I can hoping soon to see you all. I received a letter frome Dick on yesterday stating he was over to see you all as you stated in your letter which I received on last Friday. He wrote me word he had to bring Nannie over the river with him as she got so surly could not get along with her he wanted to now what she would sell for hear. Negros are veary cheap at this time owing to the Curancy as money is veary scarse now and with all people are expecting a big fight to come oft soon and they do not now what the result will be.

Mag, if you see aunt Pattey ask her the least she will take for Nannie in new Curancy and let me now and if it is not two much I will buy her myself. I do not want her to sell but to keep. I will take her to Richmond and hire her out find out and let me heare frome you soon. Mag I sent in a letter on the 5 or 6 of April a ten dollar note new Curancy and I received two letters from you since and you did not say any thing about it I thought probley you did not receive it. In my last letter I gave you a statement of what money I had on hand and what disposition I would mak of it if I should be call out so I will send you a nother one now and if I should be call out will make the same disposition turn over to Mr. or Mrs. Tignor what money and papers I have. This statement is made up to the first of May 1864—all of my matters is paid up the above date for bord and the amt is due to me which statement I will give you as neare as I can blow.

Amt on hand at this date $ 1103.00
Amt Due by T. W. Tignor for the bacon
   & lard I bought for him　　　　　183.00
T. W. Tignor to T. W. Cofer 7 lbs. of
   bacon 4.75　　　　　　　　　　　33.25
T. W. Tignor to T. W. Cofer for lead　137.75
　　　　　　　　　　　　　　　　　————
　　　　　　　　　　　　　　　　　1457.00

Mag besides the above amt I have due me the first of May—by the Govorment for last mounth work—One Hundred and Eighty Four Dollors which I will get paid to me on the 5 of this mounth ading this amt to the amt above of

.... $ 1457.00
　　　　　　　　　　　　184.00
　　　　　　　　　　　　————
making................. 1641.00

I have other small amt due me which I shall colect on the 8 when the pay oft amt to $73.00 added 73.00
　　　　　　　　　　　　　　————
making in all .... $ 1716.00

The lard I think I shall sell soon as it cominces to run out. I have been offorred Eight Dollars pr lb. in our issue for it, Mag there is nothing of such interist. I am well hoping this may find you all well. My love to all. I will send your cloth and also the leather soon. Your Husband. T. W. Cofer

Now let's interpret this letter.

When the skilled worker was not occupied with disengaging himself from the clutches of the army, and was able to devote his whole attention to the production of guns, shell, cannon, harness, shoes, or whatever, another official im-

provision was likely to foul things up. This was an organization known as the Militia of the Second Class. This bellicose body was as a rule composed of mechanics and artisans like Tom Cofer, organized into companies and battalions by shop and factory, commanded by mill owners and superannuated or disabled veterans who were serving locally as government inspectors.

Courtesy K. D. Sykes

MR. COFER "DETAILED" TO THE RICHMOND ARSENAL

Although the Southern arms industry in general had great difficulty in protecting its skilled hands from the draft, this special order to report for duty at the Richmond Arsenal shows an exception in the case of Thomas Cofer, a conscript.

Its effectiveness as a fighting force may be debatable, but there is no question of its effectiveness in bringing production to a complete standstill. Its formation and use was a measure born of desperation, and there is a slightly desperate note sounded in Cofer's letter when he mentions "being called out." Moreover, the system used to call the general public to arms was, in itself, enough to cause the staunchest to search his soul, with its death defying pronouncements of "No Surrender!—Under Any Circumstances!!!" posted about the cities.

However, lest one gain the wrong impression from the above, be it understood that on two occasions the Richmond Militia took part in extremely hard fighting, not only doing a creditable job but actually keeping veteran Yankee troops at bay until relieved by regular troops of Lee's Army of Northern Virginia. Thus, when Tom writes of being "called out," and of the general expectation of a "big fight," he is not speaking as a civilian, safe from shell fragment and minie ball, but as a blooded infantryman who had probably heard their song, and "seen the elephant."[11]

Galloping inflation insured that a mechanic's pay wasn't enough for him to live on, let alone send much to his family. Hence many became part-time merchants, and dealt in products and produce from home, sending back whatever they could pick up in exchange, as well as money. This could hardly be called "speculating," and is not to be confused with what came to be known as "Black Market" operations during World War II, although the resemblance is obvious. It was perfectly legitimate, but not highly regarded when conducted on a large scale. Tom was a small operator, judging from his letter.

Tom Cofer was an enterprising man, apparently in the thick of things and even interested in the possibilities inherent in renting out a slave. Reading between the lines of his letter, one gathers that he didn't own one himself, but thought that it might be a good business venture. Lest he seem a cold-blooded, callous wretch, in the best tradition of Simon Legree, remember that Negroes were regarded as valuable (though troublesome) property.

One can learn a good deal about a man from a letter to his wife, especially when written under the stress and strain of war's uncertainty. Cofer was worried about his family. Communications were chancy. Was his wife getting the money he sent home? He missed her—this is quite apparent. He was likely to be mobilized for active duty with his militia outfit, but didn't want her to worry. He wanted to make sure she understood the state of his finances, if anything happened to him. This leads to a most revealing personal financial statement, as well as directions as to whom to turn for help—another gunsmith named Tignor, whose activities included dealings in meat, if Cofer's note means anything—or it may be that Tignor's establishment housed numerous boarders. It's hard to tell. It is inferred that Cofer boarded with the Tignors. Cofer wrote a neat hand, he made his points, and signed his name. No more can be asked of any man.

Just one more item, and we can leave the war years. Cofer's whereabouts and activities during the war have intrigued not a few collectors, and his presence here, there, and elsewhere hopefully suggested, while uncounted attempts have been made to identify numerous unmarked weapons as having been made by him. The evidence seems plain that when Norfolk and Portsmouth were captured and all his goods and possessions with them, Tom Cofer went to work in the Artillery Work Shops at the Richmond Arsenal and remained there.

RECONSTRUCTION

When the war was over, Cofer gathered together his family and returned to Portsmouth. Penniless and without property, Cofer set to work to repair his fortunes. Within a year he had somehow managed to regain his house on Court Street, paying $650 to the same Samuel Freedley who had bid it in at the U.S. Marshal's sale.[12] It will be remembered that Freedley had paid $500. The profit may seem small by today's standards but the price was high in the post-war South, whose economy was in ruins, and, remember, Cofer's "secesh" money was worthless.

Cofer is listed as a gunsmith in the Norfolk-Portsmouth directories from 1869 through 1875, doing business first at Market Square and later 13 Union Street in Norfolk as a gun and locksmith.

On July 23, 1885, aged 57, which would now be considered an early age, Thomas Wrenn Cofer died. He is buried in old Oak Grove Cemetery, Portsmouth. Oddly enough, he is remembered by his family not for his activities as a gunsmith, but as the inventor of a clockwork device for dispersing the common housefly! Although of no significance to those of us who are accustomed to window screens, this later invention was of importance in the days preceding their use and enjoyed moderate success. One may still find them in antique shops, from time to time.

T. W. Cofer remains, in the final analysis, as a figure seen through an age-dimmed glass. He emerges from the blur only momentarily through a handful of pistols and cartridges, his patent, a few letters, his Army orders, and deeds and court notices. No one now alive knew him at an age that could produce clear impressions.

It is unfortunate that his accounts seem to be lost, that no identifiable likeness of him exists. One can only hope that collectors will exert every effort to reconstruct the work and image of this man. The fragments are fast disappearing, the grand old people who knew the men of '61 and '65 are almost gone. Time has nearly run out, and a priceless opportunity to obtain vital information is slipping away.

FOOTNOTE REFERENCES

1. Cofer's middle name was from his mother's family. The Wrenns were from Wrenn's Mills, Virginia, a hamlet now vanished. This intelligence is furnished for those hardy souls who may wish to do a little Cofer hunting of their own.
2. Colonel William Allan, "Reminiscences of Field Ordnance Service with the Army of Northern Virginia, 1863-1865," *Southern Historical Society Papers*, Vol. XIV, 1886, pp. 137-146.
3. General Gorgas's unpublished and unedited records were not available for study, and a thorough examination of the scantily indexed mass of Confederate Records in the National Archives was not possible.
4. Established by an Act of the Confederate Congress and approved by President Davis on 21 May, 1861, the Confederate Patent Office commenced operations the next day.
5. John W. H. Porter, *History of Norfolk County, Virginia* (Portsmouth, Va., W. A. Fiske, 1892). Hereafter *Porter*.
6. *Porter*, p. 133. This source also lists Robert E. Cofer and Reuben F. Cofer as members of Saint Bride's Light Artillery, later Co. I. 38th Virginia. Their relationship to T. W. Cofer is unknown.
7. Sam E. Smith, "Survival Figures for the Dance Brothers Revolvers," *The Gun Collector*, No. 22 (May, 1948), p. 178.
8. Cofer's family seems to have spent most of the war at his wife's family's home in Somerton, North Carolina. "Mag" Cofer, nee Margaret Augusta Saunders, a college graduate, had her hands full, dodging Yankees and raising children.
9. Cofer was indicted and tried *in absentia* under the provisions of a Federal law passed July 1862, "to suppress Insurrection, to punish Treason and Rebellion, to seize and confiscate the Property of Rebels, and for other Purposes." The shadow of this ominous instrument fell over all who assisted in rebellion or insurrection against the United States. It has been pointed out that no other cases of a gunsmith having been tried under it are known, and it is conjectured that Cofer was some sort of public official. However, in the absence of information to the contrary, and in view of the publicity given his invention, we feel that his "pistol factory" was responsible for Cofer's conviction. Condemnation of rebel property was by no means unusual, on scantier pretexts.
10. The U.S. deed is now in the possession of the family.
11. This contemporary expression must be understood to be appreciated. This strange bit of slang was the way veteran troops were wont to refer to having been under fire. It stems from the then popular tale of the farm lad who was asked to describe an elephant he had seen someplace or another. He couldn't—all he knew was that he had "seen the elephant"— and didn't want to see it again!
12. Freedley merely endorsed his U.S. deed over to Cofer.

NOTES

CHAPTER 10

Dance Brothers

THE activities and operations of the Dance Brothers have been well chronicled, first, and in brief, by Richard D. Steuart in *Firearms of the Confederacy*, enlarged upon by Paul C. Janke in a fine article which appeared in the May, 1948, issue of the *Gun Collector* magazine, and finally by Carroll C. Holloway in *Texas Gun Lore*. This last is a splendid book covering all arms used and made in Texas. The portion devoted to the brothers Dance is so comprehensive and well documented as to make additional writing almost superfluous. In other words, the story of the Dance Brothers has already been told and the authors of this present work can add but little to what has gone before.

This chapter then, makes no pretense of depth or scope and consists only of an amalgamated account of an operation already known to many gun collectors.

James Henry Dance, a descendant of a Revolutionary War color-bearer under General George Washington, and of Southern stock, left his home in Alabama at the age of 28 to venture into Texas. What he saw there must have pleased him for during the following year he was joined by his three younger brothers (George Perry, David Ethelred and Claudius), and his two sisters.

Jointly the family purchased 900 acres of land at Cedar Brake, now West Columbia, in Brazoria County, Texas. The plantation thus set up had its own forge and anvil for the repairing and manufacture of small metal parts as was the custom of the day. What started out as a planta-tion blacksmith shop developed, under the able management of George Dance, into a full-fledged metal working shop and a highly successful enterprise. It soon outgrew its location and was moved to Columbia near the Brazos River front. Here, a boiler and steam engine were added, and it became known as a "Steam factory." Although managed by George, the business nevertheless operated under the name of the eldest brother as "J. H. Dance & Brothers." It is possible that with their background the family still retained the English attitude that all property was owned by the oldest male child.

With the war, J. H. Dance entered the Confederate Army. Brother George was sworn in but apparently because of his mechanical abilities was never required to report for active duty. He continued the operation of the steam plant, assisted by brother David. In the meantime the other brother had died.

At about this time there came to Columbia one Jesse Parks and his brother Anderson who opened a small blacksmith shop near the Dance steam factory. It appears that the Parks and their shop were utilized to some extent by the Dances, but on an employee basis and not as partners or members of the firm.

On April 22, 1862, Governor Lubbock, who was also President of the Texas Military Board and in charge of all military contracts, was approached by letter suggesting that George Dance be advanced $5,000 which would permit him to add to his steam factory, and stating that if fifty hands were employed Dance could turn out fifty revolvers a week. This letter was signed by 26 prominent citizens of Columbia who guaranteed that if the money were granted, it would not be misapplied.

This initial request was followed by one from George Dance to the Governor, dated May 2, 1862, placing the Dance Brothers' plant at the disposal of the state to be used for "the manufacture of army revolvers and other arms." George included his own services in the offer. The suggestion was made that an advance of $2,000 to $5,000 would furnish the necessary additional machinery and stock, and that this advance would be repaid by the arms furnished. The letter is concluded with: "As I have already been sworn into the service, this whole proposition depends on the exemption not only of myself, but of other mechanics employed by me from military service."

The records indicate that Dance received no contract or advance of funds, but apparently he and his workmen were granted exemption from service on the promise that he would manufacture revolvers. This he did, assisted by cousins Harrison, James, and Spencer Dance from Grimes County, Texas.

In the latter part of 1863 a strong rumor was circulated that the Federals planned an expedition in their gunboats up the Brazos to Columbia for the sole purpose of shelling the pistol factory. To prevent its destruction the plant was moved to Grimes County, about three miles north of Anderson. Here it appears to have been consolidated with a Confederate powder and ammunition plant already there and in operation. It has never been accurately established what was produced at this point beyond cannon balls, but apparently revolvers were not included. It is believed that the entire production of these weapons was limited to Columbia during the years 1862 and 1863. After the war the Dance brothers returned to Columbia and made cotton gins.

The production figures of the Dance revolvers are not known, but the highest serial number

known (324) probably reflects closely the number made. The guns are of three varieties. Number 1 is a .44 caliber, six-shot, single-action revolver with a round barrel slightly over 8 inches in length and part octagon at the frame, rifled with seven grooves. The overall length of the weapon is 14 inches; weight, 3 pounds, 6 ounces; cylinder 1⅞ inches long. All parts are iron except

Courtesy Carl J. Pugliese

DANCE BROTHERS .44 CALIBER REVOLVER

Serial number 20.

for the brass knife foresight which was dovetailed into the barrel and a brass oval triggerguard and backstrap. Some few have an iron backstrap and some are equipped with a roller on the hammer. A notch in the hammer serves as a rear sight. Most of the known specimens follow this description.

The second variety is the same as the first, except for a full octagon barrel. It will be noted that while Dance guns are usually referred to as "dragoons" they are actually .44 caliber revolvers built along Colt Navy lines and are not nearly as large as the true Colt dragoon pistol.

The third variety is .36 caliber and is extremely rare. In general, these follow the lines of number 1 except for a reduction in size of all parts. In general the barrels are 7⅜ inches long although one specimen has been seen with a barrel only 6 inches long. Another peculiarity of the .36 caliber, and a few of the .44 calibers is a claw-shaped butt such as is sometimes found on a Dimick revolver.

All the guns, regardless of variety or caliber, are marked with a serial number in 12 places,

Courtesy Harry Brooks

DANCE BROTHERS .36 CALIBER REVOLVER

The owner has indicated to the authors that this may be the first Dance revolver made, and thus entitled to serial number 1.

but on some the basic number has been reduced to the last two digits on several parts. The serial numbers of the .44 caliber Dance known to the authors are as follows: 2, 4, 10, 20, 82, 87, 89, 91, 107, 121, 124, 131, 134, 164, 247, 265 and 324. In Navy caliber, the following are known to have survived the years: 83, 119 and 135. In addition, serial number 1 of the Navy caliber is said to be extant as is one in the army size said to be unmarked. This makes a total of 22 guns. Doubtless others exist of which we have no knowledge.

All Dance Brothers revolvers are distinguishable by the absence of the recoil shield, present

Courtesy M. Clifford Young

ANOTHER DANCE BROTHERS .36 CALIBER REVOLVER

Serial number 135.

GERONIMO AND A DANCE BROTHERS REVOLVER

A good many Dance Brothers revolvers found their way to the frontiers of Texas and throughout the West. There is a strong possibility that the Dance .44 revolver in the hand of Geronimo was "liberated" to become a prized possession.

A "FAKE" DANCE REVOLVER   *Courtesy Hugh Benet, Jr.*

A typical example of the type of forgery that tinkerers, frequently skilled but unscrupulous mechanics, attempt to foist on the unsuspecting arms collector. Resembling, to a degree, a Colt Dragoon, this monstrosity came to the United States via England. The serial number 81 and the letters CS appear on the piece, and there is a possibility that some part which bore this serial number is original.

on practically all other percussion revolvers. Several theories have been advanced for this singular departure from standard revolver design. To us, Carroll Holloway's reasoning seems most likely: "Occasionally, when firing a revolver of that era (percussion), not only the load which was indexed, but all the other unfired charges in the cylinder would shoot at the same time. This was so dismaying to the shooter that he usually, if physically able, discarded the revolver for a single-shot horse pistol."

George Dance, like other revolver manufacturers all over the world, has his own ideas on this problem. All models of revolvers were equipped with shields just behind the caps which were supposed to protect the shooter. George decided that this shield should be eliminated, on the theory that sometimes a cap, exploding under the hammer, ricocheted along the shield in fragments and burst one or more of the other caps which in turn, would ignite all charges.

He determined to his satisfaction that these fragments always traveled laterally and would not be a menace to the shooter if the customary shield should be eliminated. This theory was incorporated into the design.

In addition to their handguns, the Dance Brothers are credited with having made rifles on a very limited scale. One such was described as being a breech-loading percussion arm which could be fired by either the customary cap or a detonating ribbon such as is used in the Maynard primer. The gun is reported to have had a sliding breech which would cut off the paper end of the cartridge when it was inserted, thus exposing the powder and making the piece ready to fire. Further details on this rifle are not known.

In conclusion, let us remind any prospective purchaser of a Dance revolver to bear in mind that the old adage, "All that glistens is not gold" could be changed into "All flat framed percussion pistols are not products of the Dance Brothers." Some were made this way originally, either to facilitate the capping of the piece or for the reason advanced by Mr. Holloway. Unfortunately, still others have been deliberately altered in recent years to trap the unwary.

NOTES

CHAPTER 11

J. and F. Garrett and Company

J. AND F. GARRETT and Company of Greensboro, North Carolina, are well known to gun collectors as the makers of the Tarpley carbine. The name appears stamped in the stocks of these guns. Their other activities are not so well known.

The Greensboro *Patriot*, January 21, 1862, notes: "Southern Hat Factory. Messrs. J. & F. Garrett have established a hat factory on a liberal scale in this place, where they are manufacturing the various grades of hats, from the finest to the more common qualities."

As has been observed elsewhere, newspaper reporting of the eighteen sixties left considerable to be desired in the way of factual coverage and historians have learned to use this source only as an approximate indication of general fact and circumstance. Definite confirmation is usually necessary through other sources.

Time, Life and *Look* magazines were not published during the American Civil War, for which fact we may or may not be thankful, each according to his own views on the subject. Vaguely comparable, however, was a Southern bimonthly, DeBow's *Review*, although its reputation for factual reporting was excellent. As a reference source it rates considerably above newspapers of the period and many present-day periodicals. The historian requires fewer grains of salt in assimilating what he finds in DeBow. Early in 1862 the *Review* began a serialized article entitled "What We Are Gaining By The War." It reported State by State, advising of the general war effort in each, and specifically of what was being done in various towns and counties.

Its March-April, 1862, issue dealt with wartime activity in North Carolina and in that portion devoted to the city of Greensboro comments: "Messrs. Mendenhall, Jones & Gardner, of this place are now engaged in the manufacturing of guns for the State of North Carolina. This establishment is just getting underway, and it is the intention of the proprietors to manufacture largely so soon as they can get their machinery in operation." The *Review* continues: "The Messrs. Garretts have commenced the manufacture of sewing machines, pistols, guns, etc." Note the reference to pistols. Still continuing, "We have also a hat establishment, lately gone into operation, working several hands, with good prospects for patronage. . . ." This would hardly indicate any large-scale production of hats as claimed by the *Patriot* but nevertheless does corroborate to a degree this newspaper's account of January 21. On April 25, 1862, the daily Richmond *Examiner* reports: "Pistol factories and gun manufactories in Greensboro, two sword shops in Albemarle."

Products of Mendenhall, Jones and Gardner are well established through the existence of a number of their reasonably well-made rifles, the lockplates of which are stamped *M.J. & G., N.C., C.S.* and the date. But what of the pistols supposedly made by J. and F. Garrett? To date, none have been identified, but if the *Review*, the *Patriot* and the *Examiner* were correct as to the guns and hats, why not the pistols, and if Garrett did make pistols, where are they? Although unverified, it is the authors' strong conviction that those unusual brass-framed single-shot pistols, sometimes referred to as "Blunt and Syms" are actually the product of J. and F. Garrett and Company.

A detailed examination of such a pistol (serial number 126) reveals a .54 caliber barrel, 8½ inches long, while the overall length of the 2¾ pound weapon is 13 inches. A swivel ramrod 8⅝ inches long is affixed similar to that of the M1842 U.S. pistol, and identical in length. *G.W.* is stamped within ¾ of an inch of the rear of the barrel, with *P* underneath these initials. The

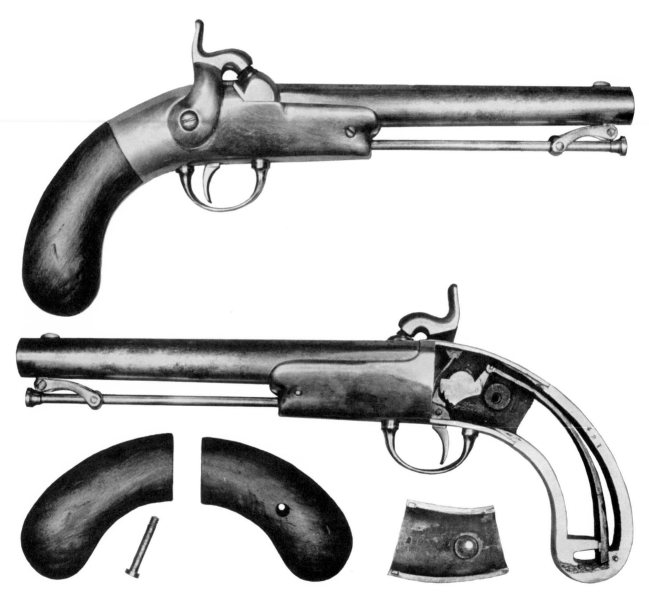

Courtesy Edward N. Simmons

J. AND F. GARRETT PISTOL

This shows the right side of the assembled arm and a left side view, partially disassembled, of serial number 427. This type of pistol is generally known among collectors as the Blunt and Syms type.

frame, fore-end and grip-straps are a one-piece brass casting, while the grips are 3¾ inches long, of walnut. The serial number is stamped on the left side of the upper strap (see illustration, serial number 427) and on the inside and upper end of a brass inspection plate in the left side of the frame. A flat spring inside the fore-end holds the rear of the rammer in place.

The highest serial number so far encountered on one of these pistols is 505, which is stamped on various places in addition to *A-3* also found on the breech end of the barrel, as it is on all 1842 pistols, and *S.R.* (or *S.H.*) at the breech itself with a *P* (proved) under these initials. At one time this particular pistol was equipped with a belt hook, this usually being a sign of sea service.

Judging from the serial numbers seen, slightly over 500 were made and with such high production it seems odd that their maker has not heretofore been identified. Some half-hearted attempts have been made to connect the gun with Ed Want of New Bern, North Carolina, who on August 12, 1861, was reported by Colonel Gorgas to have been given a "contract to make 5,000 pistols, delivery to begin in 3 months."[1] This is the only reference so far to be found of Want, and as New Bern fell to the Federals March 14, 1862, it can safely be assumed that few if any pistols were delivered from this source.

Because the barrels of the pistols in question all appear to have been originally from the Model 1842 U.S. Pistol, they may have been on hand at the Fayetteville Armory and disposed of in order to clear the establishment for the installation of the Harpers Ferry rifle machinery which was sent to North Carolina from Richmond, Virginia, in the summer of 1861. If the barrels were already at hand, and if our assumption that the production was about 500 is correct, then after the initial tooling which may have taken several months, no great length of time would have been necessary to have assembled the parts, after which J. and F. Garrett must

have looked about for something else in the way of war work.

They found it in the form of a breech-loading carbine, the brain child of Jere H. Tarpley of North Carolina who was granted a Confederate patent for his arm February 14, 1863, possibly about the time that the last of the single-shot pistols were completed.

Judging from an advertisement which appeared in the Greensboro *Patriot* of January 14, 1864, the carbine was already at some stage of production at that time. Says the *Patriot*: "Jere H. Tarpley—Tarpley's Breech-Loading Gun—This Gun has been tested by the Armory at Richmond and Raleigh, N. C., and has stood the test finely, making a favorable impression wherever it has been exhibited. We say without fear of contradiction, that it is the best Breech-loading gun in the Southern Confederacy. It can be shot with perfect safety when loaded either from the breech or the muzzle. This gun is less complicated and easier kept in order than any other gun that has been invented in this

Courtesy Smithsonian Institution
THE TARPLEY CARBINE'S BREECH
Serial number 295, shown closed and open.

THE
TARPLEY RIFLE.

We now offer the public one of the best breech-loading Rifles that has been introduced in the country. This gun was invented by **J. H. TARPLEY**, in the town of Greensboro, North Carolina, and was patented the 14th of February, 1863.

The Gun has been tested at the Armory in Richmond, and the Armory at Raleigh, North Carolina, and it stood the test fully at each place.

The barrel screws in the breech, and each gun may have a rifle and a shot gun barrel. It is the simplest and safest gun now in use.

We are now manufacturing this gun for the use of the army, and as there is a much greater demand for it where it has been exhibited and tried, than we can supply from our Factory, we propose to sell rights of all the States in the Confederacy except North Carolina. Persons wishing to make an investment in a gun that will give perfect satisfaction when tried, will do well to avail themselves of this opportunity, before the territory of States is disposed of.

Tarpley, Garrett & Co.
F. A. GARRETT, General Agent.
Greensboro, N. C., April 11th, 1863.

Courtesy Ray Riling

THE TARPLEY RIFLE, AN ANNOUNCEMENT

country. The gun was invented in Guilford County, North Carolina, and we are now manufacturing it for the State of North Carolina at our shop in Greensboro. We are ready to sell shop rights to Manufacturers in the gun business in any states in the Confederacy.—Tarpley, Garrett and Co."

It can be easily imagined by anyone who cares to consider the unique design of the Tarpley carbine, that it was not popular with the cavalrymen to whom it was issued. Without a fore-end, its barrel would be too hot to handle after just a few consecutive rounds had been fired through it. Doubtless many a Tarpley was

replaced at Yankee expense—just as fast as the deal could be made! Throughout the ages soldiers have expressed their displeasure with unsatisfactory equipment of all sorts by "losing" it, and the relatively rarity of the Tarpley may be due in large measure to its rejection by the men who were supposed to use it.

The Tarpley carbines were made with a brass frame, as were many other Confederate arms. It may or may not be significant that the brass in the Tarpley carbine is of the same quality and texture as that of the single-shot pistol in question.

Courtesy William A. Albaugh, III

THE TARPLEY CARBINE BY J. AND F. GARRETT

A full view and a detail of buttstock and breech showing the Garrett markings as well as C. S. A.

FOOTNOTE REFERENCE

1. *O.R.*, Series 4, Vol. I, p. 556.

NOTES

CHAPTER 12

The Palmetto Armory

SCARCELY had South Carolina's volunteers returned from the Mexican War when the shadows of a larger conflict gathered. Prudent legislators, realizing the state's lack of weapons, were speedily made aware of her lack of industry capable of producing them, when in the Governor's Annual Report of 1850, it was apologetically noted that arms recently supplied to the militia had necessarily been obtained outside of South Carolina.[1]

This situation was not at all unusual. At this time, not one Southern state maintained an official arms manufactory, or subsidized or otherwise supported a private arms industry and nothing that could be so designated was to be found. In New England, on the other hand, there were numerous well-established factories capable of producing rifles, muskets, pistols or whatever was needed.

The remedy was simple enough, or so it appeared to the solons. Encourage someone to start an arms factory by authorizing the purchase of so many muskets, rifles, pistols, sabers, etc., to be made within the state with local talent. This opened all sorts of avenues, political, economic and military, and pleased everyone.

Accordingly, legislation was passed for the purpose, an attractive contract was offered, and it wasn't long before a new firm had been established in Columbia to apply for it. Thus, the Palmetto Armory was born.

The guiding hand of the Palmetto Armory was William M. Glaze, a South Carolinian whose many activities serve to puzzle and confuse us by the fragmentary glimpses we catch of them through city directories, advertisements and legislative proceedings. He is first noted in 1838, when he and a John Veal became partners and operated what may loosely be called a jewelry store. Veal was an established silversmith from 1827 to 1857 and his works were highly regarded. A few pieces survive marked *Veal & Glaze*. The partnership was short-lived, for in 1844 we find Glaze operating independently.[2] From this period dates a Darling pepperbox marked *W. Glaze Patent* and *Columbia S. C. Patent 4.*[3]

In January, 1848, Glaze entered into a partnership with T. W. Radcliffe, and together they operated as silversmiths and jewelers.[4] The two men seem to have been good friends, and they were to be associated in many other ventures. Again, guns would appear to have been a part of the stock in trade. At this point the confusion starts. Glaze, the silversmith and retail jeweler, is perfectly understandable. But another source has it that by 1851 he "had an established reputation as an excellent blacksmith and saw and gin manufacturer."[5] The difference between a blacksmith and a silversmith is rather apparent and needs no comment. To further add to the confusion, Glaze was Secretary-Treasurer of the Richland Light Dragoons in 1848, and the tradition of cavalry as elite, composed of gentlemen, had almost feudal force in that era, especially since militia cavalry furnished its own mounts, so we may assume that he was of some social prominence. Moreover, Glaze, who seems to have been something of a politician, was on friendly terms with the governor, who, in 1847, gave him the impression that he could arm a proposed "flying" battery of artillery[6] and later be paid back by the state.

Here we find Glaze the businessman making what could have been a costly mistake. In brief, he imported several cannon barrels from the north, mounted them, and turned them over to the Richland Light Dragoons. Presumably, he also furnished caissons, limbers and harnesses. The record is somewhat vague on this point, but Glaze seems to have done the work in his own shops. He then tried to collect for his services. His friend was no longer governor, the Richland Light Dragoons did not have any money, and the state bluntly informed him that as far as it was concerned, the Ordnance Department knew nothing of his transactions and would have nothing to do with them. Glaze worked harder getting his money than he did mounting the guns, but was paid eventually.[7] He probably learned a lesson or two in dealing with state functionaries that served him well a few years later. But what was William Glaze? Silversmith, blacksmith, merchant, politician, soldier, manufacturer, entrepreneur? The best answer seems to be that he was all of these things.

Another accomplished individual was a partner in the new venture. James S. Boatwright was also a manufacturer of cotton gins and saw mills and had a wagon and carriage shop, to boot. Boatwright, like Glaze, was highly regarded and was considered to be quite wealthy.[8]

It is not surprising that one of Glaze's talents and experience should be awarded the state's contract. He seems to have been an energetic individual, because between the time the State Legislature authorized the purchase of locally made weapons, and April 15, 1851, when the contract was signed, he had persuaded Benjamin Flagg, an established New England manufacturer, to move his musket machinery to South

Carolina and had also negotiated the purchase of the pistol machinery belonging to Asa H. Waters and Co. Moreover, he had erected a three-story building on Arsenal Hill, with a one-story wing. The Armory buildings were approximately 64 by 154 feet. Included with the other machinery he installed was a "large fast-acting trip hammer and a steam-driven fan for the furnaces." Among the 40-odd workers he imported were machinists and iron workers, stockers and burnishers, all highly competent, many of whom brought their families with them and settled in Columbia. The net result was the largest arms manufactory south of Harpers Ferry, Virginia.[9] So much for the myth of the leisurely Southern businessman!

Actually, Glaze's efforts were simplified to some extent by a dearth of U.S. contracts in the New England area. Both Flagg and Waters were then without orders and had been since 1849, the official policy of the War Department having been radically changed, so as to confine purchases only to those arms and equipments which could not be made at the government arsenals at Harpers Ferry, Virginia, or Springfield, Massachusetts.

But this in no way detracts from the laurels due Mr. Glaze. He must have been a man of determination and rather firm convictions, because not only did he move men and machinery to Columbia and enter into a contract for muskets, rifles, pistols, cavalry and artillery sabers, including all equipments such as scabbards and bayonets, but also put up a completion bond of $260,000. This was twice the amount of the contract and was and is a substantial sum.[10]

The Palmetto Armory was located at the northeast corner of Laurel and Lincoln Streets, in the western reaches of Columbia, facing what is now the Governor's Mansion, but was then a part of the Arsenal Academy, a state military school. The area was known as Arsenal Hill because it contained the State Arsenal. How the old officers' quarters, now the Governor's Man-

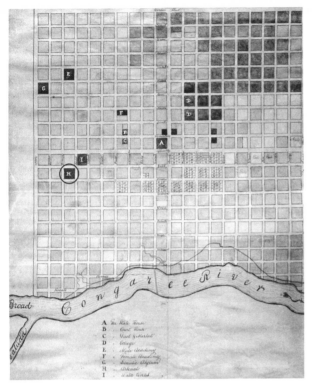

Courtesy South Carolina Archives

COLUMBIA, SOUTH CAROLINA, CIRCA 1850

Showing location (circled) of the old "Arsenal." This is not to be confused with the Palmetto Armory, which later became the Palmetto Iron Works, although the Palmetto buildings were within a few hundred yards of the site of the old arsenal on "Arsenal Hill."

sion, escaped the tender ministrations of Sherman's army is something of a mystery, when one considers what happened to the rest of Columbia in 1865.

However, we digress. With the signing of their contract, Glaze and Flagg proceeded to business. Because of its interest, as well as its simplicity, the contract is reproduced in full.[11]

The State of South Carolina

THIS AGREEMENT made and entered into between the State of South Carolina by Major James H. Trapier, Ordnance officer for the State of South Carolina aforesaid, for and in behalf of the said State, of the First part and William Glaze and Benjamin Flagg of Columbia in the said State, of the Second part. WITNESSETH,

That the said William Glaze and Benjamin Flagg agree and promise to furnish to the said Major J. H. Trapier or his successor in office for the use of the State aforesaid, the following arms to wit. Six Thousand Muskets, One Thousand Rifles, One Thousand Pair Pistols, One Thousand Cavalry Sabres and One Thousand Artillery Swords, with their equipment complete. These arms and their component parts, to be manufactured within the State of South Carolina, of the best material and workmanship, and as far as practicable, of material and by mechanics obtained in the State aforesaid.

AND the said William Glaze and Benjamin Flagg further stipulate to put their armory in operation by the first October, One Thousand Eight Hundred and Fifty-one, and to have completed and ready for inspection the said arms at the times and rate specified as follows, namely, Five Hundred Muskets, Three Hundred and Fifty Rifles, Three Hundred and Fifty pair of Pistols and Three Hundred and Fifty Swords with the equipment for each complete during the month of January, One Thousand Eight Hundred and Fifty-two. The same in February of the same year; and so on for every succeeding month of the same year, till the contract be completed. It is understood between the parties aforesaid, that all arms manufactured under this contract shall be after the patterns adopted and now in the Army of the United States; but that the State reserves to herself the right to alter all or any of said Patterns, by the direction and according to the Judgment of the said Major James H. Trapier, Ordnance officer as aforesaid, or his successor in office, or of the Board of Ordnance; and should such alteration involve an increased cost of manufacture, a corresponding increase of price to be determined by the Board of Ordnance, shall be allowed.

IT IS FURTHER understood that all arms manufactured under this contract shall in their finished state, before acceptance, be subjected to the usual inspection and tests: and also that the parts of which they are composed shall in the process of their fabrication, be subjected at all times to inspection and proof by the Board of Ordnance, or Ordnance officer, or other agent appointed by them or him for that purpose, and also that the parts shall interchange.

IT IS STILL FURTHER understood that the said William Glaze and Benjamin Flagg shall furnish the appropriate patterns and gauges for verifying the principal dimensions and forms of the different parts of the arms manufactured under this contract.

AND the said State of South Carolina, by the said James H. Trapier, Ordnance officer as aforesaid agrees and promises that the said William Glaze and Benjamin Flagg, having faithfully performed all the stipulations made by them in this contract shall be paid as follows: For the Muskets with equipments complete, Fourteen Dollars 50/00 ($14.50) per piece.

Rifles with equipments, Fifteen Dollars 50/00 ($15.50) per piece. Pistols with equipments, Fourteen Dollars and 50/00 per pair; Swords and Sabres with equipment, Six Dollars 50/00 ($6.50) each.

It is agreed also, that payment shall be made at the expiration of each month, and for the arms which shall have been received during that month.

IN TESTIMONY whereof, the State of South Carolina has caused the great seal of the State to be affixed hereto and the hand of the said Major J. H. Trapier, Ordnance officer as aforesaid, and the said William Glaze and Benjamin Flagg have hereunto set their hands and seals on this Fifteenth day of April—In the year of Our Lord, One Thousand, Eight Hundred and Fifty One.

Signed, Sealed and
Delivered in the
presence of —

/s/ J. H. Trapier
Maj. State Ordnance

(The words "with Equipments" being first interlined in the 6 & 7 lines of the 2nd page)
/s/ R. W. Colcock
    (witness to Execution by J. H. Trapier)
                    /s/ Wm. Glaze
Test
    /s/ C. O'Hanlon
                    /s/ Benjamin Flagg

It is not known why Boatwright did not sign the contract, or is it known what the state meant by "Artillery Swords." *Foot* artillery swords were then quite popular, but so was the U.S. model artillery saber. The point is unimportant as will be seen. That Flagg actually was a signatory to the contract is convincing proof that he was actually in Columbia and active in the affairs of the company. Very likely he acted as production superintendent.

From all indications, the actual delivery of arms was held up to some extent. Perhaps the contract stipulation that local people should be employed where possible caused part of the trouble. Perhaps it was a bit more difficult to relocate men and machinery than Glaze and Flagg had envisioned.

In any event, on April 30, 1852, an extension of the completion date of the contract was authorized. This most interesting document, brief and to the point, also substituted 1,000 cavalry sabers for the 1,000 artillery swords originally specified.[12] So far as is known, no artillery swords were produced. We have never seen or heard of one, at any rate, and it would seem logical to so assume. The contract is here quoted in part.

"Contract between William Glaze & Benjamin Flagg and The State of South Carolina For/ Major Trapier

The undersigned, securities for Glaze & Flagg in their contract for furnishing to the State of South Carolina, certain small arms, do consent to the extension asked by them, as to the time of completion of the contract—namely, to the

A SABER BY WM. GLAZE & CO.

Although not germane to our subject, we illustrate this excellent example of a saber and its scabbard, products of the armsmaker of our interest.

1st. December 1853—and also, to the following amendment of said contract—namely, that instead of 1000 Cavalry and 1000 Arty. Swords, they furnish 2000 of the former & none of the latter."

Regardless of the need for an extension of time for completion of the contract, the arms were delivered in due course and the state did not need to invoke the bond. However, not all of the contract was filled, as the following shows.[13]

Ordnance Department,
May 8th 1853

Messrs: Glaze & Co.
Gentlemen,

It is my duty to inform you that the remainder of the "appropriation for the defense of the State" will admit only of an allowance for the completion of the "Contract for Muskets & Rifles."

Respectfully
/s/ W. R. Calhoun
Major State Ordnance

Thus in a few lines, a contract is broken. Upon analysis, much is revealed, however. We have seen that the original contract was amended so that no artillery swords were to be furnished, and to our knowledge, no one has ever seen such a weapon that could be traced to Glaze. Now we see that the state could pay only for the completion of the contract as it applied to muskets

and rifles. By May 8, 1853, Glaze must have completed the order for 2,000 pistols, because they are to be found today, if one is lucky enough, in sufficient quantity to reinforce our belief. On the other hand, only one cavalry saber, marked *Columbia, S. C.* on the shoulder of the blade and *Wm. Glaze & Co.* on the right is known. It is to be seen in the Charleston Museum. Notice that it is a dead ringer for the U.S. M1840 and extremely well made. It may well be that Glaze had furnished a small number of sabers to the state prior to May 8, 1853, but it is certain that he did not supply 2,000.

Plain, serviceable sabers patterned after the U.S. M1840 are to be found, marked *Columbia, S. C.* These may be the product of the Palmetto Armory, but then again, they may not be. The uniformity of markings encountered in his firearms, together with his obvious pride in them, as demonstrated by the craftsmanship they show, make it seem unlikely that he would have disposed of the remainder of the state order without marking each weapon. Far more likely, the brass went into the foundry pots, and the steel blades into the furnaces to be used for something else.

But the *Columbia, S. C.* marking of the otherwise unidentified sabers appears to have been struck by the Palmetto Armory's die. *Caveat emptor!*

The products of the Palmetto Armory are among the most desirable American arms extant. They are extremely well made, and today are certainly among the rarest of any period in our history. There were fewer of the pistols produced, for instance, than were many of the so-called rare Colts, or of the M1855 pistol with shoulder stock made at Springfield. Moreover, everything about Glaze's products is top quality, be it metal or wood.

Shortly after the signing of the contract for new arms, Glaze had agreed to alter muskets for the state. The contract reads:

We, the Undersigned, do agree to promise to alter, from flint to percussion, the locks of all, or any portion of the muskets now belonging to the State of South Carolina—the work to be done in the best manner & on the same plan as that adopted by the United States.

We agree to promise further, to put all the locks in complete order—to reduce the springs so that they will work as well as if originally made for Percussion—and to put in new Springs wherever they are necessary—

Columbia, May 31 '51

Wm. Glaze & Co.

The Undersigned agrees & promises that the above named work having been faithfully & well

executed, the said Glaze, Flagg & Boatwright shall be paid for each musket, two dollars

/s/ J. H. Trapier
Major Ordnance

Charleston, May 6th '51[14]

What is considered to be one of the muskets Glaze reconditioned has been examined. It was not converted from flint to percussion. It has what was once a Springfield M1842 lock, dated 184?. This mark can plainly be seen under a magnifying glass, the lock having been dressed with a heavy file at this point, but no attempt made to disguise the fact. The customary Palmetto marks have been struck in over the original lock markings, but the rest of the weapon is straight Springfield. If this had turned up within the period of 1959-1960, it could only have been considered a poorly executed fake. However, it was found in 1952, well before fake Palmetto dies had been made. The barrel, dated 1851, has not been re-marked, or has any other part of the weapon.

An original .69 caliber Palmetto musket, showing much hard use, is illustrated. This piece has the usual M1842 U.S. musket dimensions. The steel butt plate is marked *SC* on the tang.

Courtesy Hugh Benet, Jr.

A PALMETTO MUSKET AND A RE-WORKED U. S. MUSKET

The upper musket was made by William Glaze and Company. The lower musket, a U. S. M1842, was evidently re-worked by Glaze.

Courtesy Hugh Benet, Jr.

MUSKETOON

This shorter weapon contains Palmetto parts throughout, and it is presumed that it was made up by Glaze during the war.

The barrel is marked only *VP* (Viewed and Proofed) and stamped with the small Palmetto tree which seems to have been the South Carolina Ordnance Deparment's acceptance proof. The barrel tang is marked *SC* and *1853*. The lock is heavily stamped with the Palmetto Armory mark, with *Columbia/S.C. 1852* behind the hammer. The trigger-guard is steel, the bands and fore-end cap are brass. The ramrod is shaped like the M1842 U.S. counterpart with the exception that its business end is cupped to fit over a ball. The bayonet lug is on top of the barrel in line with the sight, rather than under it, as on the U.S. model, and is marked *L*.

Musketoons were not a part of the Glaze contract, so the specimen illustrated cannot really be considered as such. However, this .69 caliber weapon is not an example of the amateur gunsmith's art. The job was too well done for one thing, and it has not been "sporterized" commercially as were so many rifles and muskets after the war. This is a little recognized fact, but in 1865 and thereafter, surplus and captured weapons were jobbed to firms that made them into extremely serviceable sporting or birding pieces.

The wood in the musketoon's stock is of unusual quality, and the piece is in almost new condition. In addition to the usual Palmetto musket markings, it is stamped *W.G. & Co.* on the left barrel flat. The ramrod has a heavy brass tip, totally unlike the standard ramrod, but it is threaded on the other end, as were most that were made for military use. This may, of course, be sheer coincidence. It may be a wartime job as William Glaze & Co. was an alternate name for the Palmetto Iron Works. A number of well-finished conversions, generally carbines, are to be found incorporating Palmetto parts, but the buyer had best beware unless he is familiar with the niceties of military minutiae.

The Palmetto rifle is the rarest of Glaze's products, which makes it rare indeed. Its scarcity is due in part to only 1,000 having been made, and to the capture and destruction of 500 of them when Sherman's army took the Citadel at Charleston.[15] It is a copy of the .54 caliber M1841 rifle which is, and was then, known variously as the "Mississippi" rifle (after Colonel Jeff Davis' Mississippi regiment which used them in Mexico), the "Winsor" after Windsor, Vermont, where many were made, and the "Jaeger." This was a remarkably effective and certainly popular piece. The specimen examined showed no signs of ever having had a sword bayonet stud, which

Courtesy Battle Abbey, Richmond, Virginia

A PALMETTO RIFLE

Conforming in many respects to the Harpers Ferry model of 1841. The lock plate is stamped Palmetto Armory C. S. in a circle enclosing a palmetto tree. Columbia S. C. 1852 is stamped to the rear of the hammer. Wm. Glaze & Co., the maker, is stamped on the left side of the breech with the view and proof markings of South Carolina and a small palmetto-tree proof mark.

A PALMETTO PISTOL

This U. S. M1842 pistol reflects the high quality workmanship of William Glaze and Company. The upper view shows the various barrel markings and the date on the tang.

is as it should be, because the U.S. model was originally issued without a bayonet. Thus, we may safely assume that no sword or saber bayonets were furnished by Glaze. The lock is dated *1852* and the barrel tang, *1853*, while the butt plate is marked *SC*. All hardware is brass. The barrels are marked *VP* and with the small Palmetto tree, and are stamped *steel* on the left barrel flat as well. The rifle is the only Palmetto arm to carry the latter marking. *SC* is stamped on the tang of the breech plug. The type of rear sight with which the rifle was fitted is not known.

Somewhat puzzling is the purchase of 2,000 single-shot horse pistols made after the U.S. M1842 at a time when many militia officers had purchased Colt pistols, and the fame of the Walker was abroad in the land. However, the explanation is simple enough. South Carolina wanted to be independent, to make its own arms. Machinery to manufacture the M1842 was within reach, but that for the more modern Colt was not. The '42 military model pistol was not patented, and was a proven, dependable weapon. As in all Palmetto weapons, the workmanship was excellent, and proofing was as strict as with the U.S. counterpart. The backstrap, trigger-guard and band were brass, as was the front sight and side plate. There was no rear sight, although added later, probably at the start of the Civil War. The steel lock was marked similarly to the rifle and musket, with most locks dated *1852* and most barrel tangs stamped *1853* and marked *SC* as well. The assumption is easily made that the parts were made in different years. The barrels were proofed *VP* with the usual small Palmetto tree, as well as *Wm. Glaze & Co.* on the left flat. They were caliber .54 and were not rifled. They faithfully followed the U.S. model in their swivel ramrods, as in all other respects.

In past years, Palmetto locks have been put into Aston, Johnson and Waters M1842 frames,

and one such hybrid with a barrel marked *Wm. Glaze and Bro.* has been seen. *Bro.* is a strange substitute for *Co.*!

As is the case with many other highly desirable martial handguns, the Palmetto pistol is now being reproduced in some quantity. The reproductions are well executed and hard to distinguish from the originals without close comparison. The die work on the Palmetto seal is particularly good, and no effort has been made to mark these weapons as reproductions. Using U.S. M1842 assemblies, old marks have been dressed off, new dies made up, new marks struck in. One admires the workmanship while deploring the motives of such people.

A close look at a fake and a genuine lock plate shows that the latter has the unmistakable ap-

Courtesy Harry C. Knode

PALMETTO PISTOL LOCK PLATES

The specimen illustrated above shows unquestioned original production stamping. The lower, which shows file or grinding marks across the face, exhibits the imprint of somewhat different dies. It is believed by the authors that the lower example is not original but a reproduction. Evidence of the existence of later-day spurious dies prompts all serious collectors to look upon any specimen deviating from the original as suspect.

Courtesy Harry C. Knode

A PALMETTO MUSKET LOCK

This lock plate shows an interesting variation from the typical pistol lock plate. This may represent the other authentic version of the dies used on Palmetto arms.

pearance of age. Most of the plates to be found are similar in this respect, even if they have recently been polished. Also, seals are usually dim, and in many cases seem to have been struck on a slight angle. The fake, on the other hand, has a deep and precise seal, and little sign of age because it was milled off before being re-marked. However, a few vestigial pits remain, and judicious use of various commercial compounds could bring the fake lock into line with the real thing in a matter of just a few days.

Notice that the slug at the rear of both plates is nice and deep. This is characteristic of nearly all Palmetto lock plates.

A closer look at the *Columbia/S. C. 1852* shows that the faker may have made a serious mistake. His lettering lacks the old-time dips of the original. His 2 doesn't have the looped top that we see. But it may be that he faithfully copied a variant of Glaze's dies. Before damning

a suspect piece (and from now on, all of them are suspect) one should check for other signs.

How new is the stock? Were inspector's marks removed from the old stock? Is the stock too worn to tell? How about the inletting? It is hard to fake the discoloration that comes from oil, dirt and age. Check the barrel marks. Are there signs of welding? Overstrikes? How about the seal on the lock plate? Here we encounter a distressing fact. Glaze made no less than 9,000 locks and probably more. He marked an unknown quantity of U.S. material—perhaps in excess of 5,000 muskets. The seal is a work of art, but easily worn and hard to reproduce so that minor variations between dies were inevitable.

Major variations exist—not in the diameter of the seal, but in the thickness of the Palmetto trunk, in the shape of its leaves, and in punctuation. Even the star is not standard. A musket lock with an asterisk instead of a star is illustrated. A detailed study of a genuine seal of what may be termed "thin leaf" design and one of the fakes will reveal notable differences in the shape and design of the foliage of the Palmettos. But was the lock dressed off and re-marked? The fakes show signs of milling and, unfortunately, so do many genuine plates. Acid or magnaflux would reveal previous marks, but acid is not looked upon with much favor and magnaflux is not easy to come by.

Perhaps the inside of the lock has something to tell us, but even this is not certain. One pistol lock was struck inside with a single punch mark. Some have initials; some, nothing.

In the final analysis, today we may be able to tell a fake from the real thing, but with a few chemicals or a winter in the compost heap, these things can be made impossible to identify.

Bayonets made by Glaze are also almost impossible to identify, but it is thought that the specimen shown is one. If it is not, it is close enough to be illustrative of the type. It is unfortunate that the little Palmetto tree proof mark used on Glaze's gun barrels was not used on his edged weapons. This bayonet is the usual M1842 type, marked only *SC* and is made to fit the Palmetto bayonet lug, which is on top of the barrel, as previously stated. A similar bayonet may be seen with a Palmetto musket in the collection at Fort McHenry, Maryland. Oddly enough, the home of the "Star-Spangled Banner" contains a rather nice collection of Confederate weapons.

The quantity of arms supplied by Glaze was remarkably small, in relation to the fantastic numbers to be used a few years later, but entirely within reason when compared to the size of the forces which participated in the Mexican War. The mere fact that preparation of some sort was begun, however inadequate it proved to be later, speaks highly of the determination of South Carolina to support her principles. It also makes plain the old maxim that it is customary to begin a war with the previous war's

Courtesy Hugh Benet, Jr.

BAYONETS FOR PALMETTO MUSKETS

These portions show, on the left, an example thought to be of the type furnished by Glaze as part of his contract for the muskets and, on the right, a U. S. bayonet, so marked and carrying also SC under the U. S. marking.

weapons was as true then as it is now, because the Palmetto Armory contract was for 6,000 smooth-bore muskets and 2,000 smooth-bore single-shot pistols, but only 1,000 rifles!

Here is a typical example of a particular type of military mind at work. If we consider that the volunteer officers of Mexican War experience were at all intelligent and capable of the most rudimentary observation, if we give them credit for the slightest knowledge of military science and tactics—not the kind one gets from books, but that learned in the campaigns in Mexico—then how can we reconcile their obvious belief that accurate aimed rifle fire capable of killing at ranges up to 1,000 yards was not as good as musketry which is really effective only to 100 yards? Strange that the lessons learned on the plains of Mexico should be so quickly forgotten. Perhaps most of the legislators weren't there.

With the completion of the state contract, William Glaze and Company found themselves with machinery and workmen but no orders for guns. An uneasy political truce prevailed, and South Carolina, in the expectation that U.S. arms would be furnished for its militia and the knowledge that a pro-southern Secretary of War (Jefferson Davis) was in charge in Washington, wasn't receptive to the idea of making further state purchases. So Glaze resumed making cotton gins, plows and other agricultural implements as well as steam engines—in short, anything that a well-equipped factory could produce. Flagg isn't mentioned again and seems to have drifted off; where, we do not know.

An odd item that crops up is mention of another contract Glaze filled in 1854. For $14,000, he "rolled back" the old statehouse in Columbia to make way for a new building! Upon investigation, one finds that he actually jacked up a substantial brick building and moved it to a new location.[16] This was accomplished with local labor, using special equipment imported for the purpose.

For years, collectors have wondered what happened to the Armory's gun-making machinery. For the most part, it could have been used for other purposes, and the filing jigs and the dies for locks, butt plates, bands, and springs could easily have been stored or sold. In any event, there should be no great mystery made over what happened to it. After all, by the time seven years had elapsed and war had finally and inevitably come, wear and tear would have taken their toll of machinery that was in daily use, and the capacity for producing weapons would have been greatly lessened. The machinery belonged to Glaze, and he was not one to see it sit idly by while money was to be made with it.

The activities of the company up to 1861 are easy to trace. Glaze was kept busy with orders, some of impressive size, as witness a $1,600, 70 horsepower steam engine delivered to Wade Hampton.[17] Having changed the name of the Palmetto Armory to the Palmetto Iron Works, Glaze further confuses historians by calling his firm William Glaze and Company on occasion. After the death of his partner in 1857, Glaze was sole proprietor, regardless of what he called his company. By 1860 he was turning out products valued at more than $60,000 each year.

With the coming of the Civil War, one would expect Glaze to have re-entered the weapon business, and that he was willing to do so is shown in a letter dated December 4, 1860, to the State Ordnance Department. "I can cast all shot, shell, heavy cannon and mortors [sic] at the same price the State pays for them. I would be able in six months or less time to furnish not less than thirty rifles or rifled muskets per day and of Pistols a much larger amount."

Notice that Glaze needed time to tool up for production, but seems to be sure of his capabilities. Nothing came of his offer, and the next we learn of his activities is through an advertisement in the Richmond *Daily Examiner* on June 8, 1861: "Notice of Thomas McNeill requesting contributions to the C. S. Armory and Foundry Company, Capital $1,000,000 to fabricate artillery of all types, rifles, pistols, swords, bayonets, rockets, and all munitions of war. Thomas E. McNeill, acting superintendent, Glaze and Radcliffe agents."

This is no doubt one of the most tantalizing advertisements encountered in our research. No other has been seen. If Glaze was serious, and there is no reason that he shouldn't have been, it is unfortunate that the plan did not mature. Glaze had proved what he could do and the South needed well-made weapons.

Another advertisement in the Charlotte, North Carolina, *Daily Bulletin* on August 26, 1862, merely states that the Palmetto Iron Works is prepared to make steam engines, mills and iron castings, etc. Weapons are not mentioned, but certainly the potential of the Iron Works for the production of less glamorous but equally important equipment existed and was used.

Odds and ends of information that tie in to what the Iron Works could logically have been expected to do appear here and there, interspersed with wild exaggerations. An elderly gentleman, a former foreman and later proprietor of the Iron Works, gave an interview to a reporter from a Columbia newspaper around 1900. Among other things, we read that the Iron Works made picks and shovels, "etc.," for the Ordnance Department and rollers for the powder mills at Raleigh and Columbia, during the war. The "etc." may refer to such items as bits, horseshoes, axle trees, artillery hardware and articles of a similar nature. The article also refers to a contract awarded Boatwright and Glaze for 250,000 breech-loading rifles.[18] This is most interesting, especially when one knows that Boatwright died in 1857. However, we also read that Boatwright and Glaze converted 5,000 flint muskets to percussion in 1852, and this has the ring of truth, although the number may be exaggerated.

Another account has the Iron Works making

Courtesy The South Caroliniana Library

THE PALMETTO ARMORY IN RUINS

An old photograph showing the devastation wrought by Sherman's army.

"bombshells, cannon balls, minie balls, and also several revolving cannons, this last being the invention of a man named 'George.' It worked something on the order of the Colt's revolver. The cylinder moved horizontally. I saw several of them tried out. They used cartridges, but it [sic] was not adopted by the government."[19]

Revolving ordnance, of sizable caliber or otherwise, seems to have been quite popular at the beginning of the war—that is with everyone but the artillery and, probably fortunately, the C.S. Ordnance Corps. What happened to the guns referred to is unknown, but a variant on the theme, made in Petersburg, Virginia, is still to be seen there.

Courtesy The South Caroliniana Library

THE PALMETTO ARMORY REBUILT

A more recent photograph taken about 1912 of the "Palmetto Iron Works."

General William T. Sherman took Columbia on Friday, February 17, 1865. He promptly burned it. What wouldn't burn, he blew up. There wasn't much left of the Palmetto Iron Works when Uncle Billy moved on, but a picture was taken of the ruins.

Let Glaze himself tell what happened.

I witnessed the burning of Columbia. I know that the city was destroyed by Gen. Sherman's army, because they were in the city at the time, and I saw persons in the uniform of the United States soldiers setting fire to the city in various places. I saw two such persons fire Mr. Phillips' auction warehouse. They opened the door and threw balls, which they had set on fire, into the building, and in less than twenty minutes the building was in flames. This building was diagonally across from the petitioner's store. It occurred about 7 o'clock, P.M. All that part of the city caught directly after that—in about one-half of an hour. I saw several other houses fired, and among them my own building. I am speaking now of what I saw myself. I saw a building back of the old City Hotel fired by balls by persons wearing similar uniforms, whom I know to be United States soldiers, for they came into my own house. They burned my machine shop. There were about one hundred soldiers there at the time. They broke up the machinery and then set fire thereto; not, however, by balls as aforesaid, but by the broken boxes, etc. and oil poured on. In the course of a half an hour the conflagration became general. Most of the burning was done from that time until about 3 o'clock next morning. I was a member of the city council at the time, and went with the mayor to Gen. Sherman, when Gen. Sherman promised the mayor that there would be no burning that night. I saw no efforts on the part of the United States soldiers to subdue the fire; but, on the other hand, I saw them endeavoring to spread it, and heard some of them remark that it was not half enough. It was on my way home from our conference with Gen. Sherman that I saw Mr. Phillips' warehouse fired. I saw a sky-rocket sent up from the State House yard, where the headquarters of Gen. Sherman were,

which I took to be the signal for the burning of the city, for immediately thereafter the fire burst out all over the city. Soldiers had been stationed at different points in the mean time.

Signature/W. M. GLAZE

Sworn to and subscribed before me, this 18th day of March, A. D., 1872.

ALBERT M. BOOZER,
U.S. Commissioner for District
of South Carolina.[20]

The subordinates of Brevet Lieutenant Colonel T. G. Baylor, Chief of Ordnance with Sherman, wrote an extremely detailed report on the ordnance stores captured and destroyed at Columbia.[21] In meticulous regular army fashion, they were careful to list where each classification was found and how many of each item there were. Their main place headings were: *Citadel, Magazine, Arsenal.* A subheading under Arsenal appears as *Armory*, still another is *Depot and Armory.*

We may assume that the Federal ordnance people who viewed the captured stores and who gave local place names to captured installations would have used the abbreviated colloquialism "Armory" for Palmetto Armory, which is what most people in Columbia still call it. Remember, too, that the Palmetto Iron Works was only a few hundred yards from the State Arsenal on Arsenal Hill and that the same report refers specifically and quite properly to 500 Palmetto rifles found at the Citadel. On the other hand, the report locates the Citadel and Magazine of Charleston in Columbia, and there was a Confederate Armory in Columbia. It would be interesting to know if the Armory entry applies to the Palmetto Iron Works or to the Confederate Armory, because at the "Armory" were found 6,000 unfinished musket barrels and stocks!

Under Depot and Armory are listed a 1½ inch breech-loading cannon (George's perhaps?)—gun carriages, caissons and a large number of sponges and rammers. It is unfortunate that such large gaps exist in Confederate and South

Carolina Ordnance Records. Documentary proof may not exist in as detailed form as we might wish, but there can be no doubt that the Palmetto Armory played an important part in the South's war effort. The life of the Palmetto Armory was of short span, but its products endure to its memory. If ever a state got its money's worth, South Carolina did.

FOOTNOTE REFERENCES

1. David Duncan Wallace, *History of South Carolina* (New York, 1934), Vol. III, p. 120.
2. E. Milby Burton, *South Carolina Silversmiths 1690-1860* (Charleston, S. C., 1942), pp. 229-231. Hereafter, Burton.
3. Samuel E. Smith, "South Carolina Ante-Bellum Pistols," *American Rifleman*, Vol. 103 (November, 1955), No. II, pp. 36-37.
4. *Burton*, pp. 218-220.
5. E. M. Lander, Jr., "Columbia's Confederate Arsenal," *State Magazine*, Sunday supplement to the Columbia *State*. August 13, 1950. Hereafter, *Lander*.
6. *MS.* Collection, South Carolina Archives Department.
7. *Ibid.*
8. *Lander.*
9. *Southern Agriculturist* (Laurensville, South Carolina, 1853), Vol. I, p. 50.
10. *MS.* collection, South Carolina Archives Department.
11. *Ibid.*
12. *Ibid.*
13. *Ibid.*
14. *Lander.*
15. *O.R.*, Series 4, Vol. XLII, p. 181.
16. A. S. Salley, *The State Houses of South Carolina, 1751-1936* (Columbia, South Carolina, 1936), p. 18.
17. *Lander.*
18. In Richard D. Steuart's voluminous notes, a number of newspaper clippings are found from which the names of the papers or dates of publication were trimmed when they were glued in scrapbooks according to subject matter. This is used only because it has been qualified in the text as doubtful, but is still an interesting comment.
19. J. P. Williams, *Old and New Columbia* (Columbia, South Carolina, 1929), p. 110.
20. W. G. Simms, *The Sack and Destruction of the City of Columbia, South Carolina* (Columbia, South Carolina, 1865). A second edition (with notes by A. S. Salley) (Atlanta, Georgia, 1937), pp. 90-91.
21. *O.R.*, Series IV, Vol. XLVII, p. 181.

NOTES

CHAPTER 13

Schneider and Glassick

MANY enigmas are to be found in even the most cursory examination of the annals of Confederate arms makers, but none greater than that of Schneider and Glassick of Memphis, Tennessee.

The only traces of these men and of a contract they are reputed to have obtained to supply revolving pistols to the South are dissimilar weapons, obviously made by two different shops and following two distinctly different models.

In the face of this, one may wonder if the firm actually existed, but exist it did. This is shown by the customary exaggerated newspaper praise which usually greeted the advent of a new, locally produced weapon. Appearing in the Memphis, Tennessee, *Daily Appeal* on December 8, 1861, the article is so short as to be terse, but also managed to overstate the truth somewhat.

"Memphis Manufacture—We were yesterday shown, by Messrs. Schneider and Glassick, of Jefferson Street between Front and Main Streets, a six-shooter Navy pistol of their own manufacture. It is a beautiful weapon, not inferior to the Colt's make in any particular. The finish of the whole, the accuracy of the parts, and the excellent working of the mechanism are admirable. Iron, brasswork and woodwork are all specimens of skill. We are proud that Memphis can turn out such splendid workmanship."

Leaving this interesting tidbit of information for the moment, we find that the firm is first listed in the 1860 Memphis City Directory as "Schneider & Glassick, guns, pistols, etc., 20

Jefferson Street." Somewhat previous to this, William Schneider and Frederick G. Glassick, gunsmiths both, operated independently, in company with numerous others in the booming Mississippi river town.

A .44 caliber derringer was considered as much a pocket accessory along the river as a penknife, and Glassick sold them. One is illustrated, marked *F. Glassick & Co./Memphis, Tennessee* along the top of its barrel. This is a somewhat cruder, heavier weapon than those emanating from Philadelphia and the shops of Deringer, Wurfflein, Evans, et al., but a sturdy, serviceable piece, nonetheless. It is not known if Glassick made it himself, but it certainly antedates the Civil War, and is of a type which is now classified as a "Southern Derringer."

Courtesy Edward N. Simmons

A STURDY DERRINGER

Probably made by F. J. Bitterlich of Nashville, Tennessee, and so stamped under the barrel. The top flat of the barrel is clearly marked F. Glassick & Co. Memphis, Tenn. The pistol is seven inches long overall.

SCHNEIDER AND GLASSICK REVOLVERS

Serial number 23 at the top, and serial number 6 below. It will be noted that the space or gap between barrel and cylinder is too great to be attributed entirely to use and wear or a loose barrel key. Poor workmanship notwithstanding, the finish and marking are of acceptable professional quality.

At some unknown date in the late eighteen fifties, Schneider and Glassick threw in together, and another Southern derringer has been seen marked *Schneider & Glassick, Memphis, Tennessee.*

With war, all gunsmiths had more work than they could handle, altering flint weapons to percussion, reboring, repairing and refinishing, even restocking all sorts and varieties of weapons for the defense of their states and nation. Despite the press of this sort of work, many cast an eager eye at government contracts.

A few actually went into limited production of handguns, rifles and muskets. Schneider and Glassick seem to have preferred revolving pistols, and hence the news clip about their "beautiful weapon." We need not belabor the fact that newsmen are given to superlatives and that the first blush of patriotism made many things look like what they were not.

Now, almost 100 years after the three surviving specimens marked Schneider and Glassick were made, none is exactly beautiful. But all were serviceable then, as now, and no doubt used for the purpose for which they were intended. The puzzling thing about these lonely survivors is that two are completely different from the other.

Number 6, to call it by its serial, is 13 inches overall, with a 7½-inch fully octagon barrel. It is .36 caliber, 6-shot, with a brass frame, trigger-guard and backstrap. Along the top of the barrel is die stamped *Schneider & Glassick, Memphis, Tennessee.* This was not marked letter by letter, and is on one line. Colt parts will not interchange, the nipples have a different screw thread, and like most of Confederate manufacture, are somewhat larger. A considerable gap is observed between the ends of the barrels and the faces of the cylinders of this model, not entirely due to wear. The serial *6* is found on cylinder, backstrap, trigger-guard, barrel, hammer and rammer. An identical weapon, serial number 23, has been found, and it is felt that this was the type referred to by the *Daily Appeal* because of their brass frames.

It is fruitless to guess at how many of this type were made. If one a week was turned out from May, 1861, to March, 1862, when Memphis was captured, then 50-55 might be a reasonable total. On the other hand, it takes time to get even one revolver a week into production, so perhaps only about 15 or 20 were made.

A third revolver is also marked *Schneider & Glassick, Memphis, Tennessee* on the top of its barrel, but this was done letter by letter. The weapon is much like the Leech and Rigdon, except for a most unusual hammer safety, which consists of a pin on the hammer which enters holes on the rear of the cylinder between the nipples. *12M* is found stamped here and there, and appears as *12 Mdl* in one spot. *Mdl* may stand for model, which is somewhat incongruous.

The backstrap and trigger-guard are brass, but the frame is iron and the .36 caliber barrel is dragoon type. It is 6-shot. In the opinion of those who have examined them, the different models were not made by the same person or persons, nor on the same design.

It would seem somewhat improbable that Schneider and Glassick would change their basic

Courtesy Edward N. Simmons

SCHNEIDER AND GLASSICK REVOLVER

Iron frame and dragoon barrel. In these respects, as well as others, it differs from serial numbers 6 and 23. This specimen is marked 12M.

design and materials after making a few weapons, so one must look elsewhere for an explanation as to why these are so dissimilar. The most logical explanation would seem to be that having obtained a contract of some sort, they subcontracted for its fulfillment. While this seems a bit far-fetched, it is true that Glassick sold pistols of others' manufacture but marked with his name before the war, one such being a Southern derringer made and marked *F. J. Bitterlich, Nashville, Tenn.*, under the barrel where it cannot be seen, while *F. Glassick & Co. Memphis, Tenn.* appears on top, to be read by all.

The Memphis *Appeal* ran Schneider and Glassick's swan song on March 7, 1862: "All persons who have left guns or pistols, or arms of any kind with us, and which have been in our store for three months past, will please call and get them, as we intend to deliver to the Government all such arms not taken away on the 15th of the present month. Schneider and Glassick, No. 20, Jefferson Street."

By March 15, Memphis was in Yankee hands, and Schneider and Glassick were out of business.

CHAPTER 14

Samuel Sutherland

So HARD pressed for arms was the South that it was necessary to repair and modernize any and everything that would shoot. The confiscated U.S. armories located below the Potomac River were pitifully few and inadequate to handle such a large task. Thus it was that local gunsmiths were called upon to show their patriotism by repairing arms not only for the private citizen but for the Confederate Government as well. Most responded gladly and the quantity and quality of their work was such that several became known in their own communities as "The Armorer of the South." One such was Samuel Sutherland who operated at 132 Main Street, Richmond, Virginia.

The Chief of Confederate Ordnance has this to say regarding the repair of arms: "A great part of the work of our armories consisted in repairing arms brought in from the battlefields or sent in from the armies in too damaged a condition to be effectively repaired at the arsenals. In this way only could be utilized all the gleanings of the battlefields. My recollection is that we saved nearly ten thousand stands of arms from the battlefield of Bull Run, and the battlefields about Richmond in 1862 gave us about 25,000 excellent arms through the labors of the armory at Richmond."[1]

Samuel Sutherland had been in the gun business in Richmond for many years before the war. Many fine quality flintlock weapons bear his name, either as dealer or maker, for he was active in both respects. In a list of Virginia gunsmiths of 1855, the Virginia *Gazetteer* of that year says: "Virginia Gun and Pistol Emporium, Samuel Sutherland, 132 Main Street, Richmond, Manufacturer, importer and dealer in every description of sporting apparatus and fine cutlery. Gunsmiths and persons from the country are requested to call and examine the most extensive stock in the state of guns, pistols, rifles in every variety, quality and size. Prices to suit all customers."

Courtesy Battle Abbey, Richmond, Virginia

SINGLE-SHOT PISTOL BY SUTHERLAND

Of the derringer type but with swivel rammer. The back-action lock is engraved and bears the legend S. Sutherland/ Richmond, Virginia, in two lines. The caliber is .45. This example has a 2½-inch belt hook on the left side.

That Sutherland was at the same location five years later is shown by an advertisement in the Richmond *Daily Dispatch* of July 7, 1859: "Southern Importing House. Samuel Sutherland, 132 Main St., Richmond, Va., importer and dealer in guns, pistols, rifles, powder flasks, shot pouches, game bags, wadding and sporting articles of all kinds. Pocket cutlery, walking canes, fishing tackle, etc., etc. Colt revolvers in any quantity and on the most favorable terms."

On December 24, 1861, he advertises in the Richmond *Daily Examiner* as being "Opposite Eagle Square on Main St."

In our files is a letter from Joel B. Sutherland, D.D.S., 1208 Monument Avenue, Baltimore, Maryland, dated December 2, 1909, and addressed to Richard D. Steuart. This was in answer to an inquiry made by Mr. Steuart concerning the wartime activities of Samuel Sutherland, father of the doctor. Says Dr. Sutherland:

"My father's first contract with the Confederate Government was for the supplying of powder and ball cartridges. These were of two kinds; the single ball tied above the yellow paper tube, and ball and three bucks, arranged in the same way. This was the ammunition of the old musket, a heavy but formidable weapon, the principal arm of the militia regiments. The emergency called for an immediate supply of this sort of ammunition, and agents were sent broadcast throughout the South to gather powder and lead from every available source. Country stores, village grocers (allowed under the law to carry from two to six kegs of powder) were besieged and their stock appropriated for a consideration. My uncle Dr. A. B. Sutherland was dispatched to Wythville, Va., the seat of the lead mines with authority to buy up the plant. Upon his arrival, he found that Northern agents had preceded him. When he reported this to Government authorities prompt action was taken and the exclusive output secured. This incident is vividly impressed upon my memory I having accompanied my uncle on that mission.

"At the Virginia State Armory at Richmond, Va., then in command of Capt. Charles Dimmock, vast numbers of muskets (many of the old flintlock type), carbines, sabers and small arms of various sorts were found stored there, and my father now having become 'Armorer of the Confederacy' immediately proceeded to alter the flint locks into percussion guns and remodel the carbines for mounted cavalry service.

"The old curved and rusty sabers renovated became much in evidence though more ornamental than useful.

"This was the first consignment of war material, delivered by my father to the Government, through the agency of the War Department. I do not recall the date, but it followed closely upon the secession of Virginia. Now I am aware that much of the above is irrelevant, but the recalling of it has served to refresh my memory on the main question viz: 'To what extent did Samuel Sutherland figure in the remaking of arms from parts gathered from battlefields by Ordnance Officers?'

"After the first battle of Bethel an order was issued from the War Department directing that all captured and abandoned arms of whatever description be gathered and turned over to the Ordnance Department, special officers being detailed for the purpose, and after First Manassas (Bull Run) vast quantities of ordnance of every description were turned in to my father, and promptly put in condition for the 'Fighting Division of the Confederate Army.'

"At the request of the Armorer for the return of skilled workmen who had responded to the early call, and were now at the front, the Secretary of War ordered a special detail, and such men as were needed, were returned to the benches. The work began in earnest and a request was made to all citizens to turn in anything in their possession that 'looked like it could shoot.' This request was responded to with alacrity, the result being the disgorging of some of the most outlandish specimens of firearms possible to conceive. Old pepperbox revolvers, single and double self-cockers, some with hidden triggers that snapped open as they were cocked, three-barrelled guns, the twin barrels for shot and one on top rifles, Derringers, Allen & Wheelock self-cockers, old Kentucky rifles with barrels five feet long, many of which bore the name of 'S. Sutherland—Maker,' were contributed by the West, and I recall that my father hailed them with special delight—recognizing

A PREWAR GUNSMITH'S SHOP

The establishment shown here, while we certainly do not represent it as the Richmond shop of Samuel Sutherland, may be considered as reminiscent of an earlier smithy where the ". . . old Kentucky rifles with barrels five feet long . . . which bore the name of 'S. Sutherland—Maker'" first saw the light of day. Rebuilt perhaps by the hands that had fashioned them, they served once more as indicated in this chapter. The above is from a signed presentation photograph of an unpublished painting by the late renowned artist, Gayle P. Hoskins.

them as old friends. He knew the stuff they were made of. The barrels were shortened and re-mounted, fine sights adjusted, and the valuable arms turned over for the exclusive use of the sharpshooters.

"The 'John Brown Machette' figured also in the furnishing of war material. Governor Henry A. Wise on the occasion of the John Brown's raid had shipped my father a large case box of that

primitive weapon, which was placed on exhibition, and so great was the demand for a 'John Brown Spike' that vast numbers were reproduced, many of which remained on hand at the breaking out of hostilities two years later. It consisted of a double edge knife about two feet long, ground to a point and secured to the end of a six foot pole. These were turned into sword bayonets and also adjusted to the short

German rifle. John Brown had built wiser than he knew.

"I must introduce to you just here a mysterious character in the person of one Williams, a man of stalwart build, standing over six feet and muscular. He reported to the Armorer by order of the Secretary of War, he was an English importation, or rather exportation, having been sent on by one of our Government agents abroad. He became my father's right arm. He was a forger of steel and a maker of gun barrels after the old English twist style. He was allotted a space apart, erected a separate forge and brought in monstrous anvils and paraphernalia, unlike anything here-to-fore known to the factory. An aura of secrecy pervaded his 'pent up Utica,' and the boys in the shop referred to him as 'the Gunmaker of Moscow.'

"He forged and hammered from early morning till way into the night, adjusting breeches and breakoffs to barrels, to be stocked in the factory adjoining. Thus was the mighty work accomplished. I know of no instance in which the pepperbox pistol you refer to was made out and out in the South, but you are correct in your surmise that this and many other arms were remade and perfected by parts gathered from the battlefields by officers of ordnance, appointed for this special purpose.

"I entered the army myself in April of 1862 and remained until the surrender at Appomattox. What I have submitted to you in this hurriedly prepared paper is authentic.

"The work in Richmond went bravely on to the end. On my return, my father told me that when the torch was applied, he locked the doors, and arm in arm with Williams, repaired to Capitol Hill where they sorrowfully watched till the flames reached the little 'Confederate Arsenal' and reduced it to ashes."

In another letter Dr. Sutherland advised that his father moved from Richmond to Baltimore, Maryland, in June or July, 1865, where he purchased the gun firm of Merrill, Thomas and Co., 239 Baltimore Street.

That he continued the repairing of firearms as well as dealing in them is evidenced by Le Mat No. 21, under the left grip of which is penciled "Owned by B. Rouger (Rouzler?), S. Sutherland, 1872." This undoubtedly was Sutherland's way of showing customer ownership of a repaired arm in 1872. Doubtless the present owner of this gun wishes that the date of the repair job lay within the war years.

Handgun specimens repaired and/or as originally issued bearing Sutherland's name are numerous. Those encountered by the authors are as follows:

1—An under-hammer percussion pistol originally made by Ethan Allen, Grafton, Massachusetts, but with a hammer and barrel put on the frame by *Sutherland, Richmond* and so stamped. The piece is 13½ inches overall with a half-octagon .31 caliber rifled barrel.

2—A .45 caliber derringer-type pistol with a 6-inch octagon barrel and a belt hook and checkered grips and a swivel ramrod. Marked on tang of lock plate S. *Sutherland, Richmond, Va.*

3—An under-hammer pistol with a .36 caliber, 8-inch, half-octagon barrel marked S. *Sutherland, Richmond, Va.*, said to have been captured from a Confederate soldier.

4—A six-shot pepperbox revolver with 3¼-inch barrels on which is stamped *Allen & Thurber, Norwich, Ct., Patented 1837, Cast Steel* and S. *Sutherland, Richmond, Va.*

5—A .31 caliber percussion Allen vest pocket pistol with a flat hammer. This is double action "self-cocking," and has a 2-inch barrel. On the left side of the hammer is stamped *Allen's Patent* and on the right side of the barrel, S. *Sutherland, Richd. Va.* upside down.

6—A bootleg type single-shot percussion pistol with a 12-inch half-octagon barrel stamped *SUTHERLAND/Richmond,/Va.* on the top of the barrel.

It is now impossible to say with any certainty which of these Sutherland guns had a connection with the Confederacy, but there is no question that some of them did.

FOOTNOTE REFERENCE

1. Ben La Bree (editor), *The Confederate Soldier in the Civil War* (Louisville, Kentucky, 1895), p. 328. Also a reprint with preface by John S. Blay (Paterson, New Jersey, 1959).

NOTES

CHAPTER 15

George Todd

A GEORGE TODD is said to have journeyed from Montgomery, Alabama, to Austin, Texas, in 1851, and to have opened a gunsmith shop there on Second Street. Doubtless this theory is grounded in fact, but George *H*. Todd seems to have been only 14 years old in 1851, and while men matured early on the frontier in the good old days, it is unlikely that a 14-year-old would do much business as a gunsmith.[1]

Without making too careful a distinction between George and George H. Todd, however, because they were one and the same, we find that he made imitations of Colt's famous 1851 Navy revolver from about 1856 when Colt's patents expired, to 1861, when the Civil War started. This is an indisputable fact. Four of his products have been seen, three closely examined and two proven not to be altered Colts by a true acid test and Magnaflux.[2] The two tested revolvers are both identically marked *George Todd, Austin* on the right side of their steel frames and *George Todd* on the tops of their barrels, apparently with the same dies.

Evidently Todd gave his customers a choice of barrel styles, because both round and octagonal barrels have been seen. Todd made his recoil shields thicker than Colt's, and it has been noticed that his barrel keys will not always interchange. Both deviations from the Colt design can be attributed to Todd's evident lack of machinery and a consequent need for much hand fitting and finishing. His revolvers are quite obviously hand made, and it is surprising to find that the highest recorded serial number is 272.

In reply to those who would have it that Todd started his serial numbers at 100, or 200, or 250, a perfectly logical rebuttal is made by Mr. Carroll C. Holloway, who personally examined two Todd revolvers. Writing in the *Texas Gun Collector,* Holloway points out that from the expiration of the Colt basic patents in 1856 to the start of the Civil War was a considerable period of time—certainly long enough for a small business to turn out one revolver a week, or in the neighborhood of 300.[3] Further, from a practical point of view, unless Todd was boosting his own ego, what good would it do him to inflate his production in this manner? The quality of his wares was self-evident—sturdy and doubtless as reliable as Colt's, they may not have been as pretty, but they spoke with just as much authority.

In accepting the Todd revolvers as genuine, one chokes slightly over the age of the gunsmith—a mature 19 in 1856.

When the war started, Todd is said to have sold his holdings in Austin, and to have joined a firm in Lancaster which proposed to make revolvers for the state of Texas. Finding that the firm was more inclined to talk than deeds, Todd quit, and at this point he becomes two people.

Mr. H. Maxon Holloway, then Director of the Montgomery Museum of Fine Arts, wrote Richard D. Steuart on March 13, 1933, that George H. Todd had secured a government contract to repair and generally recondition arms early in the war, and that he had used brass in his work because of a general scarcity of iron and steel.

It is an indisputable fact that at least one "Confederate musket, regulation pattern, brass mounted, brass lock plate stamped *George Todd, Montgomery, Ala., 1863, C.S.*" has been seen. This weapon was offered Steuart in a letter from Yoakum, Texas, dated in the early nineteen hundreds.

So far, except for the strange age which we must attribute to Todd at the beginning of his career, his history seems to have developed in fairly logical fashion. If one wonders why Todd seems to have been two people, we now introduce the statements of George H. Todd, Jr., in answer.

In 1925, Mr. Berkley Bowie, one of the first collectors and students of Confederate arms, located the son of George H. Todd, who was then proprietor of Todd's Gun Store at 11 North Court Street in Montgomery. In reply to a letter from Bowie, the following was received:

February 3rd, 1925

Dear Sir:

Your letter of January 1st 1925 to hand. My only knowledge of Fire Arms being manufactured in Montgomery for the Confederate Government is what my father told me during his life time. My father died in 1912. He often spoke of the Winter Iron Works which was located on Commerce Street in the City of Montgomery, Ala. They manufactured "The Mississippi Rifle" which was a short musket with a bore of about ¾ of an inch in diameter. Brass trigger-guard and brass mountings. The guns were well made and well rifled and were accurate shooting.

I have seen a great many of them around Montgomery in years past but don't think there are any to be had now. I may have one among my collection.

My father manufactured Revolvers and Percussion Caps for the Confederate Government at Austin, Texas, from 1860 to 1864. I have the old lathe and a lot of the old tools which he used in the manufacture of Revolvers. The lathe is in serviceable condition at present although we never use it. We have a lot of the old musket material which my father brought back to Montgomery from Texas after the war. He often told us of casting the brass frames and guards for the Colt's revolvers which they would make up into revolvers which had been captured. In one instance he tells of over a thousand Colt's revolvers being captured in transit but were not complete and the missing parts had to be manufactured, which parts were made up on this same old lathe which I now possess.

I know very little about the Carbine Factory which was located at Tallassee, Ala. Have often heard the "Old Timers" talk about it but could not get any further data about it.

I have one of the old magazines of Antique Fire Arms but will have to look it up. My relics have been scattered about for some time and there has been no care taken of them, although they are all here in my shop.

I don't care to dispose of any of my relics at any price as I cherish them very much on account of my father.

This summer when I have more time I expect to fix up a room separately for them and when I do they will be very complete.

I don't know of the "Spiller & Burr" revolver factory.

We have a lot of the Colt's revolver material which was manufactured by my father. It is quite interesting to see what nice lathe work was done in those early days. I am enclosing you a clipping from today's advertiser which might interest you and I assure you that any time I can be of any service with information I am only too glad to help you out.

This was followed by another letter to Steuart, who worked closely with Bowie.

Feb. 9th, 1925

My Dear Mr. Steuart;—

Your nice letter of 6 inst. received. For some years past we had quite a collection of Confederate Fire Arms but the writer went to his plantation after the death of Geo. H. Todd, Sr., the writer's father and left the Gun Store in charge of a brother who has let the collection "go to hell."

Courtesy C. C. Holloway

A GEORGE TODD REVOLVER

This .36 caliber example is stamped George Todd, Austin on the frame and top of the barrel. This maker also made similar revolvers with full octagon barrels.

For eight years I enjoyed the country life but my business was nearly wrecked in the meantime.

All my relics are here in the shop but are badly scattered and every now and then I run across one and put it in place.

I am placing all my relics in one room now and expect to get them back together some day.

My father manufactured "Confederate Colt's Revolvers" at Austin, Texas, in the '60s. He often spoke of casting brass frames for them and considerable of the parts were captured from the Federals. I have the lathe and lots of the old tools which my father manufactured these brass frame Colts with.

Would be pleased to have a copy of your *Confederate Veteran* and would be glad to contribute to the welfare of it anytime I can.

Despite the strangeness of the reference to a musket with a ¾-inch bore that was well rifled by someone who should have known better, George H. Todd, Jr., seems to know what he's talking about—he should have, because he too was a gunsmith.

All things considered, it would seem logical for Todd to have returned to Austin where he had made a reputation, when his Lancaster job fell through. It is quite likely that he did, and equally likely that he worked in a state or Confederate armory or laboratory, where he not only repaired arms but also made percussion caps.

The brass framed imitation Colts defy analysis. No one has identified any, but that certainly doesn't mean that they were not made. However, it is possible that Todd meant something different from our definition of "frame." He may have meant backstrap and trigger-guard. This seems logical, because if Todd senior was repairing captured Colts, the frames would be about the last part to have been damaged.

George H. Todd, Jr., was a gun collector of some repute, and owned one of the largest collections in Alabama. He shared his father's trade and interests, and presumably spent a good deal of time listening to reminiscences of the war. Since his father did not die until 1912, it is safe to say that his recollections of his father were not those of a child, but of a mature man.

How to explain the regulation pattern Confederate musket with brass lock dated 1863? The explanation may be simpler than one imagines.

Young George might have been responsible for it. Brass handles easily and he had most of his father's tools. In fact, it has been said by collectors who knew him, that he effected other "restorations" of this nature.

But how to explain the statement by the Director of the Montgomery Museum of Fine Arts? Here again, we must consider all attempts to document the senior Todd's activities in Montgomery during the war have met with a singular lack of success, and that we have only the son's word to go on. Doubtless he furnished this statement to Mr. Holloway at the time his collection was given to the museum in the early nineteen thirties.

In summary, George H. Todd seems to have made imitation Colt Navy revolvers in Austin, Texas, from approximately 1857 to 1861. During the war he appears to have worked for the Confederate Government in an armory or laboratory or both. After the war he opened a gun shop in Montgomery, Alabama. Someone, probably his son, made certain restorations which now serve only to confuse the issue, and point up the fact that such activities are nothing new to the field of collecting.

FOOTNOTE REFERENCES

1. Todd's age was arrived at by a tortuous process of deduction based largely upon letters from Todd, Jr., and newsclips in Richard D. Steuart's papers. As has been remarked previously, the latter was in the habit of gluing clippings on a given subject in a scrapbook, but not in dating them, or noting their sources, although they do seem to fall in chronological order. Hence, when we find an entry about Todd dated November 8, 1911, followed by a clipping saying the elder Todd is 74 but hale and hearty, we may assume, safely or otherwise, that he was born 1911 minus 74, or in 1837, and from 1837 to 1856 is 19 years. Moreover, Todd junior states that his father died in 1912.

    The fact that so little is actually known of either Todd, although records certainly exist on both, should encourage some on-the-spot research. Certainly all efforts by mail have been a dismal failure.

2. Hugh Benet, Jr., "Hidden Markings," *The Gun Collector* (May, 1950), No. 32, p. 444.

3. Carroll C. Holloway, "George Todd, Austin Revolver Maker," *The Texas Gun Collector* (October, 1951), No. 15, pp. 13-15.

CHAPTER 16

Tucker, Sherrard and Company

BEING very naïve, we find it easy to be impressed with self-proclaimed knowledge, even at times with misinformation that bears only a remote resemblance to knowledge. How often at gun exhibits have we seen someone with authoritative air examine an unknown pistol and with profound wisdom solemnly state the piece in question to be either European or American because, "The stock is made from European (or American) walnut." Invariably this is said with a finality that brooks no opposition. How we have admired the man who could do this and wished we had the same ability to visually determine the source of walnut. Such ability, however, must be quite commonplace, because the circle that always surrounds this oracle is quick to echo his opinion with: "Yes, it certainly is (or is not) American walnut."

Recently we obtained a single-shot pistol that had all the earmarks of a Baltimore-made Halbach flint lock, but also some earmarks of foreign manufacture. We thought that it would be easy to establish its identity by simply finding out if the stock was made of American or European walnut. With this in view we approached the gentleman who is in charge of that section of the Smithsonian Institution that deals in forestry and woods, and laid before him our problem.

We were somewhat taken aback upon being informed unequivocally that *no one* could look at a piece of ordinary walnut and tell whether it was of American or European origin. This expert expressed strong doubts as to whether such a

distinction could be determined after microscopic examination.

We further notice that fast-draw opinion artists are usually well rounded in all other branches of knowledge, their expertness extending to many aspects relative to guns, and undoubtedly to sex, politics and the weather as well. These are the persons who upon examining any flat-framed revolver, with a slight pursing of lips and knitting of brow, condescendingly announce to their followers that this is in fact a Dance Brothers revolver. Or, if the barrel frame on this particular gun contains no loading aperture it is a "Tucker and Sherrod." We wish we had the ability to so quickly distinguish black from white without being distracted and puzzled by troubling shades of gray.

At one annual gun show we saw a grouping of several revolvers, the frames on none of which contained a loading aperture. These included some with octagon barrels, round barrels, knife foresights, pin foresights, square trigger-guards, round trigger-guards, elongated cylinder stops and even some with etched cylinders. The caption attached to this display announced it to be the largest assembly of "Confederate Tucker and Sherrods" ever grouped. It was thus apparent to us that contrary to our belief, the Tucker and Sherrard operation was a sizable one and to have such a survival ratio of so many distinctive and different models they must have had a production second only to Colt.

After gazing at this display for some time we

sought the advice of an authority, never hard to find at a gun show. We questioned several of these at length as to how and why all these pieces were identified as having the same parentage. In each case we were gently informed that they all had no loading aperture in the barrel frame which made them all "Tucker and Sherrods." In our ignorance we had previously thought this feature only meant that the gun in question had not been completely finished, otherwise, how could a bullet be inserted in the chamber if the barrel frame had no accommodation for the bullet? We were told that in loading this revolver it was necessary to separate the barrel from the rest of the gun for this particular operation, but this made little sense to us, for if this was the case, why were they all equipped with a loading lever and rammer? We further fail to see any advantage in disassembling the barrel every time it was necessary to reload.

After much soul searching, thought and due deliberation we concluded that we should go to someone who really knew what he was talking about. Incidentally, in talking about these Texas guns we know of only two persons who have engaged in serious and productive research on the subject. They are Carroll C. Holloway and Victor Friedrichs. We do not refer to them as "authorities" only because we believe they would not approve of such terminology. Let us just say that we think they know more about the subject than anyone else.

Those who are not acquainted with *Texas Gun Lore* by Holloway have a treat in store. It is written with humor, gives much information, is solidly buttressed by facts, and is recommended reading to any gun collector and especially to anyone who is considering the purchase of an allegedly Texas-made revolver or shoulder arm.

Victor Friedrichs has long been a ramrod in the Texas Gun Collectors' Association, and his name has appeared over many interesting articles dealing with Texas arms in their journal.

Upon reading the section in Holloway's book devoted to Tucker and Sherrard, and an excellent and factual article by Friedrichs entitled "Trials and Tribulations of a Confederate Gunsmith,"[1] which completely verified Mr. Hollo-

Courtesy Battle Abbey, Richmond, Virginia

TUCKER AND SHERRARD WITH SQUARE BACK TRIGGER-GUARD

This arm is .44 caliber with serial number 103 on all parts. It is of true dragoon size.

AN OCTAGON-BARRELED TUCKER AND SHERRARD

way's previously published conclusions,[2] we were gratified to see that our own thoughts on the subject were not too far afield. We cannot attempt to improve or enlarge upon their thoughts, facts or conclusions, and in setting them forth we trust that both Mr. Holloway and Mr. Friedrichs will forgive us for not using quotes on just about all that follows:

In 1861, a Labon E. Tucker, formerly a gunsmith and dealer from Marshall, Texas, his two sons Argyle W. and Elihu McDonald, Pleasant Taylor, W. L. Killen and J. H. Sherrard, local blacksmiths of Lancaster and Dallas, formed the pistol-making firm of Tucker, Sherrard and Co. Note that the spelling of the last member of the firm's name is "Sherrard."

The firm secured the services of Colonel John M. Crockett as legal counselor. The colonel was a close personal friend of Governor Lubbock and had been elected Lieutenant Governor on the same ticket that placed the latter in office. It is pertinent that Lubbock headed the Military Board which passed on all contracts for arms for the state.

On April 11, 1862, a contract was drawn up between the firm in question and the state of Texas which called for 3,000 revolvers to be supplied by the former at $40 per revolver. Of the 3,000, 1,500 were to be of .36 caliber and the balance .44 caliber. The contract was signed July 21, 1862. It is noteworthy that all official documents refer to the firm by the phonetic spelling of Tucker, Sherrod and Co. rather than by their true name of Tucker, Sherrard and Company. At the time of signing the contract the firm was advanced $5,000. Correspondence previous to this inquiring of the Military Board as to revolver design and materials to be used in their forthcoming production indicates that up until this time no work had been accomplished that could not be done with pen and pencil.

Shortly after the signing of the contract, the one person familiar with revolver making, Labon Tucker, withdrew from the firm, for reasons unknown, and thereafter the venture was operated under the name of Taylor, Sherrard and Company. It was under this name that the state gave an additional advance of $5,000 in September, 1862.

Almost immediately trouble began. The Confederate States impressed so many operatives of the plant into the armed service that on November 20, 1862, the firm was forced to report that all but three of their employees had been taken from them. This complaint was followed by notification on January 28, 1863, that the firm would be unable to complete its contract unless the state furnished ample manpower and that metal must be made available to them at a price lower than the $1 per pound they were then paying. They went on to advise the Board that their factory was tooled to produce 200 revolvers a month but that they had never had sufficient workmen to realize this potential. Nevertheless, the firm stated that as of the date of writing it had some 400 revolvers "nearly finished, lacking only a few parts."

A short time previous to this they had reported 100 revolvers nearly finished, lacking only a few parts. It is obvious that some difficulty they were unable to overcome was preventing the completion of any gun and that in the meantime the firm was continuing to stockpile unfinished revolvers. Letters from the firm to the Board continued, excusing, but not explaining the delay.

On February 28, 1863, there appeared in the *Texas Almanac* of Austin, the following: "Six Shooters—We were shown the other day a beautiful specimen of a six-shooter, manufactured in Dallas by Colonel Crockett, who has a large armory now in successful operation. The pistol appears in every respect quite equal to the famous Colt's six-shooter, of which it is an exact copy, with the exception of an extra sight on the barrel which we think is a definite improvement. We learn that Colonel Crockett has now 400 of these pistols on hand, which he has manufactured within the last six months, and which he has offered to the Governor at remarkably low figures—not one-third of what they could be sold at by retail. We hope they will not be allowed to go out of the State, as it is notorious how deficient we are in arms for home defense."

The question naturally arises: if on January 28th the firm had 400 revolvers complete except for a few unfinished parts, how did it come to pass that one month later Colonel Crockett was displaying a finished revolver? There could be three logical answers to this. One, the bottleneck besetting the firm had been overcome, and the other 399 revolvers would be finished shortly; two, a crash program had been instigated to

Courtesy Paul C. Janke

DECORATION ON CLARK-SHERRARD REVOLVER

The flat development of the cylinder decoration as shown here lacks the name of the artisan, L. S. Perkins. It would normally be found over and between the two designs.

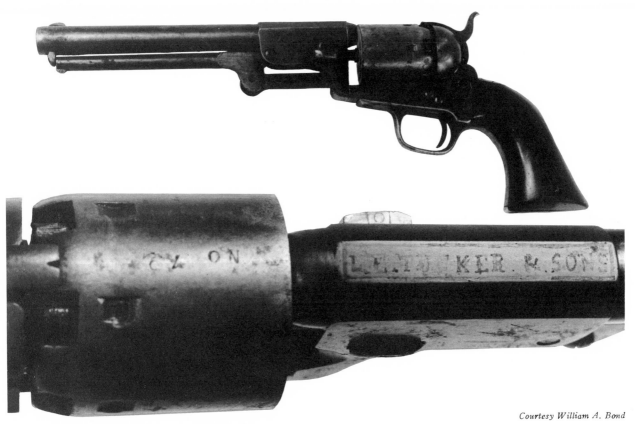

Courtesy William A. Bond

REVOLVER MARKED L. E. TUCKER & SONS

This .36 caliber iron framed specimen with brass trigger-guard and backstrap was made by L. E. Tucker of the firm of Tucker and Sherrard. The barrel and cylinder marking are shown in the accompanying detail.

make by hand sufficient parts necessary to finish this one particular gun, a not too difficult undertaking; or, three, parts from other guns were used to complete the specimen. Answer number one is out, as will be seen from subsequent facts. This leaves answer number two or three—the reader can take his choice. In either event, it makes little difference, because the gun (or guns) displayed by Colonel Crockett appears to have been the only specimen that was completed during the period of the War of Secession, and how it could possibly be identified as such is not known.

Because the firm had failed to live up to its contract and had furnished no guns to the state, their contract was canceled in the summer of 1863. The $10,000 advance was repaid to the

state with interest of $814.44. Thus died the Confederate, or Civil War venture of Sherrard, Taylor and Company (formerly Tucker, Sherrard and Company).

We next hear of the revolvers two years after the war had drawn to a bloody close. On June 1, 1867, A. S. Clark, brother-in-law of Pleasant Taylor, and foreman of the pistol factory during the period of its operations, wrote one S. W. Stone, a hardware merchant, to tell him, "We have about 400 caliber .44 old style army revolvers which we plan to embellish into high class merchandise. We are prepared to furnish you a dozen at $20 gold each." Quite obviously the "400 revolvers" were just as unfinished in 1867 as they were in January, 1863, for the wording of the letter indicates that the finishing is strictly in the future. The "we" in the letter probably referred to Sherrard, for at least two specimens of .44 caliber dragoon-sized Colt imitations have appeared marked *Clark, Sherrard & Co., Lancaster, Texas.* The further embellishing "into high class merchandise" appears to have consisted of acid etching the cylinders with figures, cannon and shields, with a large star separating the words *Texas Arms.* This etching was evidently done by one L. S. Perkins because his name is included in the design.

Of the existing specimens of "Tucker & Sherrard's" the following serial numbers are known: 2, 23, 103, 126, 160, 241 and 402. However, in the words of Mr. Holloway: "It is painfully evident that some of the numbered specimens listed above are of doubtful origin. . . . Proof that those cylinders bearing the long narrow, rectangular stops were made in Texas would be interesting to all arms students. We believe Jonathan Browning of Utah should receive credit for this type of cylinder." Mr. Holloway concludes: "The most important trait attributed to the gun is the absence of a loading aperture on the right side of the frame. Could it be that some of the barrels left the plant before they were finished? We think so."[3] So do we.

Of one gun of similar parentage there appears no doubt. That is a .36 caliber revolver with a 7¾-inch dragoon-type barrel. It has a brass backstrap and trigger-guard and the grips are cherry. It is numbered 72 on major parts, but was originally 79, having had the 9 converted into a 2 wherever it appeared. The top of the barrel housing is deeply etched *L. E. Tucker & Sons.* The barrel housing is also crudely acid etched. A partially illegible inscription on the cylinder reads *Weatherford, Parker County, 1864.*

This is the only known specimen of this type, possibly made at Marshall, Texas, by Labon E. Tucker and his two sons. It was purchased in the fall of 1950 from Hugh Dial Tucker, son of Elihu McDonald Tucker (born 1840) and grandson of Labon E. Tucker.

FOOTNOTE REFERENCES

1. Victor Friedrichs, "Trials and Tribulations of a Confederate Gunsmith," *Texas Gun Collector* (October, 1954).
2. Holloway, *Texas Gun Lore*, pp. 129-139.
3. *Ibid.*

CHAPTER 17

The Virginia Manufactory

A MONSTROUS weapon indeed is the first model Virginia Manufactory pistol, the largest in size and bore of any American military handgun. Upon first encountering a specimen, one's most probable reaction would be an exclamation of awe, not untinged with overtones of apprehension and disbelief.

Not too different was the reaction of a soldier of the eighteen sixties upon first coming face to face with the arm. To illustrate, in a letter dated June 8, 1915, Colonel John M. Payne, late Confederate States Army and Collector of the Port of Wilmington, North Carolina, recalls:

"Speaking of pistols, I will tell you an anecdote which still amuses me to think of though it occurred fifty years ago. I was the officer in charge of the Ordnance Depot at Greensboro, N. C., at the time of General Johnston's surrender. There came a young officer dressed in a brand new uniform of a Confederate captain and I saw at once that he had been a Bureau Official in Richmond where he had been used to consider himself a personage of importance. He came with a pompous self-confident air and handed me a paper signed by some cabinet officer ordering me 'to issue Captain—a pistol.'

"As soon as I had this order I made a low salaam which comported with the dignity of the occasion and called out to one of my Negro porters. 'Lawrence, get the gentleman a pistol.'

"The Negro understood me and soon appeared with a Virginia flint-lock weapon—some two feet long with enough metal in the butt end

to make it more formidable as a bludgeon than as a firearm. I made another low bow and offered it to the fellow.

"'My God' he exclaimed. 'What do you call that?'

"'A pistol, sir.'

"'I don't want that thing.'

"'I am sorry, sir, but it is all we have.'

"You could better appreciate the fun had you been on the spot like myself."

Before going into the details of these pistols, however, let us first examine their background.

In 1798 the Virginia Assembly authorized the establishment of an armory at Richmond and two arsenals elsewhere in the state. Work began

Courtesy Virginia State Library

THE VIRGINIA STATE ARMORY

This was built at Richmond, Virginia, in the early 1800's. The Virginia Manufactory arms were made here. During this time it was known as the "State" or "Virginia" armory. In 1861 it was turned over to the Confederate government and produced a large percentage of Confederate small arms and equipment.

205

on the armory shortly thereafter and by June 15, 1799, a contract for the foundation had been let to Moses Bathis.[1] By September 5, 1800, the walls of the two wings were ready to be roofed. The structure was completed in 1802, and this is the date that appears on the first arms to be turned out.

Located in Richmond, Virginia, on a narrow strip of land between the Kanawha Canal and the James River, the Armory was situated at the south end of Fifth Street facing north on the canal. Pictures show it as a very long and impressive brick structure surmounted by a huge domed cupola in its center. Two wings on either end extended back toward the river. These were joined in the rear by barracks. The square thus made was a parade ground.

Courtesy National Archives

RUINS OF THE VIRGINIA STATE ARMORY

A photograph showing destruction by fire in April, 1865. Production of Confederate materials ceased with the evacuation of Richmond.

To the immediate left was the Tredegar Iron Works, its proximity being such that the uninformed assumed it to be a portion of the Armory itself. Overlooking the establishment from the north was Gamble's Hill whose top afforded a view of the whole city of Richmond and had long been a favorite and fashionable promenade on all holidays. To the left of the Armory was the terminus of the Richmond and Petersburg Railroad.

It was here that the state of Virginia turned out quantities of arms and accouterments. The

establishment continued as an arms manufactory until the early eighteen twenties after which it fell into disuse aside from the storage of state arms and military equipment, and the housing of the "Public Guard." The "Public Guard" corresponded roughly to the National Guard of other states. In 1845, serious consideration was given to using the structure for a State Military School such as was already in operation at Lexington, in connection with the State Arsenal there, but these plans were never adopted.

Shocked by John Brown's raid on Harpers Ferry, Virginia, in 1859 and the fact that this psychotic anarchist was deified in the North rather than otherwise, an act was passed by the Virginia Assembly January 21, 1860, to refurbish the entire Armory, which by this time was in serious disrepair. Touching on this in his annual message, the Governor of Virginia was reported by the Richmond *Dispatch* of January 8, 1861: "The Act of January 21, 1860, authorized the appointment of a committee to supervise the rehabilitation of the State Armory. I appointed Col. F. H. Smith, Col. P. St. G. Cocke, both graduates of West Point and Capt. G. W. Randolph, formerly of the Navy. On the 17 of August last they reported that they had contracted with J. R. Anderson & Co. (Tredegar Iron Works) of this city to prepare the Armory for the fabrication and repair of arms. This work is now going forward with energy and success. . . ."

At the time of Virginia's secession from the Union, April 19, 1861, and her seizure of the U.S. Harpers Ferry Arsenal on the same day, the State Armory was still in process of renovation. Machinery from the Arsenal at Harpers Ferry was moved to Richmond and set up in tobacco warehouses, awaiting completion of the Armory. On July 12, 1861, George W. Munford, Secretary of State of Virginia, offered to lend all machinery and stores captured at Harpers Ferry to the Confederacy. At the same time Munford offered use of the Armory buildings in Richmond for the operation of the machinery in question.[2]

Upon the acceptance of this offer by the C.S.

Government following a bitter argument between Colonel Charles Dimmock, Virginia's Chief of Ordnance who wished to retain the property and operate it under state jurisdiction, and Major J. Gorgas, Chief of Ordnance, C.S.A., all state military stores were removed from the Armory to 7th and Cary Streets, Richmond. On October 2, 1861, the Richmond Daily *Examiner* notes: "The State Armory is at Seventh and Cary Sts. and arms should be sent there." This referred to arms which were being converted from flint to percussion. The new location was used only for storage and distribution, not for manufacture. Shortly thereafter a large portion of the Virginia State Ordnance Department moved to Lynchburg, Virginia, for it is on record that on August 12, 1862, Captain J. Hutcherson of Dublin, Virginia, was sent 93 altered percussion pistols from the "Virginia Armory, Lynchburg, Va."[3]

With its transfer to the Confederate Government the Virginia Armory building became known as the Richmond Armory and here, divorced from all state supervision, the works pursued its primary objective—to manufacture arms and equipment, but for the Confederacy rather than the state of Virginia. An extensive account of the Armory's activities after having been turned over to the C.S. Government can be found in *Confederate Arms.*

During the twenty-odd years of its early operation under state authority, the Armory was known variously as the Richmond State Armory, the Virginia Armory or the Virginia Manufactory and here were manufactured all arms and equipment necessary for the maintenance of the Virginia State Militia.

For military purposes, the state was divided into four (later five) geographic divisions. Each division was further subdivided into from four to seven Brigades, each of which was composed of approximately six regiments of infantry. A "Synopsis of the Organization of the Militia of the State of Virginia" is to be found in "Military

Laws, Adjutant General's Office" published annually by the state. An Act of January 28, 1800, made it mandatory that all arms issued Militia be marked with the number of the Regiment and/or the County to which it was issued. A complete listing follows in the hope that it may assist the collector in establishing to what part of the state his Virginia Manufactory arm was originally issued.[4]

Synopsis of the Organization of the Militia of the State of Virginia.

The 1st Division, composed of the following Brigades: 4, 11, 12 and 15. The Brigades consist of 29 regiments as follows: 4th Brig.: 1, 17, 23, 24, 29, 100, 102. 11th Brigade: 26, 42, 63, 69, 84, 101. 12th Brig.: 10, 18, 43, 53, 64, 91, 110, 117. 15th Brig.: 22, 39, 50, 66, 73, 83, 96 and 98th—totaling 29 regiments.

The 2nd Division, composed of four Brigades as follows: 1, 3, 5 and 6. These Brigades are made up of the following regiments: 1st Brig.: 3, 5, 16, 30, 34, 82. 3rd Brig.: 12, 28, 38, 40, 47, 88, 90. 5th Brig.: 25, 36, 44, 45, 85, 89. 6th Brig.: 56, 57 and 60—totaling 22 regiments. The 3rd Division composed of seven Brigades as follows: 7, 10, 13, 16, 17, 18, 19 and 20. The Brigades are composed as follows: 7th Brig.: 13, 32, 58, 93, 97, 116. 10th Brig.: 4, 76, 104, 118, 103, 123. 13th Brig.: 8, 48, 79, 80, 81, 106, 120, 121, 126. 16th Brig.: 31, 51, 55, 67, 122. 17th Brig.: 70, 72, 78, 94, 105, 112, 124. 18th Brig.: 114, 77, 14, 46. 19th Brig.: 108, 75, 35, 86. 20th Brig.: 11, 119, 107, 113, 125—totaling 46 regiments.

The 4th Division is composed of five Brigades as follows: 2, 8, 9, 14 and 21. These five Brigades are composed as follows: 2nd Brig.: 33, 68, 74, 19, 115, 52. 8th Brig.: 15, 29, 59, 62, 65, 71. 9th Brig.: 7, 20, 54, 95. 14th Brig.: 6, 9, 21, 37, 41, 61, 87, 92, 109, 111. 21st Brig.: 2, 27, 99—totaling 29 Regiments.

Total of 4 Divisions, 21 Brigades and 126 Regiments.

CAVALRY AND ARTILLERY

There are four regiments of each. They are raised within the respective divisions of the Militia, and are distinguished by the same numbers. The battalions of each also correspond with each other.

1ST REGIMENT

1st Battalion—Composed of the Troops and Companies raised within the 4th and 12th Brigades.

2nd Battalion—Composed of the Troops and Companies raised within the 11th and 15th Brigades.

2ND REGIMENT

1st Battalion—Composed of the Troops and Companies raised within the 1st and 3rd Brigades.

2nd Battalion—Composed of the Troops and Companies raised within the 5th and 6th Brigades.

3RD REGIMENT

1st Battalion—Composed of the Troops and Companies raised within the 7th, 13th, 17th and 19th Brigades.

2nd Battalion—Composed of the Troops and Companies raised within the 10th, 16th, 18th and 20th Brigades.

4TH REGIMENT

1st Battalion—Composed of the Troops and Companies raised within the 8th, 9th and 21st Brigades.

2nd Battalion—Composed of the Troops and Companies raised within the 2nd and 14th Brigades.

The following are the Regiments in Virginia arranged in numerical order with the counties in which they are located:

1—Amelia
2—Accomack
3—Orange
4—Ohio
5—Culpeper
6—Essex
7—Norfolk
8—Augusta
9—King and Queen
10—Bedford
11—Harrison
12—Flyvanna
13—Shenandoah
14—Hardy
15—Sussex
16—Spottsylvania
17—Campbell
18—Patrick
19—City of Richmond
20—Princess Anne
21—Gloucester
22—Mecklenburg

23—Chesterfield
24—Buckingham
25—King George
26—Charlotte
27—Northampton
28—Nelson
29—Isle of Wight
30—Caroline
31—Frederick
32—Augusta
33—Henrico
34—Culpeper
35—Wythe
36—Prince William
37—Northumberland
38—Goochland
39—Town of
    Petersburg
40—Louisa
41—Richmond
    County
42—Pittsylvania

43—Franklin
44—Fauquier
45—Stafford
46—Pendelton
47—Albemarle
48—Botetourt
49—Nottoway
50—Greensville
51—Frederick
52—New Kent and
    Charles City
53—Campbell
54—Norfolk Borough
55—Jefferson
56—Loudoun
57—Loudoun
58—Rockingham
59—Nansemond
60—Fairfax
61—Mathews
62—Prince George
63—Prince Edward

64—Henry
65—Southampton
66—Brunswick
67—Berkeley
68—James City and
    part of York
69—Halifax
70—Washington
71—Surry
72—Russell
73—Lunenburg
74—Hanover
75—Montgomery
76—Monongalia
77—Hampshire
78—Grayson
79—Greenbrier
80—Kanawha
81—Bath
82—Madison
83—Dinwiddie
84—Halifax

85—Fauquier
86—Giles
87—King William
88—Albemarle
89—Prince Wm. con-
      solidated with
      36th Regt.
90—Amherst
91—Bedford
92—Lancaster
93—Augusta
94—Lee
95—Norfolk Co.
96—Brunswick
97—Shenandoah
98—Mecklenburg
99—Accomack
100—Buckingham
101—Pittsylvania
102—Powhatan
103—Brooke
104—Preston

105—Washington
106—Mason
107—Randolph
108—Monroe
109—Middlesex
110—Franklin
111—Westmoreland
112—Tazewell
113—Wood
114—Hampshire
115—Eliz. City, War-
      wick and part
      of York
116—Rockingham
117—Campbell
118—Monongalia
119—Harrison
120—Cabell
121—Botetourt
122—Frederick
123—Tyler
124—Lewis
125—Nicholas

From the "Synopsis" it will be noted regarding cavalry and artillery that "There are four regiments of each. They are raised within the respective Division of the Militia and (their designation as to Regiment) are distinguished by the same numbers (as those of the Division to which they are assigned)." Thus, cavalry and artillery arms are found only with a "Regiment" number and not with the name of the County as on the infantry weapons. For cavalry and artillery the "Regiment" number is actually the number of the Division. Thus, a cavalry pistol stamped *1st Va. Regt.* means that it had been issued to a troop assigned to the 1st Division and composed of troops and companies raised within the 4th, 11th, 12th or 15th Brigades. As these four Brigades were composed of 29 different regiments it can be seen that the arm in question could have been used by someone attached to any one of these infantry regiments.

Although all types of military arms and equipment were produced at the Virginia Manufactory Armory, we are concerned primarily with the pistols made there. These were of two models and were made between the years 1805 and 1821.

The first model pistols date from 1805 through 1811 inclusive and appear to have been strictly a salvage operation; a means of utilizing otherwise unusable musket and rifle parts. The result was the largest American military handgun ever produced, varying in length from 17½ to 18½ inches overall. The .69 caliber musket barrel was 12 to 12½ inches long, held to the stock by a double fore-end band. All metal furniture was iron except the brass foresight. There was no rear sight. The lock was the rifle lock stamped in the center *VIRGINIA* with *Manufactory* beneath. *Richmond* with the year of manufacture is stamped behind the gooseneck hammer. The ball (or flat) headed iron ramrod is held in the stock by friction and in addition by a spring spoon attached to the bottom of the barrel and inlet into the stock. Except for minor variations such as an absence of the barrel band retaining spring on some, all the early model pistols were the same.

Coincident with the War of 1812, and possibly because of it as well as for other unknown reasons, all Virginia arms were redesigned at about this time. The musket dropped its gooseneck hammer in favor of one which was reinforced. The rifle, except for retaining its full stock, became very similar to the Harpers Ferry Model 1803, even to the substitution of brass for the previously used iron furnishings.

The greatest changes, however, were in the pistols. The new (or second) model in general conformed to the Harpers Ferry Model 1805, being half-stocked, all brass-mounted, with a .54 caliber 10-inch barrel and an overall length of 15½ inches. This was definitely no salvage operation and no spare parts went into its making. The heavy iron butt-cap of the early model was replaced by one of brass whose arms extended up the grip. The entire weapon was a handsome and graceful piece, although somewhat heavier overall than the Harpers Ferry it copied.

The lock on the new arm was considerably smaller than the one previously used. It is stamped in the center *VIRGINIA* with *Richmond* and the date behind the reinforced hammer. The word "Manufactory" was omitted. In 1815 the markings were changed once again, this time to *RICHMOND* in the center of the lock and only the date behind the hammer. This applies also to those dated 1816, and presumably thereafter.

It has been generally believed that 1816 was the last year of manufacture for pistols, none having turned up bearing a later date. However, a quick look at the records shows such a belief to be erroneous. Their manufacture continued as long as the Armory was in operation.

On March 3, 1821, the Virginia General Assembly passed an act to the effect that as of January 1, 1822, all manufacture at the Armory would cease, and thereafter the premises would be used as an Arsenal for the storage of arms. Further, no new work was to be started and activities would be confined to the completion of arms whose manufacture had already begun.

The report of the Armory Committee, dated December 20, 1821, for the year 1821, reveals that during this last year of operation the Armory produced 2,508 muskets with bayonets, 206 rifles, 2,063 swords and 18 pistols. As there are rifles and muskets extant bearing the date 1821, it must be assumed that the 18 pistols would also bear this date, but none have as yet appeared to prove this point.

The Armory Committee also reported that as of December 20, 1821,[5] the arms on deposit in

Courtesy William M. Locke

TWO MODELS OF THE VIRGINIA MANUFACTORY PISTOL

Two exceptionally fine specimens are shown. The upper one is the first model with the 1805 date on the lock plate. The lower is a second model bearing the date of 1813 on the lock plate and with a swivel ramrod.

Courtesy William A. Albaugh, III

A FIRST MODEL CONVERSION

Showing the first model Virginia Manufactory pistol converted to percussion. The overall length of this weapon is nearly 18 inches. The lock is dated 1808. See detail view of conversion.

the Armory were as follows: 31,703 Virginia muskets with bayonets, 2,531 muskets furnished by the Federal Government under state quota, 2,213 rifles, 5,387 swords and 836 pistols. Judging from this, it would appear that about 40 muskets were made for each pistol and each 14 rifles.

In addition to lock stampings, most parts of both first and second models show what appears to be a serial which usually takes the form of the same number stamped twice, such as 33, 55, 88, etc. In some cases under the barrel and on the inside bow of trigger-guard a number has been observed to have been repeated four or five times.

The converted 1808 first model pistol illustrated bears innumerable stampings: No. 88 is on the underside of the barrel, and on the stock under the backstrap. A raised *W* in a sunken cartouche is to be found in the metal on the underside of the backstrap. *UII* appears on the left side of the barrel and inside of the lock plate which also contains the letter S. No. 1 is also stamped on the underside of the barrel

inside of the butt cap, and inside of the counter plate. The lock plate and ramrod are marked with Roman numerals. The barrel is stamped *P* (proved) at the breech, this being noted only occasionally on the Virginia arms.

The 1808 flint pistol illustrated is original throughout and is marked as follows: *33* on the outside of the counterplate, top of the barrel, trigger-plate, trigger-guard, butt cap, fore-end band and on the stock near the hammer. The inside of the counter plate, the underside of the butt cap and barrel are stamped with *99* over *22222*. The inside of the trigger-guard bow is stamped *99*. The inside of the lock plate is stamped with *W* and a fancy raised *S* in a sunken cartouche. All lock screw heads bear what appears to be a small half moon. The ramrod has two sets of unrelated Roman numerals.

Another pistol of this same date, also an original flint, was stamped with *20* on various parts in addition to *66666* under the barrel, inside the bow of the trigger-guard and behind the counter plate. The barrel top on this gun was stamped *3, V, a REG,t*. Still another original flint pistol is marked on most parts with *111* followed by *JJ*. The barrel top is stamped *P* (proved) and *2, V, a REG,t.*

A controversial feature on the second model is the ramrod. Some collectors insist that all second models were made with a swivel ramrod. The authors have personally examined a sufficient number which were never made with a swivel so as to question whether any were ever originally made in this manner. Bearing in mind that these guns were almost a direct copy of the Harpers Ferry Model 1805 (1806) which took a wooden rod, it seems unlikely that any such radical departure in design as the addition of a swivel rod would have been made. Also bearing in mind that these pistols were primarily for cavalry, it seems more likely that while furnished originally with a wooden rod, a swiveled metal rod was added later to lessen the danger of losing an unattached rod while attempting to load on horseback. Still another theory has it that those without swivel rods were for infantry and that the cavalry pistols were made originally with the swivel. The reader can take his choice until later research shows which is correct.

The U.S. Ordnance Manual of 1850 describes the alteration of flint to percussion arms as follows: "The Barrel is altered, 1st by closing the vent in the side, and boring a new vent on the upper part of the barrel, and putting in a percussion cone. The screw thread of the cone is a little shorter than for newly-made percussion arms, so that it may not project into the bore.

"The lock is altered; 1st by removing the cock, the battery, battery screw; 2nd, by cutting off the pan, near the face of the lock plate, filling up the hollow of the remaining part with brass, soldered in, and dressing off the upper surface even with the top of the lock plate; 3rd, replacing the cock by a percussion hammer; 4th, filling up the holes of the battery screw and the battery spring screw with pieces of these screws, rounded on the outer end, and filling in the pivot hole of the battery spring with wire."

This was the early and simple alteration, although the finished job added no beauty to the arm and to our eyes, 100 years later, appears rather unprofessional. The U.S. Ordnance authorities seem to have felt much the same way, because in the mid eighteen fifties this type of alteration was stopped and a more complicated method adopted: cutting off the breech end of the barrel and supplying a forging with a bolster as a nipple seat which was either brazed onto or screwed into the breech end of the barrel, the effect being to supply the piece with an

Courtesy William A. Albaugh, III
DETAIL VIEW OF CONVERSION

This illustrates the form of alteration of the first model Virginia Manufactory Pistol, from flint to percussion.

entire new breech. The external parts of the flint lock were removed and the top of the lock plate filed to conform to the shape of the new bolster.

As of September 30, 1860, the state of Virginia had the following arms on hand: 422 muskets, rifled; 2,659 muskets, percussion; 53,988 muskets, flint lock; 56,014 bayonets; 80 cavalry musketoons; 90 artillery musketoons; 31 sappers' and miners' musketoons; 725 carbines; 1,020 rifles, percussion; 3,293 rifles, flint lock; 94 rifles, Sharps; 246 rifles, Colt; 185 rifles with sword bayonets; 1,317 revolvers; 3,675 cavalry swords; 703 artillery swords and 1,347 horseman's pistols, flint lock. These arms were divided between the State Militia, in Depot (for service in emergency), in the Lexington Arsenal and the Richmond Armory. Of the pistols, 1,021 were in the hands of the Militia, 210 in Depot and 116 in the Richmond Armory.[6] Once again the ratio will be noted as approximately 40 muskets to each pistol.

In 1861 and 1862, thousands of Virginia manufactory rifles, muskets and pistols were altered from flint to percussion. Those sufficiently interested can go to our National Archives and scan Volume 116, Captured Rebel Ordnance Records, which gives in detail the number of pieces altered, the dates, and by whom the job was done.

Small individual gunsmiths such as S. Sutherland and Thomas Addams, did a portion of this altering and the work done by this type of contractor is characterized by the early method alteration (screwing a nipple into the barrel and adding a percussion hammer) or by screwing a drum with attached nipple into the original vent and cutting just enough off the top of the lock plate so that it would fit snugly around the drum. In some instances the external parts of the old flint lock were not removed. Records show that for such conversions the smiths were paid about $3.17 apiece.

The largest contractors for alterations were S. C. Robinson, the Union Manufacturing Company and F. Persignon, and W. B. and C. Fisher of Lynchburg. This work began in 1861 and continued through 1862. The following examples give some idea of its extent. The Union Manufacturing Company altered 3,080 arms during the months of August, September, October and November, 1861, of which 172 were

rejected because of defective cone seats, or loose hammers. During the same period of time, S. C. Robinson altered 3,444 with 205 rejected. F. Persignon is noted to have altered 181 pieces with seven rejected from October 17 to November 28, 1861.

These larger contractors used the later and more professional appearing-type alteration involving an entire new bolster for the nipple seat, but unlike the U.S. Ordnance Department which cut off the end of the barrel and inserted a new breech, the Southerners used only a new bolster which was borax welded to the breech end of the barrel, and the top of the lock cut out to fit snugly around the bolster. There are several distinctive shapes to these bolsters and undoubtedly additional study and research will ultimately link the various shapes to the proper contractor.

Existing records of the Civil War contain innumerable references to "repair" and/or "alteration" of arms by both North and South. Such work was done by the government, by State Armories, or by individual gunsmiths and the methods used in the North or the South were similar if not identical. Thus, holding an early model Springfield altered from flint lock to percussion, we have no way of knowing where or exactly when the gun assumed its present form. Had it been the custom to sign and date such conversions, those with Southern markings would be gladly accepted today by collectors as secondary Confederates. Unfortunately, this is not the case, and we know of only one type of altered weapon that can be accepted as Confederate on face value. These are the products of the Virginia Manufactory. As a matter of fact, even in original flint, practically all saw active service in the war. In the case of the altered arms, it should be remembered that most conversions were made in 1861 or 1862 for the sole purpose of having a more modern arm to point northward.

Thus it is that Virginia Manufactory products share with those made at the Palmetto Armory, Columbia, South Carolina, the status of being the most desirable of the secondary Confederate single-shot pistols.

FOOTNOTE REFERENCES

1. Calendar of Virginia State Papers, Vol. 9.
2. *O.R.*, Series 4, Vol. 1, p. 469.
3. *C.R.O.R.*, Vol. 105, 8-12-62.
4. *Military Laws, Adjudant General's Office* (Richmond, Virginia, 1820).
5. Journal and Documents of the House of Delegates, 1821-1822.
6. *O.R.*, Series 4, Vol. 1, p. 387.

PART IV

CHAPTERS 18 and 19

PERSONS AND PLACES

A listing of Persons and Places associated with the Southern arms industry, and presenting a selection of illustrations of arms in the Associate class as defined in the Introduction

BIBLIOGRAPHICAL NOTES

Concise Bibliographical data and concluding with an Addendum comprising the Confederate patent records as they apply to "Firearms including Implements and Machinery of War, etc.," for the years 1861 through 1864

CHAPTER 18

Persons and Places

THIS chapter includes reminders and cautions. In addition to the numerous persons definitely known to have been engaged in the repair, production, procurement or sale of those Confederate arms which actually saw service in the great conflict, a number of others are worthy of mention. All of these are known to have had some connection with Confederate handguns. A miscellany of the weapons repaired, made or purveyed by them is illustrated in this chapter, together with some pertinent comments on the persons and places involved.

Unfortunately, it is all too easy to allow enthusiasm to outweigh logic when a weapon of known connection to a maker, who was active within the period of our interest, comes to hand. Thus the pitfall of "authenticity by association" is ever present and must be avoided at all costs. Unless the piece in question has a documented history of use in the war, or can be accurately dated by some other means, such as the period during which its serial number falls, it cannot be considered to have "Civil War" association, regardless of whose stamp it bears.

Since such a bewildering variety of arms was used, it often requires a good deal of will-power to prevent the heart from mastering the head.

In addition, it must be borne in mind that many of these gunmakers, importers and dealers were active before and after the 1861-1865 period, as well as during the hostilities. Any arm made, altered or sold by them may be very attractive as a true Southern arm, a desirable collector's item for a number of reasons, but

should not be considered a true Confederate *war* item unless the foregoing criteria apply.

The authors have viewed specimens or photos of arms by many of the following persons or companies and have used in this directory only those illustrations that were thought to best serve as visual references for collectors in this special field.

The listing which follows, therefore, should be considered with these facts in mind.

ADAMS REVOLVERS

John Adams of Dalston, England, patented a .44 caliber double-action revolver on November 7, 1857. Those made by the London Armoury Company, London, England, are thought to be Confederate. On November 6, 1860, Adams assigned his patent to Thomas Poultney of Baltimore, Maryland.

On January 21, 1861, the Virginia State Ordnance Department received 999 "new Adams revolvers" made by the London Armoury Company to equip its State Troops. (Virginia Calendar of State Papers.)

For further reference to the London Armoury Company, see Part II, Chapter 8.

ADAMS, SOLOMON

Solomon Adams came to Virginia from Massachusetts in 1860 to accept the position of Master Armorer of the state of Virginia. In 1861 he was sent to visit the Harpers Ferry and Springfield Armories to copy patterns to use at the Richmond Armory, permission having been granted by the U.S. Secretary of War. On January 14, 1862, Adams was commissioned Master Armorer in Confederate Ordnance, and remained in charge of the Richmond Armory throughout the war. (Acts of C. S. Congress, Vol. 1, p. 671 and Official Records Series III, Vol. 1, p. 9.)

ADDAMS, THOMAS, JR.—Richmond, Virginia

A gunsmith of Richmond, who was paid $910.52 on July 2, 1862, by the state of Virginia for altering 91 Virginia rifles, 41 Deringer rifles, 59 muskets and 94 pistols. He received $788 on August 1, 1862, for altering 188 Virginia rifles and 12 Deringer rifles.

ALLEN AND DIAL—Columbia, South Carolina

Gun dealers of Columbia, South Carolina, who on January 3, 1861, advertised in the Richmond *Daily Examiner*, "Rifles and pistols. Mounted men solicited to buy from our stock."

ALLEN AND HILLE—New Orleans, Louisiana

Gunsmiths located at 79 Magazine Street, New Orleans, Louisiana (1853 New Orleans City Directory), who are believed to have made a limited number of pistols. Principal in the firm was Joseph Allen.

APALACHICOLA, Florida

Site of a U.S. Arsenal until seized by the state of Florida on January 5, 1861. It then operated as a Confederate Ordnance Station. At the time of its seizure the Arsenal contained 57 flintlock muskets, 7 flintlock rifles, 110 percussion muskets, 103 percussion rifles, 118 Hall's carbines and 98 pistols.

BAILEY, D.—New Orleans, Louisiana

Name found on an English-made Tranter-type revolver.

BAILEY, THOMAS—New Orleans, Louisiana

An English gunsmith who came to New Orleans and made fine rifles which closely followed the English pattern. Also made a 5-shot percussion .36 caliber revolver with 4½-inch barrel marked with his name. After the capture of New

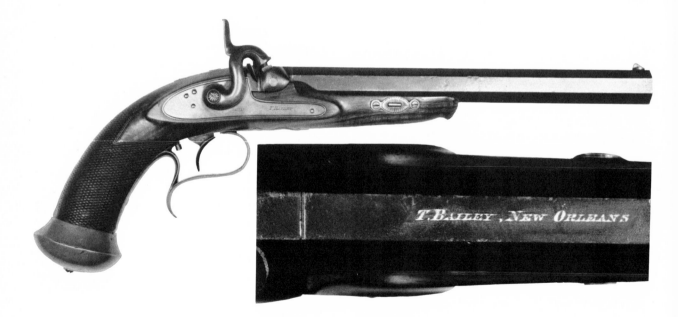

Courtesy Miles W. Standish

SINGLE-SHOT PISTOL

The lock is stamped T. Bailey and the top flat of the barrel T. Bailey, New Orleans, as shown in the enlarged detail.

Orleans by U.S. forces in 1863, no record can be found of him.

The 1853 New Orleans City Directory lists Bailey as operating from 160½ Chartres St.

BEARDEN, L. J. E.—Galveston, Texas

A gun dealer whose name appears on a large silver-mounted derringer-type pistol with 2¾-inch barrel made by Van Wart and Son Company.

BEAUMONT-ADAMS REVOLVERS—England

"Shipped impartially to both sides during the Civil War." (J. N. George, *English Pistols & Revolvers.*)

BEAUREGARD AND SLIDELL—Charleston, South Carolina

It has long been reputed that G. T. Beauregard and his brother-in-law John Slidell formed a partnership in the early part of the war for the purchase of arms and that they were the Southern agents for Butterfield revolvers.

BEAUVAIR, R.—St. Louis, Missouri

A gunsmith of St. Louis who reputedly supplied arms to Southern sympathizers during the war, and may possibly have made brass-framed revolvers of the Whitney model.

BECHTLER, CHRISTOPHER—Rutherford, North Carolina

Made a .28 caliber "end over end" pistol with two hammers and triggers with the two barrels extending in opposite directions. The triggerguard formed a main spring for each barrel. Overall length 5 inches. Frame of brass with *Christopher Bechtler* engraved on one side and *North Carolina* on the other. Circa 1850. Bechtler was better known for gold coins which he minted and which bear his name.

BITTERLICH, FRANK J.—16 Deaderick St., Nashville, Tennessee

A gunsmith who made derringer-type pistols marked with his name and address, and who also supplied various dealers, in which case the dealer's name was frequently stamped on the barrel or lock and Bitterlich's name and address was stamped on the underside of the barrel. It is possible that Bitterlich supplied some of the so-called Schneider and Glassick revolvers.

BOURNE, WILLIAM—Savannah, Georgia

Reports persist that this individual made imitation Colt and Remington revolvers stamped *W. B., C.S.A.* This marking is more likely to be found on a faked piece.

BOURON, P., AND SONS—New Orleans, Lousiana

A gunsmith and dealer who, in 1853, according to the New Orleans City Directory for that year, operated from 259 Bayou Road, but later moved to 534 Chartres Street. His firm was composed of himself and his son, Louis L., and their names are to be found on various guns and pistols. Philipe Bouron had a contract with the Confederate Ordnance Department to remove the Maynard primers from a number of guns captured from the Federal Government.

BURTON, JAMES HENRY

Born at Shennondale Springs, Jefferson County, Virginia, of English parents, August 17, 1823. Educated at Westchester Academy until the age of 16 when he entered a Baltimore machine shop as an apprentice. In 1844 went to work at Harpers Ferry Arsenal and was appointed a foreman the following year. He later became Master Armorer and held this position until 1854 when he left to become Chief Engineer of the Royal Small-arms Factory at Enfield, England. In 1860, he returned to this country where he was commissioned a Lieutenant Colonel in the Ordnance Department of Virginia. He was placed in charge of the rebuilding of the Virginia State Armory. When Harpers Ferry was captured, Burton superintended the removal of all machinery to Richmond. In September, 1861, he was commissioned a Lieutenant Colonel of the Confederate Ordnance Corps and placed in charge of the Richmond Armory. In the summer of 1862 he was ordered South to establish a permanent Armory for the Confederacy. Macon, Georgia, was chosen as the site, and by the end of the war a large and handsome Armory was almost completed.

During the war Burton was active in several arms-making enterprises, being an active partner in the pistol manufactory of Spiller and Burr.

After the war he was employed by the firm of Greenwood and Batley of England who were engaged to supply machinery for a small arms factory at Tula, Russia, for the manufacture of the Berdan rifle.

Burton returned to Virginia in 1873 and engaged in farming until his death on October 18, 1894.

BYINGTON, J. S.—Nashville, Tennessee

On September 27, 1861, sold to Lieutenant M. H. Wright, the Commanding Officer in Nashville, Tennessee, 25 "Navy repeaters" at $45 each. (Volume 19, Captured Rebel Records, Archives.)

CALHOUN, W. H.—Nashville, Tennessee

The barrel of a *Deringer Philadelphia* pistol is also stamped *Manufactured for W. H. Calhoun,* Agent, Nashville, Tennessee.

CLARK, F. H.—Memphis, Tennessee

Gun dealers who were agents for Henry Deringer of Philadelphia and whose name is to be found on such pistols. One such is 8 inches overall, .45 caliber, silver-mounted with a 4⅝-inch barrel, the top of which is stamped *F. H. Clark, Memphis.*

CLARKSON, ANDERSON AND COMPANY—Richmond, Virginia

Advertised in the Richmond *Dispatch,* June 13, 1861, "Bowie knives and pistols for sale. 106 Main St." On December 31, 1861, Clarkson and Company, 106 Main Street, advertised in the Richmond *Daily Examiner,* "Virginia made bowie knives at reduced prices."

COCKE, S. B.—Richmond, Virginia

A gunsmith whose name is occasionally found on Kentucky rifles and altered Virginia Manufactory pistols.

COX AND SON—Atlanta, Georgia

A .36 caliber percussion under-hammer single-shot pistol stamped *Cox & Son, Atlanta, Ga., 1847,* with an 8½-inch, part-round, part-octagon rifled barrel with an open rear and hooded front sight was offered in 1847. The grip was of the saw handle type and the trigger-guard acted as a main spring.

DEANE AND ADAMS REVOLVERS

According to Colonel William Couper, page 50, "One Hundred Years of the VMI," 999 Deane and Adams revolvers were purchased by the state of Virginia and received January 21, 1861. Colonel Couper is evidently referring to the "999 new Adams revolvers" already mentioned.

In a private collection is an Adams, Deane and Adams revolver stamped on the underside of the barrel, *F. Hainline, 8 Ky. Cav., C.S.A.* Hainline is reported to have been a member of General Morgan's cavalry.

DEVISME REVOLVERS

Made in .36 and .45 caliber, 12 inches long, six-shot 4½-inch octagon barrel. Loading tool in butt, false hammer (cocking lever) on side. Left side of frame marked *Devisme, bte;* on top of barrel, *Devisme à Paris.* Cylinder, frame and other parts elaborately engraved. Belgian proof marks.

As Devisme of Paris was the maker of the exquisite sword carried by General Robert E. Lee, it is reasonable to assume that some of the Devisme revolvers went South, although they are not Confederate *per se.*

DIMICK, H. E.—St. Louis, Missouri

A maker or dealer in imitation Colts, Dimick had absolutely no connection with the Confederacy.

DIMMOCK, CHARLES—Richmond, Virginia

A Northerner who came South as Commanding Officer of the Virginia State Armory. Remained in this capacity during the war with the rank of Brevet Brigadier General.

DONNAN, W. S., AND COMPANY—Richmond, Virginia

This firm was in the hardware business for years before the war. Flintlock rifles, shotguns and pistols appear with the firm name stamped on the lock plate. After World War II, a case of flint pistol locks was discovered in this firm's warehouse, having been there for over 100 years.

ERICHSON, H.—Houston, Texas

A name appearing on derringer-type pistols.

EYLAND AND HAYDEN—Charleston, South Carolina

Jewelers and importers, 250 King Street, Charleston, South Carolina, 1833 to 1835. Upon the death of Eyland, Augustus H. Hayden and one Gregg operated under the trade name of Gregg and Hayden until about 1850, when it became Hayden and Whilden (A. H. Hayden and William G. Whilden). The firm imported many fine English pistols and swords.

Courtesy William A. Albaugh, III

LARGE SINGLE-SHOT PISTOL

The top flat of the barrel is engraved: Imported by Eyland & Hayden, Charleston, S. C. The hammer safety thumb-piece and the ramrod and pipe are missing from this English-made pistol.

FISHER, W. B. AND C.—Lynchburg, Virginia

Gunsmiths and agents who operated from a shop on Main Street in Lynchburg. According to

a letter from Mrs. S. O. Fisher to E. Berkley Bowie, dated September 8, 1925, the Fishers were originally from Strasburg, Virginia, but moved to Lynchburg before the war. The family consisted of the father, eight sons and two daughters. The father and four of the sons (Levy, William B., Cyrus, and George) went into the gun business, of which apparently William B. and Cyrus were the principals. The youngest son, S. O. Fisher, worked at a bench in the gun shop. During the war the firm manufactured percussion caps.

On August 14, 1862, the firm was paid $336.19 for altering 101 Virginia flintlock muskets and an additional $484.88 on September 22, 1862, for altering 152 Virginia muskets.

The firm's name is occasionally encountered stamped on Colt revolvers as agents. A .36 caliber single-shot percussion pistol with 3-inch half-round barrel, flat-top hammer and checkered walnut grips is stamped, *W. B. & C. Fisher, Lynchburg, Va., Patented 1845 Etc.*

FOLSOM, H., AND Co.—St. Louis, Missouri and New Orleans, Louisiana

A gunsmith who, while in St. Louis, Missouri, in the eighteen fifties, was connected with H. E. Dimick and possibly Charles H. Rigdon (of Leech and Rigdon). No guns bearing his name with the St. Louis address are known although a few swords so marked have appeared. Being of strong Southern sympathies, Folsom left St. Louis in the late eighteen fifties and proceeded to New Orleans where he went into the gun business at 55 Chartres Street. Various English imports have been found bearing his name. One such is a 5-shot, double-action .40 caliber English-made revolver with no cocking spur on the hammer. It is engraved *H. Folsom & Co., Chartres St., N.O.* on the right side of the barrel. The grips are checkered walnut and the frame and trigger-guard are nicely engraved. The gun bears Birmingham (England) proof marks. *See also* Kitterage and Folsom.

GERALD, J.—Alabama

A cutlass pistol of the Elgin type, but English-made, has been observed having *J. Gerald, Alabama, C.S.A.* engraved on the top of its octagon barrel.

GODWIN, THOMAS W., AND CO.—Norfolk, Virginia

The Macon, Georgia, *Telegraph* of June 26, 1861, states, "Thomas Godwin, an ingenious mechanic of Portsmouth, Va., has invented a revolver which fires nine times, each barrel discharging separately at intervals. The machinery is much more simple than that in the Colt's repeater. A Bowie-knife is also attached which may be unshipped or retained in service at pleasure." No specimen of this revolver is known to have survived. Godwin was the operator of the Virginia Iron Works at Norfolk.

GRATIOT MANUFACTURING COMPANY—St. Louis, Missouri

Reputedly made .44 caliber percussion revolvers. Nothing further is known.

GREGG AND HAYDEN—Charleston, South Carolina

See Eyland and Hayden.

GRISWOLD, A. B., AND COMPANY—New Orleans, Louisiana

A gunsmith-dealer operating from 15 Chartres Street, New Orleans. English Tranters have been found marked *A. B. Griswold & Co., New Orleans*. Griswold was first a clerk in the firm of Hyde and Goodrich and then a partner in the firm of Thomas, Griswold and Co. who made many fine swords for the Confederacy.

GUIGNARD—Columbia, South Carolina

See Radcliffe and Guignard

GUION AND SON—New Orleans, Louisiana

A gunsmith and dealer. An English Tranter is known to bear the name of *F. T. Guion, New Orleans, La.*, and a Wurfflein derringer is marked the same on its lock plate.

The New Orleans City Directory of 1861 lists a Thomas Guion at 20 Saint Charles, as a dealer in "guns, rifles and sporting apparatus."

HAPPOLDT AND MURRAY—Columbus, Georgia

A gun and sporting goods dealer in the late 1850s. The firm was composed of J. H. Happoldt and John P. Murray.

HAPPOLDT, J. H.—Charleston, South Carolina

Son of J. M. Happoldt. Entered the gunsmithing business with John P. Murray in Columbus, Georgia. At least one percussion single-shot pistol is known, bearing the name of J. H. Happoldt. He is also believed to have made breech-loading arms.

HAPPOLDT, J. M.—Charleston, South Carolina

A dealer and gunsmith operating from the northeast corner of Meeting and Cumberland Streets in the mid-eighteen fifties, he made a general line of percussion sporting arms, single-shot pistols and cased dueling pistols with accessories. His pieces were finely made and are much sought after today.

HARPERS FERRY, VIRGINIA (now West Virginia)

Site of the U.S. Arsenal and Armory whose activities have been so fully documented by other sources that only brief mention is necessary here. The flintlock pistols made at Harpers Ferry were used as a pattern by the state of Virginia for those made at the State Armory in Richmond from 1812 to 1821.

HARTLEY, MAJOR

Connected with the Colt Arms Company, and on December 17, 1859, was in communication with the Governor of Virginia regarding the construction of an Armory for the manufacture of Colt revolvers within the state of Virginia. (Virginia Papers, Doc. No. 7, No. 14462, page 509.)

HAWES AND WAGGONER—Charleston, South Carolina

This name and address appears on a Philadel-

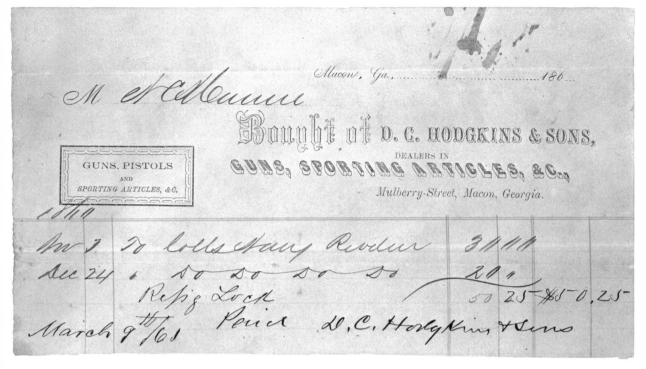

RECEIPT FOR COLT'S NAVY REVOLVERS

This receipted bill from D. C. Hodgkins & Sons, Macon, Georgia, is evidence that Colt revolvers were available in the deep South, at almost the beginning of the War years.

phia-type derringer single-shot percussion pistol of about .41 caliber and 3-inch barrel with engraved German silver mounts. Nothing further known of this company.

HAYDEN, AUGUSTUS H.—Charleston, South Carolina

Senior partner of Hayden and Whilden, importers and military outfitters at 250 King Street, Charleston. Formerly a partner in the firm of Eyland and Hayden.

HENLEY, W. H.

This name appears on the top of a Confederate-made dragoon revolver with a 7-inch .44 caliber part-round barrel (⅓ octagon). The weapon has a brass backstrap, trigger-guard and fore-sight. *C.S.* is stamped on the right side of the frame. The unique feature of this revolver is that the cones are set flush with the back of the

cylinder and cannot be seen except from the rear. Nothing further is known.

HODGKINS, D. C. & SONS—Macon, Georgia

"Dealers in Guns, Pistols, and Sporting articles, etc." at Mulberry Street.

HOFFMAN, LOUIS—Vicksburg, Mississippi

Imitation derringer pistols are sometimes found marked *Louis Hoffman, Vicksburg* on the barrel and *L. Hoffman* on the lock plate. Hoffman was reputedly in business about a year prior to the start of the Civil War.

HUNTER, JAMES—Falmouth, Virginia

Proprietor of Hunter's Iron Works and manufacturer of Rappahannock Forge pistols.

HYDE AND GOODRICH—New Orleans

The 1853 New Orleans City Directory lists this firm as dealers in guns, pistols and military goods, located at 15 Chartres Street. The firm imported a number of English Tranter pistols which are engraved *Hyde & Goodrich, agents, N.O.* or *W. Tranter's Patent, Hyde & Goodrich, Agents for the United States South.* In 1861 the firm changed its name to Thomas, Griswold and Co. and continued as military outfitters until New Orleans fell to U.S. forces in 1863.

JOHNSON, FELIX—Memphis, Tennessee

The Memphis *Appeal* of September 18, 1861, carried the following: "A home made Colt's repeater. On Saturday morning last we had the pleasure of examining a Colt's repeater which was made by the Rev. Felix Johnson. This weapon was complete in all its details and appointments and as well calculated to do damage as Mr. Colt's best. Every calculation necessary to a perfect fitting of all parts were made with the utmost nicety. The Reverend inventor of this valuable weapon was on a mission from the Governor and Military Board of Tennessee to make arrangements with Messrs. Wright & Rice, of this vicinity, for the procurement of suitable machinery to aid in the manufacturing of this

weapon. We earnestly hope this enterprise may be a success. Florence (Alabama) *Gazette,* September 14."

KAPP, ALFRED—Sisterdale, Texas

Son of Dr. Ernst Kapp and at one time an employee of the Colt revolver factory at Hartford, Connecticut, who returned to his father's farm at Sisterdale, Texas, shortly before the outbreak of hostilities and reputedly made six revolvers. Kapp's guns vaguely resembled Colt's but had Remington's solid frame and utilized Smith & Wesson's outside hand and overhead cylinder stop. The grips are flared in a manner similar to those of Rogers & Spencer. A revolver attributed to Alfred Kapp is on display in New Braunfels, Texas, at the Sophienburg Museum.

KERNAGHAN, D., & Co.—New Orleans, Louisiana

An English-made 5-shot .36 caliber revolver is marked on the top of the barrel *Made Expressly for D. Kernaghan & Co., New Orleans.* Left side of the cylinder is marked *Patent A840.* The ramrod has a peculiarly shaped end and also an odd fastening similar to that on the Colt Walker. The gun is double action only and has check-

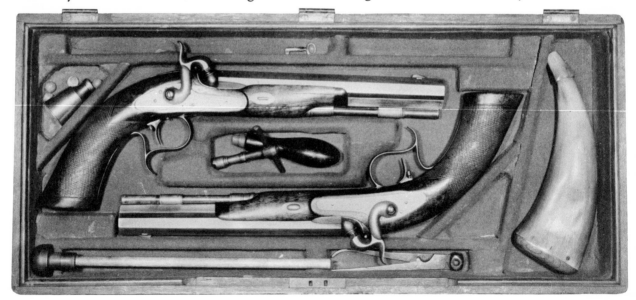

Courtesy Harry C. Knode

CASED PAIR OF PISTOLS

A sturdy pair of pistols with a number of the proper accessories. These are marked Peter Kraft, Columbus, S. C.

ANOTHER SINGLE-SHOT PISTOL

Courtesy Harry C. Knode

Made by C. Kreutner, showing also a detail of the barrel marking.

ered wooden grips. It is evidently a Birmingham trade piece sent to a New Orleans dealer.

KIRKMAN & ELLIS—Nashville, Tennessee

Name appearing on flintlock holster pistols of the 1800 period very similar to English dragoon pistols. Some have brass locks. Some percussion rifles are marked similarly.

KITTERAGE & FOLSOM—New Orleans, Louisiana

Listed in the New Orleans City Directory of 1861 as dealers in "Guns, rifles and sporting apparatus," at 55 St. Charles.

The "Folsom" is evidently H. Folsom.

KRAFT, PETER W.—Columbia, South Carolina

The Richmond *Daily Examiner* of January 3, 1861, carries an advertisement: "Bowie knives, fine English, French and German double guns, Colts, Smith & Wessons, Allen & Wheellocks and Adams English repeaters. Double barrel guns, rifles and pistols made to order. Mounted men solicited to buy from our stock." Kraft was also a principal in the sword making firm of Kraft, Goldschmidt and Kraft of Columbia, which operated from 184 Main Street.

KREUTNER, CHRISTIAN—Montgomery, Alabama

Operator of a small gun factory at 14 North Perry Street, near Dexter Avenue, and had a contract with the state of Alabama for Mississippi rifles at $35 each. During the war served as Captain at the Montgomery Arsenal in charge of repairing arms. He also made pistols, one of which is a large affair some 15 inches overall, with a .58 caliber single-shot 9-inch octagon barrel. The weapon has a silver fore-end cap and barrel escutcheon. Lock and barrel bear his name and in addition, *Montgomery, Alabama.*

LEFFLER—Memphis, Tennessee

A gunsmith located at 90 Main Street, Memphis, Tennessee, who made derringer-type pistols before the war. During the war he was employed by a J. G. Schmidt who had a contract with the Confederate Government to repair arms at 120 Main Street.

LEGG, T. C.—Columbia, South Carolina

Name appears on percussion dueling pistols with English barrels.

LEONARD, CHARLES—Petersburg, Virginia

On June 28, 1861, advertised in the Richmond *Examiner* "everything connected with the gun trade, 56 Sycamore Street." On May 27, 1861, the Richmond *Dispatch* advised that Charles Leonard, Agent, had received Colt's pistols, army, navy and belt size. Numerous rifles and shotguns are to be found bearing his name. A single-shot percussion pistol with 8-inch octagon barrel is engraved *C. Leonard—Petersburg.*

LESSIER, P.—Selma, Alabama

Partner of C. Suter and Company, makers of Mississippi rifles for the state of Alabama, and derringer-type pistols.

LIBEAU, V. G. W.—New Orleans, Louisiana

A gunsmith from about 1835 to 1847 who sold derringer-type pistols usually marked *New Orleans* on the barrel and *V.G.W. Libeau* on the lock plate. Also made a .36 caliber percussion revolver on the order of the Texas Paterson with a 4⅜-inch barrel and folding trigger.

LIGON, E. T.—Demopolis, Alabama

Was issued Confederate patent number 24, September 24, 1861, on a breech-loading pistol. None are known.

LONARD, C., JR.—Charleston

A four-barreled pepperbox pistol is marked *C. Lonard Jr., Charleston, Pat. 1849, cast steel.*

LULLMAN & VIENNA—Memphis, Tennessee

Dealers and agent for Henry Deringer and whose names also appear on imitation derringers.

McNAUGHT, JAMES—Richmond, Virginia

A gunsmith and dealer who in 1821 advertised pistols and rifles.

MENDELHALL, (?)—Marshall, Texas

In 1864 one Mendelhall was engaged in pistol-making activities for the Confederate Government at the C.S. Arsenal at Marshall. The extent of his activities is not otherwise known (*Tyler, Texas, C.S.A.,* page 124).

MILLS, BENJAMIN—Harrodsburg, Kentucky

Assistant Armorer at Harpers Ferry, he followed the machinery from this Armory to Fayetteville after its capture by the South. His father, F. M. Mills of Charlottesville, North Carolina, was a gunsmith who learned his trade from Henry Leman of Lancaster, Pennsylvania. Various types of pistols are found marked *B. Mills, Harrodsburg, Ky.*

MILLSPAUGH, A.—Washington, Louisiana

A dealer whose name appears on a pair of fine Philadelphia derringer pistols with gold escutcheons engraved *Doct. T. Steel from J. M. Cooper.* The barrels are marked *Manf. for A. Millspaugh, Washington, La.*

MONROE, NORTH CAROLINA

In speaking of Monroe, North Carolina, DeBow's *Review* of March-April, 1862, says: "Some pistols have been manufactured from rifle barrels; several hundred bowie knives have been manufactured—200 or more. Many guns repaired and one model centrifugal gun proposing to shoot 2,000 balls per minute, constructed of wood."

MOORE, P. T., & Co.—Richmond, Virginia

The Richmond *Examiner,* August 2, 1861; "Importers and wholesale rifles, pistols and shot guns, 141 Main St."

MORRIS, WILLIAM AMBLER—Indiantown, Virginia

Orange County, Virginia's only gunsmith, known locally as "Gunsmith Billy." Born June 18, 1828 and died June 19, 1912, he operated a small repair shop for the Confederacy near Chancellorsville. His name is found on rifles and has been seen on at least one under-hammer pistol.

MORRISON, MURDOCH—Richmond County, North Carolina

In speaking of Morrison, DeBow's *Review* of

March-April, 1862, says ". . . Is engaged in making bowie knives and has made a few pistols, but his operations are on a small scale."

MURRAY, JOHN P.—Columbus, Georgia

Advertised in July, 1862, as being successor to Happoldt and Murray, 46 Broad Street, maker and dealer in shotguns, rifles, pistols, knives, etc. During the war Murray did considerable repair and altering for the state of Georgia and Confederate Ordnance, and was connected in some capacity with Greenwood and Grey's Rifle Factory. After the war he lived in Charleston, South Carolina, dying there in 1910.

NICHOLS, H. E.—Columbia, South Carolina

Advertised in the Richmond *Dispatch* of March 10, 1863, as having just received from England six "Tranters' fine revolving pistols, 80 and 120 bore, price $220 each."

POINT OF FORK, VIRGINIA

In 1781 the Virginia Public Gun Factory of Fredericksburg was moved to Point of Fork, situated some 50 miles west of Richmond at the mouth of the Rivanna River where it empties into the James. Here ordnance activities were carried on for the state of Virginia until the plant was absorbed by the Virginia Manufactory in Richmond in 1803.

PORTER, PATRICK W.—Memphis, Tennessee

Gunsmith and pistol maker of the eighteen fifties.

POYAS, F. D.—Charleston, South Carolina

Circa 1845, made fine percussion dueling pistols.

PRESCOT, D. L.—New Orleans

Name and address found engraved on the top of the barrel of a Tranter revolver.

PROUDFIT, W. P.—Memphis, Tennessee

The Memphis *Appeal*, October 31, 1861, carried the following: "All servicable double bar-reled shotguns, Sharp's carbines and Maynard rifles, Colt's Navy pistols or the single barrel Dragoon pistols and common rifles. Persons knowing the whereabouts of the above described arms are earnestly requested to assist me in the collecting. Terms, cash on the spot. W. P. Proudfit, 33 Front St., Agent for the Confederate States."

RADCLIFFE, THOMAS W.—Columbia, South Carolina

An importer and dealer in watches, guns and military goods. His name is to be found on imported English Tranter revolvers. Operated at the northeast corner of Richardson and Plain Streets. Just before the war formed the Chicora Rifles and as their captain went with the company to Charleston at the start of hostilities but returned to Columbia after a reorganization. He then was put in charge of the training camp at Lightwood Knot Spring with the rank of major. During the war, Radcliffe and William Glaze, owner of the Palmetto Armory, considered the establishment of a large armory and arsenal, but whatever plans were made evidently fell through. After the fall of the Confederacy returned to gunsmithing and continued until the early nineteen hundreds.

RADCLIFFE AND GUIGNARD—Columbia, South Carolina

This name and address is sometimes to be found on percussion fowling pieces and particularly on small single-shot pistols of French type with deeply fluted ebony handles and floral engraving on the frames. These pistols are center hammer types with folding triggers and no proof marks. The tops of the barrels are marked in three lines; *Radcliffe & Guignard, Columbia, S. C.*

RAPHAEL REVOLVER

A 6-shot, double action, cartridge revolver, with a $5^{15}/_{16}$-inch round barrel of .41 caliber; smooth round cylinder, center hammer, steel trigger-guard and walnut grips. The cylinder has a revolving shield with a loading gate in which to insert the center fire cartridge. There is a lanyard ring in the butt. This weapon was used by Confederate officers to some extent early in the war until the lack of cartridges caused them to be discarded.

RAPPAHANNOCK FORGE—Falmouth, *Virginia*

Established by James Hunter about 1775 on the north side of the Rappahannock River at Falmouth, Stafford County, Virginia. John Strode was superintendent of the plant during the Revolutionary War, later becoming connected with George Wheeler, a musket maker of Stevensburg, Virginia. Various types of arms were made, including pistols, until the plant was closed December 1, 1781. Pistols made at this establishment are excessively rare, only four or five genuine specimens being known, in addition to one or two out-and-out fakes.

One of the genuine pistols is described: Caliber .62, 8½-inch round smooth-bore barrel without sights. Total length, 14½ inches. Brass mountings. The barrel and thimble are pin-fastened to the full length walnut stock which extends to the end of the muzzle. The somewhat fishtail shape butt is reinforced by a brass butt cap, similar to the Harpers Ferry, with short, round extensions reaching into the stock on each side. The brass trigger-guard forks at the rear to complete the oval. The trigger ends in a curl. The flat bevel-edged lock plate ends in a point at the rear and is marked behind the hammer *RAPa FORGE* in two lines reading vertically and to the rear. The barrel is marked *J. Hunter.* The hammer is of gooseneck variety.

REARDON, R. R.—Nashville, *Tennessee*

Sold 66 pistols at $42.50 each to Lieutenant M. H. Wright, the Confederate Commanding Officer at Nashville, Tennessee, on October 10, 1861. (Captured Rebel Records, Volume 19, U.S. Archives.)

REVOL, J. R.—New Orleans, *Louisiana*

A gunsmith from 1850 to 1890, he was located at 346 Royal where he made fine target rifles, a few breech-loading rifles, duck cannon and an occasional single-shot pistol marked *J. R. Revol, N.O.*

ROBINSON AND LESTER—Richmond, *Virginia*

References to the Robinson and Lester "Pistol Factory" actually refer to Spiller and Burr during the time they operated in Richmond and leased the building which belonged to S. C. Robinson. Robinson had a contract with the state of Virginia to manufacture revolvers in 1861 but turned over plans, machinery and building to Spiller and Burr. He and his foreman, one Lester, then engaged in altering Virginia Manufactory flint locks to percussion and later in making carbines patterned after the Sharps.

ROGERS AND BOWEN—Augusta, *Georgia*

E. H. Rogers and William Bowen were gun dealers and hardware merchants whose names appear on sporting arms. The firm was dissolved when Bowen entered Confederate service and Rogers continued the business under his own name, advertising in local papers, "A good supply of Navy pistols always on hand of Colt's pattern—a good durable article and well finished. For sale low, E. H. Rogers." (Augusta *Constitutionalist,* July 31, 1864). The fact that he does not advertise these guns as "Colt Navy pistols" but Navy pistols of Colt's pattern might indicate they were imitations, possibly of his own manufacture.

SAGET, S.—New Orleans, *Louisiana*

Hand hammered soft thin sheets of lead made to be cut into cushions for holding the flint in a flintlock hammer are sometimes found stamped *S. Saget, New Orleans.*

SCHMIDT, E., AND CO.—Houston, *Texas*

A dealer's name encountered on derringer pistols.

SELMA, ALABAMA

Site of a large and extensive Confederate Ordnance works. Reports of revolver making at this point are not supported by any documents yet found. However, several authorities highly respected by the authors are of the definite opinion that handguns were made there. One such attributed to Selma is styled somewhat along Tranter lines but with an open frame and egg shaped trigger-guard. Its serial is 6, and the weapon is otherwise unmarked.

Courtesy Battle Abbey, Richmond, Virginia

UNNUMBERED REVOLVER BY AN UNKNOWN MAKER

This open framed specimen is believed by several authorities to have been made at Selma, Alabama.

SHEETS, M.—Shepherdstown, Virginia (now West Virginia)

A descendant of a line of gun makers that antedates the Revolutionary War and who made a .31 caliber percussion revolver with a frame and center hammer, the four-inch octagon barrel being marked *M. Sheets.*

SISTERDALE, TEXAS

Site of the revolver-making activities of Alfred Kapp.

SPRATLEY, WILLIAM S.—Norfolk, Virginia

Gunsmith in the mid 1850s who operated from 14 Union Street. A single-shot pistol, whose parts apparently came from a Harpers Ferry pistol, contains a lock which is stamped with his name. A cased 1849 Colt has Spratley's label in the lid as dealer.

STRODE, JOHN—Falmouth, Virginia

Manager of the Rappahannock Forge.

STROHECKER, H. F.—Charleston, South Carolina

Made and imported fine dueling pistols. One such has a heavy octagon .44 caliber barrel and an overall length of 14 inches with checkered grips and high quality finish. Although Birmingham proof marks are under the barrel the top is engraved *Strohecker, Charleston, So. Ca.*

SUTER, C., AND CO.—Selma, Alabama

Had a contract with the state of Alabama for Mississippi rifles at $37.50 each. Between October 1, 1863 and November, 1864, delivered 50 rifles. His partner was P. Lessier. His name is also observed on a Philadelphia derringer-type pistol.

TARVER, JAM—Searcy, Arkansas

The above was referred to as an "inventor of a repeating pistol" who wanted a patent. (Contract Book, Chapter VIII, Volume 371, page 26, April 5, 1861: Letters to C. S. Secretary of War, U.S. National Archives.)

THOMAS, HENRY, JR.—New Orleans, Louisiana

An employee of Hyde and Goodrich, and later a partner in the military outfitting firm of Thomas, Griswold and Co.

THOMAS, JOSEPH—Memphis, Tennessee

The Memphis *Appeal* of June 12, 1861, carried the following: "We were shown, by Mr. Jos. Thomas of this city, a pair of bullet moulds of his own make, for moulding the Minie balls. He can make them of any desired size, to suit the bore of any kind of gun, from the smallest pistol to the largest bore musket or shotgun. His charge is three dollars which is less than half the ordinary charge. Give him a call, near the Armory, on Clinton Street."

TIGNOR, THOMAS W.—Richmond, Virginia

The 1859 Richmond City Directory lists the

above as a gunsmith on "Main Street between 17th & 18th Streets." As a dealer, his name appears on sporting arms and single-shot pistols. Aided in the conversion of Virginia Manufactory arms from flint to percussion.

TRANTER REVOLVERS

William Tranter of Birmingham, England, patented a revolver which became very popular in the South and many were supplied to Southern gunsmiths and dealers prior to the war. Many of these were stamped with the dealer's name. Tranter is not known to have had a contract with the Confederate Government, so perhaps only those weapons bearing a Southern dealer's name can be tentatively considered as secondary Confederate.

TYRER, THOMAS—Richmond, Virginia

A cased set of dueling pistols marked *T. Tyrer, Richmond, Va.* on their locks, and engraved *Charles Bruce* on the tops of their octagon barrels; has a decorated label pasted in the top, bearing the legend: "Thos. Tyrer, Importer & Manufacturer of: Guns, Pistols & Rifles." The guns have Birmingham proof marks on the undersides of their barrels.

VIRGINIA IRON WORKS—Norfolk, Virginia
See Thomas W. Godwin and Co.

VIRGINIA PUBLIC GUN FACTORY—Fredericksburg, Virginia

Erected by order of the Convention of July, 1775, for the fabrication of small arms to equip

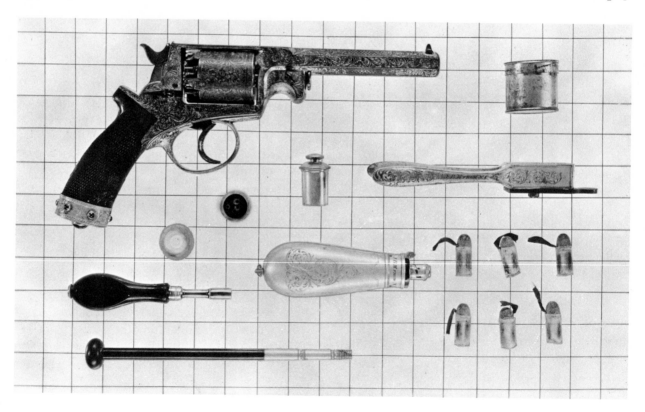

Courtesy Dr. S. Traner Buck (deceased)

AN ORNATE ADAMS

This is one of the exceptionally attractive arms of known provenance of the Confederacy. Of British manufacture, with complete accessories, it is beautifully styled and executed. Presented to General J. B. Magruder, C. S. A., by Nelson Clements and so marked, with the legend "J.B.M. from N.C." A jeweled and engraved band at the base of the butt adds special appeal to the piece. This model embodies the F. B. E. Beaumont improvement, British Patent No. 374 of February 20, 1855.

Courtesy Richard T. Brady (deceased)

REVOLVER BY AN UNKNOWN MAKER

A dragoon type arm bearing C S A marking on barrel. This was dug up many years ago on a Tennessee battlefield.

the Continental soldiers of Virginia. The extent and type of manufacture is not known, although it probably included pistols. The establishment was closed in 1783 and its equipment transferred to Point of Fork Arsenal where the State owned some 100 acres of land.

WALSH, JAMES—Richmond, Virginia

A gunmaker, dealer and importer who advertised in the Richmond *Dispatch* of May 3, 1861, as having Colts of all sizes for sale. The same source, July 8, 1861, stated that he had just received 40 Colt's Navy pistols, 20 Colt's pocket size and 4 Colt's army pistols. He converted Virginia Manufactory arms from flint to percussion and, in so doing, stamped his name on the lock plates. Cased Colts bearing his label have been found. He was located at 60 Main St.

WATSON, WALTER—Fayetteville, North Carolina

Advertised November 7, 1864: "Guns and pistols made and repaired with dispatch. Members of Reserves and Home Guards can have arms repaired at half price." According to a personal

letter from Watson in the early nineteen hundreds, he came to this country from England, and throughout the war was employed at the Fayetteville Armory. After the war he continued privately as a gunsmith.

WELCH, JAMES—Richmond, Virginia

The Richmond *Dispatch* of March 25, 1861, advertised Welch as a "gun importer, 7 doors above the St. Charles Hotel" and that he had just received from the "manufacturer a further supply of Colt's celebrated five-shooters in navy and pocket sizes. Also on hand a large assortment of dueling, self-cocking and rifle pistols. . . ."

WESTHAM ARMORY (or Arsenal)—Westham, Virginia

About the time of the Revolutionary War there was an Armory, or Arsenal, located a few miles out of Richmond (near the present Pump House) at a site called "Westham," not to be confused with Westham Station, which is located some miles west. Arms belonging to the state of Virginia were made or stored there. Ruins of the brick structure were still standing, in recognizable form, as late as 1930.

Courtesy E. M. Hubbard

ANOTHER REVOLVER BY AN UNKNOWN MAKER

The only mark on this revolver of Confederate origin is the serial number 51.

Wolfe and Durringer—Louisville, Kentucky

A fine pair of derringer pistols are marked: *Deringer, Philadel'a* and *Wolfe & Durringer,* *Louis'e, Ky., Agents.* These weapons belonged to Robert E. Lee, the shield-shaped German-silver plate on the back of the stocks being engraved *R. E. Lee, Va.*

Finally, your attention is called to the pictures of two revolvers, shown in this chapter, which may be considered as representative of that large number of Southern handguns whose origin it is impossible to trace, but whose interest to the collector and historian is undeniable. The specimen dug up on one of the battlefields in Tennessee can certainly be considered as having seen active service. While there may be a strong presumption that the other piece, with the serial number 51 as its only mark, was also used in combat, no proof of this exists. The unsolved mysteries surrounding these and so many similar pieces provide one of the greatest charms and challenges of collecting.

CHAPTER 19

Bibliographical Notes

IF IT is to be at all useful to the collector, who plans research of his own, a book such as this should contain a bibliography. Perhaps a word of explanation is in order as to why the listing which follows is relatively concise.

In the entire field of collectors' weapons, which we suppose means those which are small enough to be carried about by one man, so little has been written over the ages that a select bibliography of almost 3,000 listings can easily be published in 434 pages, and has been.

When one considers Confederate weapons, one is dealing principally with the period 1861-1865—four short years.

From a state of almost total unpreparedness, the South converted existing manufactories into new industry—to build for war. For four years factories were shifted about, not always one jump ahead of the Union Army and Navy.

By the end of the war the destruction of the Southern economy was almost total. Such machinery as had survived the torch was worn out, railroads inoperable, mines shut down, and an industrial system, which had been created by necessity, was smashed. Capital cities were in ashes, armies disbanded, reports and returns scattered. Records of all sorts were lost, destroyed, hidden away and forgotten.

Because the participants and observers of the conflict were more concerned with the military and political aspects of their times, few made more than casual, passing references to weapons when they wrote their memoirs or apologia.

While it would no doubt be of impressive length, the authors have no intention of listing all of the works they have examined in hopes of discovering clues to the subjects of this work.

Instead, we offer some practical advice. For general purposes, one could concentrate on reviewing the state archival material of South Carolina, North Carolina, Virginia, and Georgia, later branching out into the other states which comprised the Confederacy, and one could not go wrong. To the best of our knowledge, a thorough, exhaustive review of the various state archives has never been carried out.

The National Archives in Washington are a mother lode of material. Here are the captured ordnance records and other documents that amplify, explain and complement the material found elsewhere.

Historical societies, and this applies to many in the North, are replete with material, much of it not indexed or catalogued.

Museums, including the Battle Abbey and Confederate Museum in Richmond, the Charleston Museum in South Carolina, and the Montgomery Museum of Fine Arts in Alabama, all have excellent collections of arms and in many cases, documents. The Smithsonian Institution should not be overlooked; its Bulletins are priceless, its collections, in many respects, unequalled.

From time to time, we have referred to books which we here classify as "local history" or "personal reminiscence." By and large these works are not footnoted and seem to rely on their authors' memories. Many, in fact, were based upon contemporary documents and the accounts

THE PRINTED WORD

Here shown is a small section of a private library of books dealing with weapons and their role in history. Of the more than five thousand volumes in this entire library, only about thirty-five are of basic value for Confederate weapon data. This indicates the difficulties which the authors faced in accumulating and verifying data on Confederate handguns.

Courtesy F. Theodore Dexter

A PROFUSION OF COLLECTORS' ARMS

As we have stated in the text ". . . it should be obvious that a good bit of what we know is based upon detailed information supplied by the examination of hundreds of weapons in many collections." The arms are as important in research as the printed word. This collection, enjoyed in years past by the R. M. Staggs of Los Angeles, California, may have included a specimen mentioned in this book.

of eye-witnesses, but it is impossible to document the latter. While of dubious historical accuracy in some instances, a good many of these works are extremely accurate. Most important, they give us the feel and flavor of the times. They corroborate, they amplify, and they bring the men they discuss into focus, clothing them with flesh and blood.

The Official Records, 128 volumes, incorporating many, but by no means all of the records

of the Union and Confederate Armies and Navies, are to be found in most public libraries of any size. While an index exists, it is not exactly comprehensive or accurate. The Official Records should not be overlooked as source material.

By the same token, the 10-volume *History of the South*, edited by Dr. E. Merton Coulter, should be of general interest. Particularly valuable is Dr. Coulter's "Critical Essay on Authorities," found in Volume VII, entitled *The Confederate States of America, 1861-1865.* Other histories mentioned in the footnotes are of slight interest and little value, the references shown being almost the only ones on weapons to be found.

Newspapers are valuable for a variety of reasons, chief among them being indications of manufacturing activity. They are not always accurate, but should not be overlooked. Large collections exist and are listed in standard catalogues and library bibliographies. Magazines of the period are also useful.

Modern magazines generally are given to the publication of undocumented supposition, but four stand out as sources of carefully researched facts. Three of them, unfortunately, are no longer published. The latter are *The Gun Collector, The Texas Gun Collector* and the *American Arms Collector.* The fourth is *The American Rifleman,* official publication of the National Rifle Association.

The personal papers and manuscripts of men who actually witnessed events, or participated in them, are the greatest prize that one can win. Unfortunately, they are extremely difficult to find.

While *Confederate Handguns* has drawn upon all of the sources noted for its information, it should be obvious that a good bit of what we know is based upon detailed information supplied by the examination of hundreds of weapons in many collections.

Thus we have an extremely practical marriage of the written word of yesterday to the artifacts of today.

The works consulted:

William A. Albaugh, III, *The Confederate Brass-Framed Colt & Whitney* (Washington, D. C., 1955).

William A. Albaugh, III, *Confederate Edged Weapons* (New York, 1960).

William A. Albaugh, III, and Richard D. Steuart, *The Original Confederate Colt* (New York, 1953).

Colonel William Allan, "Reminiscences of Field Ordnance Service with the Army of Northern Virginia, 1863-1865," Southern Historical Society Papers, Vol. XIV, 1886.

William W. Bradbeer, *States Currency* (1915).

Beauregard Papers. 106 volumes and 815 items in The Manuscript and Archival Collection of the Department of Archives, Louisiana State University, Baton Rouge, Louisiana.

James D. Bulloch, *The Secret Service of the Confederate States in Europe,* 2 volumes (New York, 1884).

E. Milby Burton, *South Carolina Silversmiths 1690-1860* (Charleston, 1942).

Marjorie Lyle Crandall, *Confederate Imprints, A Check List Based Principally on the Collection of the Boston Athenaeum,* 2 volumes (Boston, Massachusetts, 1955).

Document No. XL—*Message from the Executive of the Commonwealth transmitting a Report of Wm. H. Peters, commissioner, appointed by the Governor to make an Inventory of Property taken from the United States Government at the Navy Yard, Gosport, and in and near Portsmouth, Virginia.* Gosport, Virginia, October 19, 1861.

This explicit and meticulously detailed report was requested by Governor John Letcher of Virginia. The document contains 128 pages pertinent to the Navy Yard supplies and properties, plus 24 pages titled *Inventory of Musket Machinery taken at Harpers Ferry and now in the Armory at Richmond.* It also includes, in addition, 16 pages titled *Inventory of Rifle Machinery sent to Fayetteville, North Carolina.* The document is thoroughly itemized and appraised with group and sort totals indicating various disbursements to various Confederate commands and stations. Many of the items listed could, and probably did, find their way into the manufacturing of handguns for the Confederacy. The executive message states "The property is in the possession of the Confederate Government, for use during the war."

Clement A. Evans, ed., *Confederate Military History*, Georgia (Atlanta, Georgia, 1899), 10 volumes.

Claud E. Fuller and Richard D. Steuart, *Firearms of the Confederacy* (Huntington, West Virginia, 1944).

W. W. Greener, *The Gun and Its Development;* with Notes on Shooting (London, 1881, first edition).

Charles B. Hall, *Military Records of the General Officers of the Confederate States of America*, Vol. 1 (New York, 1898). Although another volume or volumes were intended, Vol. 1 was the only volume produced. The portrait of General Gorgas, appearing as a frontispiece in *Confederate Handguns,* is an etching extracted from unpublished second volume of this work.

Richard Harwell, *More Confederate Imprints*, Vol. 1, Official Publications; Vol. 2, Unofficial Publications (Richmond, Virginia, 1957).

Helen Kohn Henning, *City of Columbia, 1786-1936* (Columbia, South Carolina, 1936).

Carroll C. Holloway, *Texas Gun Lore* (San Antonio, Texas, 1951).

Ben La Bree, ed., *The Confederate Soldier in the Civil War* (Louisville, Kentucky, 1895). Also a reprint of same, 1959, at Paterson, N. J.

E. M. Lander, Jr., "Columbia's Confederate Arsenal," State Magazine, Sunday supplement to the Columbia State, August 13, 1950.

W. L. Lipscomb, *History of Columbus, Mississippi, in the 19th Century* (Birmingham, Alabama, 1909).

F. T. Miller, *The Photographic History of the Civil War*, 10 volumes (New York, 1911).

Colonel James W. Morgan, *Recollections of a Rebel Reefer* (Boston, 1917).

John W. H. Porter, *History of Norfolk County, Virginia* (Portsmouth, Va., W. A. Fiske, 1892).

Ray Riling, *Guns and Shooting*, a Bibliography (New York, 1951).

Ray Riling, *The Powder Flask Book* (New Hope, Pa., 1953).

A. S. Salley, *The State Houses of South Carolina, 1751-1936* (Columbia, South Carolina, 1936).

W. G. Simms, *The Sack and Destruction of the City of Columbia, South Carolina* (Columbia, South Carolina, 1865). A second edition (with notes by A. S. Salley) (Atlanta, Georgia, 1937), pp. 90-91.

Southern Agriculturist (Laurensville, South Carolina, 1853), Vol. I.

U.S. National Museum Bulletin—No. 42, 1891 (Washington, D. C.).

Frank E. Vandiver (editor), *The Civil War Diary of General Josiah Gorgas* (University of Alabama, 1947).

Frank E. Vandiver, *Ploughshares Into Swords,* Josiah Gorgas and Confederate Ordnance (Austin, Texas, 1952).

David Duncan Wallace, *History of South Carolina* (New York, 1934).

War of the Rebellion: A compilation of the Official Records of the Union and Confederate Armies (Washington, D. C., 1880-1901).

Charles F. Wells, MS in Macon Historical Society; letters to the authors, 1959.

J. F. Williams, *Old and New Columbia* (Columbia, South Carolina, 1929).

ADDENDUM

Official patent records of the Confederacy classified under "Firearms, including Implements and Machinery of War, etc.," for the years 1861 through 1864.

In obedience to the requirements of the Act "To Establish a Patent Office," etc., approved May 21, 1861, Rufus R. Rhodes, Commissioner of Patents of the Confederate States Patent Office, presented, over date January, 1862, a first list of the patents issued from his office "prior to the first instant." A resolution of the Confederate Congress resolved that "300 copies of the Reports of the Commissioner of Patents be printed, to be paid for out of the Patent Fund, 50 of which shall be retained in the office of the

Commissioner of Patents, 100 to be distributed to the present Congress, and 150 to the Congress under the Permanent Constitution." From the foregoing quote one will understand the extreme rarity of the patent reports of the Confederacy.

There were no small arms patents per se in 1864 nor a record of any in 1865. The list of Number, Invention or Discovery, Patentee, Residence, and Date of Patent, from the original pertinent classifications are reproduced on the following four pages, we believe, for the first time in their entirety. It will be noted that other items, in addition to the handguns of our interest, have been necessarily included to complete the record under the Confederate Classifications.

THE FOLLOWING LISTS ARE
EXACT TRANSCRIPTS
FROM THE OFFICIAL CONFEDERATE RECORDS

FIREARMS INCLUDING IMPLEMENTS AND MACHINERY OF WAR, ETC.

CLASS XIII.—Firearms and Implements of War, etc.

No.	Invention or Discovery	Patentee	Residence	Date
34	Bullet-mould	Joseph Thomas	Batesville, Arkansas	Oct. 15, 1861
29	Cannon	James Lynch	Petersburg, Virginia	Oct. 4, 1861
19	Cannon, manufacture of	James H. Harkut	Natchez, Mississippi	Sept. 3, 1861
35	Cannon, breech-loading	Daniel Oswalt	Cubahatchie, Alabama	Oct. 15, 1861
12	Cartridges	Frederick J. Gardner	New Bern, North Carolina	Aug. 17, 1861
26	Cartridges, paper	John R. Spillman	Warrenton, Virginia	Oct. 1, 1861
27	Cartridges, device for making	"	"	Oct. 2, 1861
40	Cartridge boxes	John P. Gorman	Charlestown, Virginia	Oct. 2, 1861
24	Firearm, breech-loading	E. T. Ligon	Demopolis, Alabama	Sept. 27, 1861
23	Fuses, percussion	Ed. Gotthiel & R. Mott, assoc'd	New Orleans, Louisiana	Sept. 19, 1861
8	Gun automatic, breech-load'g	Phidello Hall	Springfield, Texas	Aug. 10, 1861
21	Gun, breech-loading	James P. Rankin	Marion, North Carolina	Sept. 14, 1861
1	"	James H. Van Houten	Savannah, Georgia	Aug. 1, 1861
54	"	John M. White	Citruille, Alabama	Dec. 7, 1861
11	Lance or pike attach'g to guns	Armand Preot	Gravel Hill, Virginia	Aug. 15, 1861
9	Pistol, revolving	Thomas W. Cofer	Portsmouth, Virginia	Aug. 12, 1861
18	Sword bayn't attach'g to g'ns	E. Boyle, T. Gamble, E. Macfee	Richmond, Virginia	Sept. 2, 1861
5	Sabre lance	R. W. Habersham	Beaufort, South Carolina	Aug. 6, 1861

FIREARMS INCLUDING IMPLEMENTS AND MACHINERY OF WAR, ETC.

CLASS XV.—Firearms, including Implements and Machinery of War

No.	Invention or Discovery	Patentee	Residence	Date
70	Percussion fuse	R. Archer	Richmond, Va.	Jan. 7, 1862
125	Breech-loading cannon	M. Bridges	Memphis, Tenn.	Nov. 20, 1862
111	Breech-loading firearms	A. J. M. T. O. Clanton	Panola, Miss.	Oct. 3, 1862
91	Breech-loading firearms	J. W. Howlett	Greensboro, N. C.	May 10, 1862
106	Projectile	Lucien Hopson	Lampasas, Texas	Sept. 25, 1862
108	Breech-loading firearms	George Henry	Columbus, Miss.	Sept. 27, 1862
58	Breech-loading gun	Carl Laquequist	Macon, Ga.	Jan. 21, 1862
79	Bullet machine	C. V. Littlepage	Austin, Texas	Mar. 11, 1862
109	Instrument for leveling cannon	J. A. LeToudal	Mobile, Ala.	Sept. 29, 1862
88	Mode of manufacturing scabbards	Augustus McBurthe	Richmond, Va.	Apr. 14, 1862
92	Fuse	C. A. McEvoy	"	May 1, 1862
93	Fuse	" " "	"	Apr. 23, 1862
123	Fuse	" " "	"	Nov. 15, 1862
129	Army canteen	Nathaniel Nuckolls	Russell Co., Ala.	Dec. 11, 1862
84	Instrument for sighting cannon	Chas. E. Stuart, J. C. Owing and J. H. C. Taylor		Mar. 21, 1862
112	Bullet machine	Wm. Spillman	Alexandria, Va.	Oct. 3, 1862
96	Firearms	G. J. Peterson	Prattsville, Ala.	May 31, 1862
113	Projectile	Wm. S. Winfield	Marion, N. C.	Oct. 11, 1862
121	Breech-loading cannon	D. R. Williams	Springfield, Tenn.	Nov. 5, 1862
132	Machinery for traversing guns	Jos. A. Yates	Richmond, Va.	Dec. 30, 1862

FIREARMS INCLUDING IMPLEMENTS AND MACHINERY OF WAR, ETC.

CLASS XIII.—Firearms and Implements of War

No.	Invention or Discovery	Patentee	Residence	Date
163	Breech-loading firearm	C. W. Alexander	Moorefield, Va.	Apr. 18, 1863
143	Projectile	R. H. Barrett	Murfreesboro, N. C.	Jan. 26, 1863
160	Projectile	Thomas H. Bacon	Hannibal, Mo.	Apr. 15, 1863
174	Fuse	Wm. Le Roy Browne	Ivy Depot, Va.	May 25, 1863
182	Fuse, gauge, and cutter	Albert Bloomer	Richmond, Va.	July 15, 1863
187	Torpedo	A. Barbarin	New Orleans, La.	Aug. 5, 1863
133	Projectile	Alonzo C. Chinn	Mobile, Ala.	Jan. 3, 1863
181	Explosive apparatus	Benjamin M. Cook	Kinston, N. C.	July 10, 1863
191	Projectile	H. Conner	Mobile, Ala.	Aug. 22, 1863
192	Breech-loading cannon	"	"	Aug. 22, 1863
197	Torpedo	Robert Cresezbaur	Austin, Texas	Aug. 31, 1863
176	Fuse	Isidor P. Girardy	Augusta, Ga.	June 5, 1863
178	Revolving firearm	Asa George	Charlotte, N. C.	June 10, 1863
149	Breech plug	D. W. Hughes	Don Juan, Arizona Ter.	Feb. 18, 1863
151	Revolving firearms	A. Legden	Atlanta, Ga.	Mar. 10, 1863
185	Projectile	Philip E. Love	Augusta, Ga.	July 22, 1863
135	Fuse	C. A. McEvoy	Richmond, Va.	Jan. 7, 1863
198	Torpedo	Z. McDaniel	Glasgow, Ky.	Sept. 8, 1863
199	Breech-loading firearm	Thos. Morse	Richmond, Va.	Sept. 10, 1863
202	Torpedo	Z. McDaniel	Glasgow, Ky.	Sept. 21, 1863
154	Breech-loading firearms	N. T. Read	Danville, Va.	Mar. 20, 1863
200	Torpedo	E. C. Singer	Port Lavaca, Texas	Sept. 15, 1863
209	Cap-filling machine	W. H. Smith	Richmond, Va.	Oct. 24, 1863
148	Breech-loading firearm	J. H. Tarpley	Greensboro, N. C.	Feb. 14, 1863
194	Bullet machine	R. J. White and Geo. H. Lenher	Richmond, Va.	Aug. 25, 1863
203	Machine for casting friction tubes	B. H. Washington	Hannibal, Mo.	Sept. 24, 1863
212	Bullet swaging machine	"	"	Oct. 29, 1863
213	Machine for cutting and senating [serrating] friction wires	" " "	" " "	Oct. 31, 1863
214	Machine for finishing cannon	" " "	" " "	Nov. 5, 1863
218	Machine for casing [casting] cannon	" " "	" " "	Nov. 23, 1863
161	Machine for filling cartridges	Ellison Yerby	Richmond, Va.	Apr. 15, 1863

FIREARMS INCLUDING IMPLEMENTS AND MACHINERY OF WAR, ETC.

CLASS XV.—Firearms, etc.

No.	Invention or Discovery	Patentee	Residence	Date
245	Torpedo	A. Barbarin	New Orleans, La.	May 20, 1864
257	Torpedo	Richard M. Harvey	"	Oct. 5, 1864
253	Projectile	Jas. D. Layton	Memphis, Tenn.	Aug. 25, 1864
248	Clock torpedo	Wm. Moon	Richmond, Va.	July 11, 1864
232	Breech-loading cannon	Geo. W. Powell	Clay Hill, Ala.	Feb. 29, 1864
236	Torpedo	J. C. Patton & E. Cuthbert	Petersburg, Va.	Mar. 30, 1864
260	Torpedo	J. C. Patton	"	Oct. 26, 1864
259	Gun powder steaming barrels	Geo. W. Rains	Augusta, Ga.	Oct. 25, 1864
226	Projectile	John Scott	Ocala, Fla.	Jan. 27, 1864
231	Instruments for fixing sights to cannon	C. E. Stuart, Owings & Taylor	Richmond, Va.	Feb. 26, 1864
262	Projectile	D. M. Somers & H. Dabney	Lynchburg, Va.	Dec. 17, 1864
266	Percussion cap rammer	W. N. Smith	Richmond, Va.	Jan. 6, 1864
233	Projectile	R. H. S. Thompson	New Orleans, La.	Sept. 6, 1864
255	Torpedo	C. Williams	St. Louis, Mo.	Sept. 7, 1864
256	Torpedo	C. Williams	"	Sept. 7, 1864

Index

FIRST REGIMENT, SOUTH CAROLINA VOLUNTEERS

This woodcut, from a contemporary publication, shows Gregg's First Regiment being reviewed at Fort Moultrie about 1861, in the presence of the wife and daughter of Governor Pickens. We consider it a suitable *Endpiece* to this record of the guns, the men who made them, and the times of their use.